PRAISE FOR

Ted Conover's *Whiteout*

"Conover spent two years . . . hobnobbing his way into the heart of a city most outsiders think has no heart. He had loads of fun, almost lost his soul, and managed to escape the experience to write [this] fascinating book."

—*The New York Times Book Review*

"Impudent and comic . . . There's more than snow on Aspen's hills in this saucy travel guide."

—*People*

"A thoughtful, piercing look into the town we call Glamour Gulch . . . sure to be hailed as the first serious look at a town that has become an icon of wealth, fame, self-infatuation and hedonism."

—*Rocky Mountain News*

"A funny, caustic view of life among the . . . lotus-eaters."

—*Business Week*

"It's not often that you read a travel book in which you worry that the author's soul is in danger. The result is Conover's funniest book yet, and one that has much to say about our country in the 1990s."

—*San Francisco Chronicle Book Review*

"A fine, entertaining ode to the new ski season . . . Aspen's hypocrisy, ostentation and plain old weirdness are . . . hilariously documented. For the reader, it's a ride worth taking."

—*Dallas Morning News*

"Conover is one of our most original and intelligent journalists. . . . Even as [he] takes on the Aspen icons who made the town into the circus it now undeniably is, he finds himself getting sucked in. It's the easy life that hooks him, the skiing and the women, the mountain biking and the hard-edged, new-age affluence, the 'specialized world offering much that the outside world did not.' "

—*L. A. Reader*

Ted Conover *Whiteout*

Ted Conover was raised in Colorado and lives in New York City. *Whiteout, Coyotes,* and *Newjack* were named Notable Books of the Year by *The New York Times. Newjack* won the National Book Critics Circle Award for Nonfiction and was a nominated finalist for the Pulitzer Prize. His writing has appeared in *The New Yorker, The New York Times Magazine,* and many other publications. Further information about Ted Conover is available on his web site at www.tedconover.com.

Also by Ted Conover

Newjack: Guarding Sing Sing

Coyotes: A Journey Through the Secret World of
America's Illegal Aliens

Rolling Nowhere: Riding the Rails with America's
Hoboes

Whiteout

Whiteout
Lost in Aspen

Ted Conover

To Rick,
With warm wishes —
Ted Conover

Vintage Departures

VINTAGE BOOKS

A DIVISION OF RANDOM HOUSE, INC.

NEW YORK

 FIRST VINTAGE DEPARTURES EDITION, JANUARY 1993

Portions of this work appeared in different form in *Smart* magazine and *Aspen Magazine*.

Grateful acknowledgment is made to the following for permission to reprint previously published material:

HENRY HOLT & COMPANY, INC.: "Nothing Gold Can Stay" from *The Poetry of Robert Frost* edited by Edward Connery Lathem. Copyright 1923, © 1969 by Holt, Rinehart and Winston. Copyright 1951 by Robert Frost. Reprinted by permission of Henry Holt & Company, Inc.

CHRISTINE LAVIN: Excerpt from the lyrics to "Nobody's Fat in Aspen" from the album *Future Fossils* (Philo/Rounder Records, One Camp Street, Cambridge, MA 02140). Copyright © 1985 by Christine Lavin, Flip-a-Jig Tunes/Rounder Music ASCAP. Reprinted by permission.

MCA MUSIC PUBLISHING: Excerpt from "A Pirate Looks at Forty," words and music by Jimmy Buffett. Copyright © 1974, 1978 by Duchess Music Corporation. Rights administered by MCA Music Publishing, a division of MCA Inc., NY, NY 10019. All Rights Reserved. Reprinted by permission.

WARNER/CHAPPELL MUSIC, INC.: Excerpts from "Take It Easy" by Jackson Browne and Glenn Frey. Copyright © 1972 by Swallow Turn Music. All Rights Reserved. Reprinted by permission.

Library of Congress Cataloging-in-Publication Data
Conover, Ted.
Whiteout: lost in Aspen / Ted Conover.—1st Vintage departures
p. cm.—(Vintage departures)
ISBN 0-679-74178-X
1. Aspen (Colo.)—Social life and customs. 2. Aspen (Colo.)—Social conditions.
I. Title.
[F784.A7C66 1993]
978.8'43—dc20 92-56366
CIP

www.vintagebooks.com

Printed in the United States of America
10 9 8 7 6 5 4 3 2

TO MY MOTHER, KATIE CONOVER

and

TO MY FATHER, JERRY CONOVER

Nine days I drifted on the teeming sea
before dangerous high winds. Upon the tenth
we came to the coastline of the Lotos Eaters,
who live upon that flower. We landed there
to take on water. All ships' companies
mustered alongside for the mid-day meal.
Then I sent out two picked men and a runner
to learn what race of men that land sustained.
They fell in, soon enough, with Lotos Eaters,
who showed no will to do us harm, only
offering the sweet Lotos to our friends—
but those who ate this honeyed plant, the Lotos,
never cared to report, nor to return:
they longed to stay forever, browsing on
that native bloom, forgetful of their homeland.
I drove them, all three wailing, to the ships,
tied them down under their rowing benches,
and called the rest: "All hands aboard;
come, clear the beach and no one taste
the Lotos, or you lose your hope of home."

—HOMER, THE *ODYSSEY,* BOOK NINE,
TRANSLATED BY ROBERT FITZGERALD

There were not so many of these homeless people in your time. But now they are part of life here. Do they frighten me? On the whole, no . . . It is the roaming gangs I fear, the sullen-mouthed boys, rapacious as sharks, on whom the first shade of the prison house is already beginning to close. Children scorning childhood, the time of wonder, the growing time of the soul.

And on the other side of the great divide their white cousins soul-stunted too, spinning themselves tighter and tighter into their sleepy cocoons. Swimming lessons, riding lessons, ballet lessons . . . children of paradise, blond, innocent, shining with angelic light, soft as *putti*. Their residence the limbo of the unborn, their innocence the innocence of bee grubs, plump and white, drenched in honey, absorbing sweetness through their soft skins. Slumbrous their souls, bliss-filled, abstracted.

—J. M. COETZEE, *Age of Iron*

Acknowledgments

This book had many midwives. Above all I wish to thank Margot Guralnick, Jay Leibold, and Lanette Smith for their time and care in helping me choose the words. David Rosenthal, my editor, was wise, profane, and indispensable, as usual. Mary Eshbaugh Hayes, Gib Gardner, Karen Chamberlain, Lauretta Bonfiglio, Elizabeth Kaplan, and Terry McDonell found or gave me work, for which I'm grateful. Other help in Aspen came from Paul Andersen, Paul Chesley, Tina Collen, Jill Uris, Leon Uris, Jody Guralnick and Michael Lipkin, Don Stuber, Tukey Koffend, Bo Persiko, Janie Bennett, Fritz Benedict, Hal Clifford, Robin Scarlett, Stacy Standley, Julie Peters, Nancy Pfister, and Bruce Berger and his sweet piano. I also greatly benefited from the ideas of Rick Larson, Seth Lloyd, Simon Boughton, Margo Conover, Mark Stevens, Jacquelyn Wonder, Melora Wolff, John Thorndike, and Rand Cooper. Raymond and Moana Beim, Elizabeth and David Beim, Estelle Guralnick, Brad and Ruth Segal, Judy Stein, and Rebecca Buechler aided me in other generous ways. Sterling Lord, my agent, has been behind me from the start.

Much of this book was written at The Writers Room in New York City; I and numerous others are grateful to the people who support it.

To protect their privacy, I have changed the names and a few particulars of the stories of others I got to know in Aspen. Theirs is still, in many ways, a small town. Neither they nor any of those listed above bear responsibility for the pages that follow; mistakes, in fact or judgment, are mine alone.

Whiteout

*They Call Me
Mellow Yellow*

The snow fell. The wind blew. Gusts from over the frozen hedge carried the sounds of people having fun and the smell of a hot tub. Young men made jokes and young women laughed; all I could see over the hedge was steam rising through a spotlight. But I could imagine them, naked, surrounded by bubbles, perspiration on their foreheads, warm except for the wind on their faces and the beer in their hands.

I bent over the engine of the cab. The daytime driver, Herb, had parked away from a streetlight, so under the hood it was completely dark. Checking the oil before beginning my shift was a nightly ritual, but normally I could see and my hands weren't frozen. The dipstick eluded me, and the engine still felt hot: Herb must have worked the full twelve hours.

The flashlight was missing, which meant that Richard, who leased us the Chevy Suburban, had borrowed it again. I tried to light a match, but the wind blew it out. Over the hedge, somebody popped open another beer can. The oil check was an operation you couldn't perform with gloves on. Finally, I located the dipstick. I wiped it off with some newspaper, spent another five minutes relocating the hole, and then stuck it back in for the measurement. Next, opening the driver's door with one hand to turn on the dome light,

I leaned inside with the dipstick—down two quarts, as usual. There was a case of oil in the back deck.

I couldn't find anything to protect my hand from the hot oil filler cap, so I sacrificed the end of my parka sleeve. I got a grip on the cap, unscrewed it, and—shit—dropped it. Somewhere into the engine. I tipped in the first quart of oil and started feeling gingerly around the distributor cap, the spark-plug cables, down by the alternator. Nothing. I looked under the cab, onto the packed snow of the parking space. Not there. I would have to reach back further, which effectively sacrificed the front of my parka to the accumulated grime of the front grille.

I didn't know what these parts of the engine were, but I knew my numbing hands might not be able to register if they were hot, and this worried me. I moved them around lightly and tentatively, blind. In the meantime, I could hear splashing and the slapping of bare feet on wet concrete—the action was picking up poolside. More beer cans were popped open, though the smell of oil on my hands made it harder to imagine drinking one. *"Here, Sally, catch!"* From the corner of my eye I saw a Frisbee thrown from a balcony and heard it skitter across the deck. Moments later, a voice from the balcony seemed to be calling to me.

"Hey, bro'! Can you toss us the Frisbee?"

I straightened my back and looked around. The Frisbee had traveled over the hedge, maybe carried by the wind, and landed not far away. I considered the Frisbee. In weather as cold as this, I happened to know, a tap from above can shatter a Frisbee. The Frisbee looked wet, and it was probably warm, from having been in the tub, but in a couple of moments it would be very cold.

Stalling, I cupped my hands and blew in them to warm them up, trying not to touch my face because they were dirty.

"Dude! The Fris'!"

With my half-frozen claws, I got a clumsy grip on the disk. I thought about it for a moment and then sent it flying back over the hedge, motor oil around the edge.

"Thanks, blood." Young white people, on vacation. You were their driver. You worked for them, and were best off to remember it.

I gave up on the oil filler cap and stuffed a wad of newspaper tightly into the opening. With more newspaper and my pants leg,

I wiped my oily hands, then started up the car and turned on the heat. It was 6:30 P.M., time to go to work, and I was a mess. I turned on the cab radio and was reassured to hear the voice of my favorite dispatcher, the link between me and the others of my trade.

"K-ninety-one, signing on," I said, grasping the microphone with some difficulty.

"Hello, stranger," said Susan. "Why not shoot the Port?"

"Ten-four." Another night in Aspen.

From the beginning, I had some ill intent. Not a grudge, really, because there was nothing personal between me and Aspen, but a bad feeling, let's call it, about the town and what it represented. To be skeptical about Aspen, it seemed to me, was to take a position against hype and elitism. It was to endorse traditional values of my state, like neighborliness and a dislike of pretension, and to eschew trendiness, in-crowds, and the influence of cities like New York and Los Angeles.

I grew up skiing at a publicly owned area, an hour and a half from Denver, called Winter Park. My ski club, with hundreds of kids in it, was called the Eskimos, and the Eskimo train left Denver every Saturday morning during the season for Winter Park and returned at night. The train was hot and crowded and noisy, but we learned how to ski. Aspen was for people with their own ski houses, for people from out of state, for people of means.

Downhill skiing, at the time, was still a fairly new sport. Whether in Aspen or Winter Park, it was about the outdoors, about exercise, about speed and discipline and fun. Those were days of Arlberg straps, wooden skis, and lace-up boots. As years went by, though, skiing changed. Those who promoted skiing—the resorts, the developers, the equipment manufacturers—came up with a couple of different ideas to attach to skiing. One had to do with life-style and status: A certain *kind* of person skied, we learned—a leisured, up-scale person. And another was eternal youth. A full-page advertisement placed in a magazine by the newly constituted Colorado Tourism Board pictured a guy riding on a double chair lift with his husky. "Your request for a return to childhood," read the headline, "has been granted."

It may be hard to imagine this seductive advertisement irritating anybody, but I grew up in Colorado. Colorado, at some point during my teenage years, came to recognize that in skiing and ski promotion lay riches; and Colorado, a state barely a hundred years old that until recently had been concerned with mining, farming, ranching, and some summer sightseeing, decided it was going to be about fun. Colorado became tourist-hungry.

In the sixties, seventies, and eighties, Aspen and I, both young, developed and grew older. Aspen during these years became a sort of paradigm for Rocky Mountain tourism: a small mountain town that built on its mining roots, kept its soul, promoted the arts, and attracted skiers from around the world. People in other parts of Colorado, including many of my parents' friends, were *worshipful* of Aspen: its tastefulness, its reputation. It seemed to be that rarest of things, a cosmopolitan small town. Having a stake in Aspen said something about you that was good.

But Aspen was hyped, and hype distorts. Whereas I grew up and learned about a larger world during those years, Aspen, it seemed to me, never did. Though open to the outside, Aspen remained childlike, concerned with itself, spoiled with lots of money and attention. A core of caring Aspenites banded together in the seventies and tried to gain some control over what was happening to their home, but the ethos of Aspen—what Aspen promoted—was anti-responsibility. The town was, in essence, a resort; it was about pleasure and escape. In Aspen, Peter Pans could find a Never-Never Land.

If Aspen was the paradigm, I thought, was this where we all were heading? By the early 1980s, the perennial trickle of movie stars swelled into a flood, and the town was drawing the very, very wealthy. In 1983, as I returned from several months of freight-hopping around the West and sat down to write a book about life among railroad hoboes, I read in *The Denver Post* that in Aspen, a town of six thousand full-time residents, more million-dollar homes had been sold in the past year than in Denver, a city of 1.8 million. In 1986, when I returned from a year of work and travel among illegal immigrants from Mexico, I noticed that Aspen had gained equal billing with Denver on *USA Today*'s national weather map. Over Christmas a year or two later, sixty to sixty-five private jets were crowding Sardy Field, Aspen's tiny airport. People I met on trips out of state, or out of the country, would say things like, "You're from Colorado? Oh, we ski in Aspen!" as if Aspen had anything to do with life in the rest of the state.

At the same time, I was curious. Aspen was like a pretty, rich girl with a reputation for being bad. Though unsuitable for the long term, you might want to go out with a girl like that. In 1988, I was struggling with a first novel in Denver and looking for distractions. When I heard that my friend Alex had bought the Mellow Yellow Taxi Company, an Aspen institution, I thought perhaps I'd found one. Now, there was a way I could see myself in Aspen, I thought— as a working stiff, a witness to the seamy underside. Nighttime cab driving would be even better (i.e., worse), and nighttime cab driving during high season would be better yet. As a friend of mine who had lived there liked to say, "Winter is when the toilet bowl of Aspen overflows and fertilizes the town for the next year." He was referring to all the money that businesses took in, but it seemed to me the metaphor had a broader meaning.

I kept my apartment in Denver, in case things didn't work out. But the thought of Aspen had me hooked. Maybe I could write about it; but if not, I would still have had some fun. I went to Aspen on a blind date, to see how far I could get. I went to sample an exotic and unknown flavor. The possibility that such an adventure could cost me scarcely entered my mind.

"Shoot the Port" meant go to Sardy Field, where cabbies spent much of their day (or night). The airport was Aspen's front door, the ceremonial entry to the town. For years the main gateway was Highway 82, the two-lane road from downvalley. But Killer 82, so named because of the narrow, treacherous curves that claimed several lives a year, now functioned mainly as a service entrance. Sky-rocketing housing prices in Aspen had turned most workers into commuters, forcing them to live downvalley, in towns like Basalt and Carbondale. The long lines of workers' cars and pickup trucks clogged the uphill lane of 82 at dawn, the downhill lane at dusk, while overhead passed the commuter planes and private jets carrying tourists, absentee owners, and locals of the employer class.

In fact, the two entryways came uncomfortably close to touching at the runway's western end. There, incoming planes, having just passed, by the reckoning of most passengers, rather too near to a mountain on one side of the narrow upper valley, buzzed Highway 82 seconds before touching down. If you happened to be in a car at the wrong time and hadn't seen it coming, the shadow and the roar would make your heart race. At night, you could usually see the lights of the plane from a distance, from down the valley, eerily slow until the instant they flashed overhead and revealed the fuselage. It was like a visitation of the future on the past, this strafing of the highway by pricey small planes—and in the high season it happened, on the average, every five minutes.

Awaiting me curbside at the front of the taxi queue were two women and perhaps twelve pieces of Louis Vuitton luggage. "Staying a long time?" I asked with a smile. The bags, fifty cents additional each, were fine with me.

"Just a week," one of them replied in a soft French accent. I opened the door for them.

Ingratiating yourself with customers is easier in a resort town, because there is a mutual understanding that they know little and you know a lot. As the first local they encounter, you can become a sort of one-man welcoming committee. They would tell you the name of their condo, and you would say, "Where are y'all from?"

"Los Angeles," they replied. They were blond, lovely, foreign.

"You are French?"

"Yes, we work for Chanel. It is all right that we wear our furs here?"

"All right?"

"Yes—zere is no law?"

I laughed and then they laughed. "No, you don't have to check your furs at the airport. The referendum failed, and it was only over whether furs should be *sold* here, anyway. Some people don't like them, but there is no law."

"Oh good. You know the Paradise club?" I couldn't tell which one was asking, because neither was really in the rearview mirror, but it didn't matter.

"Sure, the High Altitude Paradise. Do you want to go there?"

"Oh yes," she said emphatically. "Our friends told us all about it." I pictured them at the Paradise, your basic downstairs dance club except for the fact it was in Aspen. They would, I felt, be a sensation at the Paradise. "What else, where else should we go?"

I told them their other choices and about some of the restaurants.

They wanted to know everything about Aspen, from snow conditions (*three inches yesterday*) to which areas we were passing (*Buttermilk Mountain is on the right—it's for beginners and intermediates—and up behind it is Aspen Highlands, a bit tougher. Aspen Mountain rises directly above town, where we're headed—locals call it Ajax, after an old mine up there*) to what elevation we were at (*8000 feet*).

"Oh, and every alcoholic drink you have up here counts for about one and a half drinks at sea level—they're about 50 percent stronger at this altitude, which is about the only way you're going to save any money staying in Aspen."

It was the Aspen primer, which I repeated maybe a dozen times a day. "To the left and back, uphill a ways, is Starwood—that's where John Denver lives, where Claudine Longet—French, right?—shot her lover, Spider Sabich, the ski racer in '76." We were driving up the Roaring Fork Valley, at the top of which Aspen is perched. Highway 82 continued on through town, snaking its way up to the 12,095-ft. summit of Independence Pass. But the pass was so treacherous—with the road barely twelve feet wide in spots, and huge drop-offs that made it subject to avalanches—that it was closed from November to May or so, turning Aspen into a cul-de-sac and adding to the sense of Shangri-la.

Driving up 82, you wound through a couple of small canyons, passed across large meadows, spanned chasms with Maroon and Castle Creeks far beneath and, at the city's limit, passed Aspen's most pretentious little sign: The town's sister cities, it announced, were Chamonix, France; Davos, Switzerland; and Garmisch-Partenkirchen, Germany. Immediately, then, you found yourself, with a sudden zigzag of the road, on Main Street, Aspen, Colorado. It was beautiful at night, and my passengers aahed.

Before us lay a wide concourse, gently sloping down, snow-packed white and glittering with old-fashioned gas-style streetlights, which someone thought it wouldn't be too hokey to wrap in white lights and pine boughs. "The miners who founded Aspen had great hopes," I noted; Aspen had a main street fit for a metropolis. It was the longest street in town and by far the widest, a sort of Park Avenue of the Rockies. Main Street, in fact, had been laid out to line up exactly with majestic 12,953-foot Mt. Sopris, the peak at the end of the Elk Range that could be seen the length of the valley.

When it wasn't too polluted, that is. Yes, even Aspen had air pollution, among the worst of any city in Colorado. At night it became invisible, but in daylight you could see it from up on the mountain, looking down from the slopes. It was polluted in the old days, too, with all the silver smelters and coal-fired steam trains. But modern Aspen had pollution of a unique and appropriate sort. Some of it was car exhaust, but a bigger part was smoke from condominium fireplaces, dust kicked up by the gravel used on icy roads and, most pungent, restaurant grill emissions. On one block it was the smell of steaks, the next one, mesquite or Chinese. This was a town where the dirty air could make you hungry.

We saw a police car, and I told the women about the passenger I had from Michigan who lost twenty dollars on a bet to his friend that the police car they'd passed *couldn't* have been a Saab. He was wrong. The department had seven of them, Saab 9000's, about $30,000 each. He had neglected to realize that on entering Aspen, he was really entering a sort of fourth dimension. Yes, those city buses were free, and the racks on the side were for skis; in the summer, they put bike racks on the front. The British Aerospace 142 jet they had arrived on looked just like a Boeing 767 shrunk down to about one fifth of the size. It was a parade of toyland vehicles.

Finally, I pointed out to my passengers other landmarks: the historic Hotel Jerome, at Main Street and Mill, Aspen's main intersection and site of its first traffic light, in 1973; the post office—important, like the airport, as a link to the outside world and similarly equipped with solar-energy panels; the headlights of Sno-Cats grooming the runs way up Aspen Mountain, which met the town at the gondola building and Little Nell Hotel. That was the main stuff, and certainly enough of an introduction for the moment. Other things, they would soon learn for themselves. How icy-cold the water came out of the taps, for example—mountain-stream cold. How fast the sun could burn at this altitude, with everything white. How men and women would not be afraid to look at each other on the street here: so often, I had found, women in Aspen would hold your gaze, instead of breaking it. How they would love it here and want to belong.

It felt good to offer information, to feel like a friend of two such pretty women. I drove them first to a real estate office, where they picked up their condo keys from a guy who knew two or three phrases of flirtatious French and offered to show them around later, and then on to the condo. They were crestfallen to see it was not a very nice building. It was on a busy corner, and they were on the top floor, without an elevator. I offered to help carry the bags up, which was beyond the call of duty. "Oh no!" cried Nicole when she opened the door. The room was minuscule, a studio. They had gotten it from a travel agent. The beds were the fold-out type and would just about fill the available space when extended. They had been misled, but had paid in advance. I said not to worry, they'd be spending all their spare time at the Paradise club anyway. They gave me a small tip.

I called in 10-7 and decided to cruise downtown to the cab stand. It was disappointing, back in the cab. Eager newcomers could elevate a "local" like me, make him feel important because of all he knew. But now, even if I were to meet them in the Paradise, offer to buy them drinks, they would know I was just a cab driver. And they did not overdraw their accounts in L.A. to come to Aspen and meet a cab driver. Working in Aspen encouraged you to be unrealistic, by dangling beautiful treats in front of your face, like carrots in front of horses. And somehow, in Aspen, you were dumb enough that the carrot would make you go.

To be an Aspen cabbie is to be, in one sense, an official voyeur. No one else sitting in his car at the end of one of Aspen's cobbled pedestrian malls, lights out, night after night, would be above suspicion. But as a cabbie, it's your business to be parked where the people are, waiting for a fare, and if you've got nothing better to do than sit back and stare through the windshield, nobody's going to fault you for it. An occasional flick of the wiper button kept the windshield free of evening snow, and the warm wind of the defroster kept everything clear and cozy.

It wasn't simply people-watching—it was more like spectating at a parade, Aspen at night. During season it was mainly the tourists walking by, and many had come to be somebody else for a while. Here, the part of the stockbroker that really wanted to be a ski instructor came out; here, the lawyer could shed the corporate straight-lacing and try another role. It showed in their clothes: outrageously bright colored, outrageously revealing, or outrageously expensive, clothes that would be hard to wear anywhere else. *Recreation* comes from the Latin *recreare*—to re-create (one-self). From the taxi, you got to see people as they thought they ought to be.

The Beach was a nickname that carried over from the summer season, when a gurgling fountain, shorts, and tanning oil made the taxi stand into something like a lifeguard post. Winter or summer, from there you could see them all: the rich and famous, the rich and obscure, the young and the restless, the domestic and the foreign, the blond and the bleached blond. As a taxi driver, the Beach was a good place to find yourself midevening as the people you had taken to dinner beginning around 6 P.M. reemerged in search of a ride home.

The watching got better later—at around ten or ten-thirty, by which time the more sedate couples were headed home to heal the wounds of the day's skiing and the restless were preparing to drink and dance. As the clubs geared up, sidewalks and pedestrian malls came alive. Moderate cover charges made switching back and forth between clubs popular, and all the best ones were within about three blocks of each other: the Paragon, the Paradise, Andre's, Club An-diamo, the Tippler, the Caribou Club.

On the Beach, to a driver, there were two worlds: the outside world, of people on the mall, and the inside world—the world through your cab radio. The radio was where your mind was: You got to hear who else was on duty, where they were going, what the roads were like there. It bound drivers together, in a loose way: our names became numbers (K-91, K-10, K-24—up to fifteen of us or so on a busy night), and other familiar words turned into code, which only the drivers, never the passengers, could understand.

As a driver, you always listened to the radio, no matter where you were. And time at the Beach, between fares, was always best if Susan was the dispatcher.

A San Francisco debutante and daughter of a diplomat, Susan had come to Aspen in the sixties, when doing so was still an act of rebellion. She purchased a Checker cab, painted it a blue metal-flake, and became the first female driver in town. Now a good-looking forty-five or so, she was the grande dame of Mellow Yellow cab drivers, a sexy sort of mother-figure with a raspy smoker's voice and quick wit. A fixture at places like the Midland Bar in Basalt, a working-class bistro where she collected cover charges and improved the general atmosphere, she was, as dispatcher, sympathetic, efficient, and knowledgeable, anything but all business. She was the first person in Aspen I liked.

"I need some vitamin C and a new psyche," she announced to all the drivers. Somebody radioed in to tell her of a magazine called *New Psyche*. "Then maybe there's hope," she said.

An hour or two later, she came on the air again, laughing. "I'm sorry—it's Letterman," she explained. "He's got the guy from the zoo on again. Big birds." A small TV kept the dispatchers amused between calls. There was a brief silence as one of the drivers radioed in a thought. "Yeah, the mating call of the turkey, we hear it every day," she agreed. *Turkey* was the old tourist-town word for tourist.

"Anybody coming by the office? I'm hungry. I want a Hershey bar . . . What kind? A male Hershey bar, one with nuts."

Aspen cabbies had a more specific argot, unique to the job. Mainly it consisted of puns on the pretentious names of certain restaurants or condos, or anything else you could do something funny with. If Susan said, "K-7, shoot to Chocolate Éclair, 205," she wanted cab K-7 to speed to Château Eau Claire, a condo on the river, and knock on the door of room 205. "Pick up at Krab's" meant a fare was waiting at Krabloonik, a game restaurant located at a large husky kennel, where you could go for dogsled rides during the day. "Poor Old France" was Pour La France, a popular cappuccino-and-croissant place. The Grand Aspen Hotel was often called the "Grahnd Ahspen," in mimicry of the pronunciation of its wealthy Palestinian owner, the developer Mohammed Hadid. Snowmass Village was sometimes "Silly Little Village." "Have you dropped?" meant, of course, "Have you gotten rid of your passengers?" but it always evoked for me a large pregnant mammal about to give birth. And if, late at night, a "DVD" was "DFR," the dispatcher would understand that a "downvalley degenerate" was "down the fuckin' road"—or off the roster and headed downvalley, to a worker's town like Basalt, to get some sleep.

And then there were cab codes. 10-4 meant, of course, "got it," or "okay," or "I understand." 10-5 meant you were free, available to accept a run. 10-7 or Code 7 meant you were out of the cab and away from radio contact—going to the bathroom, for example. 10-20 or

"What's your 20?" meant a request for your location. And 10-55 or "I'm on a 55" meant you were busy with a walk-up, a nondispatched fare.

With the opening of a back door—it always seemed abrupt—the parade would enter your cab.

So, partner, can you take us to Snowmass? The middle-aged couple was holding hands, the woman in a mink and the man in a cowboy hat and long, fleece-lined leather coat.

Hi, do you know where the Boomerang Lodge is? The red-haired woman wore a tight black miniskirt, black nylons, heels, and nylon racing jacket, the man, blue jeans, a Western shirt, and black leather jacket. The budget lodge was a short ways away. "You're almost home," I said. "By the way, how do you stay warm in that?" *Oh. The skirt? It's winter weight.* She smiled.

Hey, can you fit eight over to the Aspen Club Lodge? The group appeared to be some sort of package tour, minus their leader. "Aspen Club Lodge is only three blocks away—you still want a ride?" *It is?*

We're going up Red Mountain. We'll show you the way. The couple, in their fifties, was dressed in furs and soft leathers. They didn't say another word until I turned into the circular drive of their multimillion-dollar house, just, *Left here. Next right. Keep a dollar.*

Hey, pal. The young man, maybe twenty, climbed with difficulty into the front seat opposite me. He tried reaching into the front pocket of his jeans, hard to do when you're sitting down. Finally, he extracted two wadded-up dollar bills. *Can you take me home? This is all I got. I'd really 'preciate it.* The base fare, before the ride ever started, was $1.75 and charity a hard call in a place like Aspen. He seemed like a good guy, if exceedingly drunk. "Where you going?" It was nearby. *Hey man, you're the greatest. You know what? I'm gonna get you a Bud. Don't go away, okay? A Bud. You wait here.* He stumbled inside, and I expected him to return with a can of Budweiser. Instead, he had a minuscule Ziploc bag. It contained a "bud" of marijuana. *Enjoy, man, enjoy.*

Three-twenty-nine Snowbunny St. The next passenger was a local; something about the presence said so, as well as the use of a street address instead of a lodge. *Whew—that's a long fuckin' day of work. I just flew in from L.A. today. Left for there yesterday.* "What do you do?" *I rep. Ski repped for years, but now I do clothing. I'm just switching to a new line, out of Finland. It's called Eero—good stuff. This jacket's one of theirs. I don't know you, do I?* "No, just moved here." *Yeah, well, good luck. This town's goin' to hell. I've lived here seven years, and I've done everything. Worked on tours, worked in stores, worked for the ski company, man, I've done it all. And still I can barely make my payments. Everybody's in my situation . . . 'cept the trust-funders. I figure, if you can make it for seven years, you deserve to live here.*

Between these walk-up fares, your name would periodically make it to the top of the dispatch list. Every cab had a number.

"K-ninety-one, you free?"

"Yep."

"Table 5, Charlemagne."

I sped over to the ornate, pricey restaurant on Main Street. It occupied a big yellow restored Victorian house, and much of the dining room was within an unusual octagonal room in the front of the house; billowy fabric hung from the ceiling, giving the whole thing a boudoir feeling. Dinner for two could easily exceed $200. Nobody was waiting at the curb, so I parked and went in.

I sat myself on a little bench in the foyer, to await the maître'd. Finally, the tuxedoed man bustled in, spotted me, picked up a menu, and approached. "Dessert for one, sir?" he asked.

"Excuse me?" I said. I was in my ever-dirtier parka, gloves sticking out of its pockets, scuffed Sorel boots, jeans, and a jean jacket under the parka. A certain sort of paranoid driver could have taken it the wrong way, figured the guy was making fun of him, and told him to go fuck himself. But Aspen was still informal—in what other town could a taxi driver be mistaken for an upscale diner? "Mellow Yellow, for table 5."

"Ah yes, of course."

My passengers were three women from Ohio, headed to Snowmass with large numbers of shopping bags we retrieved from the coat check. They were well dressed, prosperous, and having a ball.

"Such great shops here!" enthused one to me, as we drove from the restaurant. "We'd planned to go home and freshen up, but then Jean said, 'Heck, girls, let's just go straight through to dinner!' And we did." There was laughter. They were in Aspen alone, the three of them. They didn't ski. They were glad to be away from their husbands. They were pleased with everything.

"Isn't this a fun town?" said Jean. "Everyone here has such a fun attitude. It's so positive. Upbeat!" They wanted me to agree, so I did. These women were in heaven.

On returning, I was sent to a fancy sporting goods store on Mill St. The passenger was a salesperson, and she jumped right into the front seat—a sign of working-class solidarity. Usually, workers at the end of their shift were exhausted, but she had so much pent-up emotion I could tell things hadn't gone well. She had that lemme-outta-here attitude.

"Not a great night?" I asked.

"I could scream," she said. "I just spent hours with a bunch of Greyhound people. You know, from Bumfuck, Iowa, or someplace. They asked every little thing: 'Will this be on sale?' 'Could I try on that one instead?' God! And it was like that all night."

I wondered if my ladies from Ohio had been in there. If so, no doubt they had seen a salesgirl who was cute as pie. But privately, Aspen sales- and waitpeople often adopted an upper-class impatience with customers. Or a sense of entitlement: If the customer paid for a nine-dollar fare with a hundred-dollar bill and then tipped me only a dollar, I would sometimes feel outraged: I knew people were spending a fortune to stay in Aspen, and saw no reason why they should skimp on me. My best tips, in any case, always came from the workers.

I dropped off my fare, stopped for gas, and called Susan on the radio. "K-ninety-one, back in the hack."

"You're number eight, 91." Seven drivers were ahead of me in the wait for passengers, and there was more than an hour till the bar-closing rush. I parked, sat back, closed my eyes.

Susan came back on the air. "K-ninety-one, how many Aspenites does it take to screw in a light bulb?" I sat up and thought about it.

"Um, tell me."

"None, they screw in hot tubs."

Other drivers radioed in their laughter. Back in the hack.

The source of these broadcasts, the Mellow Yellow office, was one of three centers of my Aspen cab world, the other two being the Beach and the Port. I hazarded my way upon the office after trying for two weeks, from Denver, to get through on the phone. Alex had said to call then, to see when I would start driving. But by early December it was too late: The phones were tied up, constantly.

It wasn't easy finding the office. Most Aspen businesses that aren't restaurants, hotels, or retail shops—first-line tourist services—are conveniently kept out of the way in a planned development called the Aspen Business Center. Opposite the airport, this labyrinthine development contains offices for everything from Federal Express to pool-and-Jacuzzi maintenance companies to KSPN, "Your Higher Elevation Station." I circled for about an hour, past the conveniently located office of the competition, High Mountain Taxi, with its well-kept cabs painted with clean logos and an easy-to-recall phone number (925-TAXI), looking for the Mellow Yellow office. Then finally, noticing a motley gathering of dirty cabs with a sixties-style logo emblazoned, in yellow, green, and red, on the doors—MELLOW YELLOW TAXI, it read, in Old West lettering arching in a semicircle of sun behind snowcapped peaks—I started trying the unmarked doors.

One of them opened, revealing something not unlike a large, long closet in a state of pandemonium. Several whiskery guys, in dirty clothes and wet boots, were maneuvering past each other with cash and papers in their hands. One short one wore a huge button, about eight inches across, that said MELLOW YELLOW. The voice of Patsy Cline sang from a tape player. This was the place.

At a desk behind them, doing her nails, sat a woman who told me her name was Kim. She was a bleached blonde dressed in black and, somehow, in the midst of the turmoil, managing to look bored. Later I would learn she was a driver doing a stint as receptionist while the matter of a few traffic tickets got worked out. Alex, she said, was in another room and too busy to attend to me just then. She didn't think she could help me, either. A huge mongrel dog, named Buster, put his head in my lap, depositing a soggy ball. "I think he wants you to throw it," Kim suggested. I smiled wanly, flicked the ball off, and watched Buster go after it.

At this moment, an intelligent, friendly-looking mustachioed albino blew in the door.

"This is McGarry, the field supervisor," said Kim. "He can probably help you."

I held out my hand to shake, but the field supervisor, steadfastly avoiding eye contact with anyone, only stamped his snow-covered Sorel boots on the carpet and announced he didn't want to talk to anybody. And he wanted to pass by where I was standing. It was the door to the bathroom. I got out of the way.

Kim, idly removing lint from her black tights with tape from the dispenser on her desk, explained that he was "just in a bad mood." I heard a voice call for Buster from the open door at the end of the office and thought, Thank goodness, it's Alex. I poked my head through the door—it was the dispatch room, not Alex's office, and in there was a bald guy using one hand to massage his forehead while the other pressed down the talk bar on the microphone in front of him. KEEP OUT, said a sign on the door. I backed away.

"That's Steve Clark," said Kim. "He gets bad headaches." He had suffered from them, she explained, ever since he made his first parachute jump and the chute didn't open. He fell two thousand feet, landing on a soft field. The only ill effects, she said, had been these headaches.

I wondered how he could be sure, though, given that he worked at Mellow Yellow. Who wouldn't get a headache here? Buster, blocking the narrow aisle, was cursed by McGarry as he exited the bathroom. Alex, in a brief appearance, opened a door to chew out Kim and said to tell all callers that he wasn't there. There was a constant ringing of phones, which never seemed to get answered. From the boom box atop the file cabinets Patsy Cline sang, "I Fall to Pieces."

"This is Kim's theme song," yelled Steve Clark from the dispatch room.

"Crazy" was Clark's, Kim said to me.

"Clark who?" I asked.

"Steve Clark's. *Steve's.*"

The minutes went by, more than an hour, and I tried to soak it all in. There was a newspaper clipping on the wall: A Mellow Yellow driver had recently been arrested following an altercation with a limousine driver who he felt was jumping the line at the airport. The KEEP OUT sign on the door to the dispatch room was universally ignored. On a counter, a sign had been set up requesting donations for the treatment of Mellow Yellow's accountant, who had been critically injured in a wreck on Highway 82 the week before. The scene in the office was crazed, hilarious, sobering.

Aspen taxi driving had long been on the lunatic fringe. It all started with Natalie Gignoux's Little Percent Taxi Company, a two-car enterprise that promised customers its profit would be only a "little percent" of the fare charged. Briefly, there had been a company called Quick Silver. Mellow Yellow, named after the Donovan song, had come along a few years later. The founders, three transplanted New Jerseyans, salvaged old Checker cabs from taxi companies in Texas and spent their evenings drinking beer and fixing them up. CBS *60 Minutes* correspondent Mike Wallace was said to have put his foot through the rear floor of one rusted old Mellow Yellow taxi; another time, an unsuspecting driver drove a passenger who hailed him outside the county jail all the way down to Glenwood Springs, from which the escaped prisoner fled into the wilderness.

The situation had changed dramatically, though, with the appearance in 1980 of High Mountain Taxi. David Hyman, a former Mellow Yellow driver, had seen the quaintness of the company as a vulnerability, in business terms, and started his own company. With Aspen growing and public patience waning with the laid-back "hippie" approach, the aggressive High Mountain gained quickly on its older, funkier rival. It soon became clear to old-timers that Hyman wanted not simply to live and let live, but to make money and even wipe out the competition.

Anywhere else this would not seem novel, but in Aspen, for years a haven for those wanting out of the rat race, it seemed horrifying, a betrayal. Mellow Yellow had always been a chummy, seat-of-the-pants operation, never organized to make anyone rich. High Mountain, by contrast, was corporate-minded and uptight: it charged higher fares than Mellow Yellow, required drivers to report every fare to the dispatcher, and enforced tight standards of cab maintenance and appearance.

The birth of High Mountain had sparked the "cab wars," a period of taxi vandalism and radio sabotage that had left some drivers still not on speaking terms. And for old-time drivers and others, it mirrored a more general trend in the history of Aspen, the progressive spoiling of paradise by "greedheads," there not simply to enjoy the laid-back life-style but to exploit it by making money.

"Whose cab did you say Alex told you to drive?" Kim asked me during a lull in traffic.

"Richard Schwartz's."

"Richard Schwartz? Oh, I know him."

"He looks like one a them sucker-fish you pull out of a stream when you're fishing—it's that funny mouth of his," offered Steve Clark from around the corner in the dispatch room.

"No—you know what he looks like? Like a baby bird before it gets its feathers."

These people didn't like Richard Schwartz, but they did know how to find him. "Sure, I've got his beeper number right here," Kim said. Now she tells me, I thought. I made the call, he returned it, and half an hour later I was standing at the Woody Creek International Raceway.

Though Aspen, by this time a fast town, was home to famed race car drivers Janet Guthrie (first woman in the Indy 500) and Danny Sullivan, the oval dirt raceway, a few miles out of town, was old and funky. Executive Security International, an Aspen firm that trained bodyguards and did a brisk mail-order business in things like remote listening devices, staged fake kidnappings of executives there as part of its regular curriculum. Other days, I had seen adults in big go-carts racing circles in the dust. On the utilitarian side, it had a garage that was rented to guys like cab drivers who wanted to work on their cars.

Richard Schwartz was in there in coveralls. Kim and Steve had been right: He did look an unhappy mix of fish and fledgling. He was in a bad mood. Though I had spoken to him less than an hour before, he seemed hardly to remember who I was. He complained about Mellow Yellow, complained about Alex, and complained about the cab. It wasn't ready to drive yet, he whined. It didn't have snow tires because he couldn't afford them. More serious, because Alex hadn't provided them, it didn't have any light on top, radio, or meter, much less the glorious four-color Mellow Yellow door decal. The underlying complaint, I would later appreciate, was that he was missing out on the start of the season.

But the cab was ready a few days later, and I drove over to Richard's place for my first taxi lesson. It was an old ten- or twelve-foot pull-behind trailer, parked on a dirt road at one edge of the airport. He was surprised to see me there, having again forgotten our appointment, but he turned off the huge TV, put out a joint, finished some Cheez-Whiz and crackers, and got into his eyeglasses, jacket, and boots. There was barely room for two people to move inside the tiny trailer. As he got ready, I read on the counter a notice from the county, advising him he was parked illegally. "They say I'm illegal, but that's a crock of shit," he explained. "They're just tryin' to keep me from getting a phone." Thus, the beeper.

We went outside and climbed in. The cab, like most others in Aspen, was a Chevrolet Suburban, really more truck than car. It was so high off the ground, there was an aluminum running board to step on to help you in. The height helped when snow was deep, however, as did the four-wheel drive and just the sheer weight of the thing. There were spacious, bench-style front and back seats, plus a third seat, for two, which was accessed via the middle seat. It carried eight comfortably, and often a few more uncomfortably.

In addition, the cab was outfitted with some standard Aspen cab gear—a big metal luggage rack welded to the roof, jumper cables ("Make sure you charge ten or fifteen bucks for that," Richard advised), and a chain for towing stuck cars out of snowbanks (worth even more).

Cab 91 was a veteran, with dysfunctions to show for it. The speedometer light, for instance, had burned out sometime over the course of the car's first hundred thousand miles, so as the night driver, you could never be sure exactly how fast you were going. Nor could you always be sure when the high beams were on, because that indicator was out, too. The windshield squirter didn't work, which could be murder in the spring, when roads were all covered with melting snow and mud. The locking gas cap would freeze, and admit the key only when you poured hot water on it. And occasionally, when you were shifting into four-wheel drive, the whole transmission would lock into neutral.

And one other thing: Cab 91 reeked of patchouli oil. The only use of patchouli oil I was familiar with was as a mask for the scent of marijuana smoke. Richard swore he knew nothing about it. Most passengers were polite enough not to mention it; they probably thought it was my cologne. One night, though, a drunken guy from the Eagles Club, having sat quietly for two blocks, blurted, "Ted, why does your cab smell like a rich fag?"

Richard, busy lecturing me on the need to drive carefully on the icy streets, backed into a rusty Red Camaro as he pulled up next to a gas pump in town. We stopped with a crunch: the grille. The driver, though aggrieved, was just into town and didn't want to hassle with it. He let Richard off the hook.

At this moment, a handsome, dark-haired young guy walked up to Richard and asked if it was him. "Yeah. Who are you?" Richard demanded. Bruce was the driver Richard had found to drive on days when I couldn't, but he had forgotten what he looked like. He had also forgotten an appointment to teach him the workings of the cab, two hours earlier, according to Bruce. When Richard was on the radio, I asked Bruce, "How did you know that was Richard in the cab?"

"I don't know. Intuition. I'm very spiritual," said Bruce. He was from Massachusetts and told me he didn't pay taxes because he didn't want to support the war machine. When he quit, Richard hired Herb, a quiet guy who did little but drive and sleep. He would never talk about himself, but one day I saw an ad in the paper with Herb's name in it: It was an exhibit of woven textiles, and Herb was one of the artisans. When the exhibit closed, Herb disappeared. Richard then hired Martin Ryan, whose alter ego I discovered one day listening to KSPN. It was a show "with the latest in today's music. And I'm your host, Modern Marty Ryan."

Richard had dropped off Bruce and eventually taken me to the big taxi oval at the Port. I would later realize that much of my anxiety about arriving at the Port stemmed from that first night.

"Turn off the lights, turn off your lights!" Richard had screamed as we arrived at the end of the line of cabs. "That's really bad, to come in with your lights on. It'll piss off the guy in front of you. And out here, there's always somebody that's pissed off about something." He had tried, that night, to handle the other cabbies with kid gloves. The cab in front of us, for example, was temporarily abandoned; perhaps the driver was having coffee inside. As the line moved up, I suggested we go around him, but the protocol about that was evidently strict, too: "He'll have a fit," said Richard. Finally, after a four-cab gap had opened up in front of him and passengers were waiting, Richard let me move up.

But then he was out of the cab in a flash, tucking pieces of our passengers' luggage under his arms and frantically loading them into the back. I, trying to stay relaxed, had begun lashing their skis to the roof rack when the driver behind us leaned out his window and yelled, "Hey, let's move it!" Our ten seconds were up; he wanted to load his fare; time was money.

For what I'd thought would be a laid-back job in a resort town, Aspen cab driving was proving very contentious. The main reason seemed to be the gold-rush mentality that infected workers during high season. Tourists were the mother lode, and there were only so many of them to go around. Drivers who worked year-round felt they paid their dues during slow periods and deserved preference during flush times; to them, seasonal drivers like myself (who were hired so the companies could answer all calls in high season) were like claim-jumpers. The attitude seemed to be, You were late on the scene and there will be less for me now, so fuck you.

Inside the airport, things weren't much better. If you were between planes and bored with jealously guarding your place in the queue, you could wander inside to grab a gourmet coffee and croissant at Pour La France. Or you could try to hustle the airline baggage agents.

These guys, in what was probably Aspen's worst job, presided over the daily bumper crop of late-arriving luggage, caused by bad-weather flight delays, cancellations, and apparent incompetence. Rows and rows of this luggage usually ringed the two baggage-claim areas. Irate tourists, not finding their bags in the piles, went over to browbeat the baggage agents. The agents didn't take it lying down.

"Goodbye, sir, I need to argue with the other people now," I heard an agent named Clyde say one night.

"Friend, I know Frank Lorenzo, and the next time I'm back through town, you're not gonna be here," threatened the customer, unimpressed by Clyde's scary broken bicuspid.

"Frank's my uncle," snarled back Clyde, gesturing the next complainant to the front.

When they could escape the angry hordes, the baggage agents attempted to parcel out the suitcases to cab drivers, who delivered them to condos, at seven to twelve dollars per item.

Friction between the drivers of Mellow Yellow and those of High Mountain Taxi also upped the stress level. That first night at the airport, Richard revealed that he had until recently driven for High Mountain. He left, he said, after a disagreement with David Hyman had come to fisticuffs. "I told him, 'You're the kind of guy that gives

Jews a bad name!' " Schwartz said to me. And then, apparently in his own defense, he added, "And I'm Jewish!" Why was Richard discharged? Certainly his combative attitude didn't help. "People either love me," explained Richard, "or they hate me and think I'm a real asshole." At least half of that, I could tell, was true.

On other nights, with Richard gone, I tried to make friends with some of the drivers. The airport queue seemed a good place to do it: Most were, after all, doing nothing more than sitting in their cabs, reading the paper. But my friendliness brought suspicion. They looked at me guardedly; they answered my chatty questions but asked none of their own; they froze me out. When I arrived in Aspen, I had expected these would be my working-class allies, comrades-in-arms against the elite, but it wasn't working out that way.

Susan, the dispatcher, had become sort of a friend. She seemed sharp and trustworthy, and I had told her about my idea of writing about Aspen and loaned her my two books. "Is there something wrong? Is it because I'm a temporary driver?" I asked one evening.

We were alone in the dispatch office. She leaned back in her chair with a cigarette. On the desktop she nursed an ice-filled glass of, probably, vodka. Through the smoke I saw her face, lined by the mountain sun, somehow sage. Asleep on the couch behind her lay her huge husky. You could see she'd been in Aspen a long time.

"I think it's time you came clean," she finally said.

"About what?"

"About what you're really doing here."

"I am coming clean. As I get to know people, I'm telling them."

"No, I mean come clean faster."

"Why?"

"Rumor's out that you're undercover for the DEA."

"What? You're joking! Why me?" Several new drivers had begun the season with me, and I couldn't see how I in particular had given any cause for suspicion.

"No facial hair, no earring," she said. "You're new. They're nervous."

"They think a narc wouldn't have facial hair?" I asked. "Are narcs that dumb?"

"Yes, narcs are that dumb," she replied with unnerving certainly. For a moment she appraised me through cigarette smoke. I nodded. It was a favor to me, not a point to be argued. I started telling them.

Slowly, things changed. Not everybody came around, but some did. A worry over the DEA didn't mean they all were dealers; drug use, even in the late eighties, was a fact of life in Aspen and most people had some contact with it. I pointedly avoided starting conversations on this topic, though non-drivers constantly would ask, "Hey, is it true you can score in a Mellow Yellow cab?"

Among the other drivers were some remarkable characters. Many had been drawn to Aspen because, especially in the sixties and seventies, it was a good place to be a character. Mellow Yellow's "working-class" drivers numbered such dropouts as a former pilot for Pan Am, a disillusioned psychiatrist, a former Playboy bunny, and a woman associated with the Chicago Seven.

Many, like Alex, the owner, an Ivy League graduate, were reformed overachievers. John Marshall caught my interest at the airport because of the lengths he'd gone to to have his 1977 Checker cab converted into a four-wheel drive—"the only 4 x 4 Checker in the world." The job, which left his taxi standing a good six inches higher than any other Checker, had cost the forty-seven-year-old Middlebury College graduate $12,500. Chronic back problems could not dissuade Marshall from a calling that was not good for his health, though the tall man often seemed in pain. He had come to Aspen twenty-five years before, he told me, on the heels of an Olympics-bound ski-racer classmate he was enamored of. When she left, he stayed on. Unmarried, he spent summers in a cabin near Silverthorne, Colorado; if he was careful, the winter taxi receipts would last him the year.

The interior of Marshall's cab was pasted with currency notes from seventy-five countries, all donated by foreign passengers. His yellow business card reflected well the spirit of the enterprise. JOHN MARSHALL, it read, EXPLORER—LOVER—GOURMET. THE ADVENTURESOME GIRL'S FRIEND. A list of services followed, including: WARS FOUGHT; GOVERNMENTS RUN; BRIDGES DESTROYED; UPRISINGS QUELLED; GULFS CROSSED; DAMS DESTRUCTED; SALOONS EMPTIED; VIRGINS CONVERTED; HOT OIL MASSAGES; ELEPHANTS BRED; WHISKEY, GUNS, MANURE, BUILDING MATERIALS, LAND, FLY SWATTERS, RACING

FORMS, DIRTY LINEN, REPOSSESSED COFFINS, GOLD MINES, EXTENDED TOURS. There was a small note at the bottom: NO AUTOGRAPHS PLEASE.

Sometimes I also talked to Jon Barnes, proprietor of the amazing disco cab. Barnes had spent hundreds of hours, and seemingly all his spare cash, turning his Checker into a rolling discotheque. I spotted this piece of impressive seventies kitsch parked at the Beach one night when I was with friends from out of town. "Cover charge tonight?" I had asked. "Climb in!" he yelled. Four of us squeezed into the back, ducking so as not to dislodge the revolving mirror-ball hung from the ceiling. Barnes hit the master switch, to the gasps of my friends. There were 160 lights, including the required black light and the laserlike beam that hit the mirrored ball, sending dots of light whirling around like in a planetarium. Next came the music. Turning in his seat to afford a position in front of two keyboards suspended on his right, he pulled a ceiling-mounted microphone to his mouth and launched into a rendition of "Back in the USSR." Drums and bass parts came in as soon as he had time to bring the synthesizer on-line, and a background tape, run through a little mixing board near the floor and thence through at least four speakers, filled out the experience.

We were dancing sitting down. A crowd started gathering outside the quaking cab; and as he launched into the more pensive "Hey, Jude," Barnes threw the lever on the fog machine. Mist wafted up around our legs, onto our laps. Barnes picked up an electronic saxophone, tilted his head back, and improvised. He wasn't a bad musician.

Despite the subfreezing temperature, it got too hot inside, so we rolled down the windows; this also let the spectators outside in on the fun. Before long members of the crowd, who appeared to be mainly middle-aged businessmen and their wives, were dropping rolled-up bills through the window into Jon Barnes's lap or foisting them into his hand, when it was free. Some tried to ask him questions and—probably because he had answered the exact same questions thousands of times and was thus prepared—he had a repertoire of quick ripostes.

"Why did you do it?" asked my friend Kate.

"I'm just trying to make a dull job more interesting," he answered.

"How much did it cost?" asked Liz.

"Who cares?" he answered. We tipped him ten bucks. "Thanks for not being another insurance salesman," said Liz as we climbed out. It seemed to me a sentiment even an insurance salesman might agree with.

Twelve-hour days behind the wheel had resulted in a small paunch problem and an increasing curiosity about the lives of my more prosperous passengers. To alleviate both, I decided to enroll in a health club, and of the five in the area, I joined the most popular and talked about.

You could see why the Aspen Club was so popular: It was almost perfect. Located on six wooded acres at the edge of town, the sprawling complex was well designed, well lit, and well run. The seven outdoor tennis courts and sandy beach–style volleyball court were, of course, unusable in the winter, but that still left six racquet-ball and three squash courts, nonstop aerobics classes, a swimming pool, a Nautilus room, a free-weight room, a room with StairMas-ters, treadmills, and other machines, a full-size gym for basketball, and a little natural-foods café overlooking three indoor tennis courts. To get from the parking lot to the front door you took a path that led through aspen groves and across a footbridge that spanned a burbling brook. The towels they gave you were big and fluffy and many people didn't bother to lock their lockers. The Aspen Club, being in Aspen, was like a club within a club, if you will, and things seemed pretty safe.

But this seeming perfection was itself a problem because it led the Aspen Club to think rather highly of itself. Ads it ran for locker-room attendants, in fact, bid the umemployed to "work for Aspen's best." Best club, did they mean, or best people? Large photos on the wall inside the lobby featured Martina Navratilova following through on a forehand, John McEnroe at the net, ski racer Phil Mahre, and actor Jack Nicholson, all photographed at the club. The best people, in the best club. The Aspen Club seemed to be institu-tionally conceited.

I went in for a tour and then visited the membership office. They had found somebody cute to give the bad news: A year's member-ship, with initiation fee, came to $1100—actually not as much as I'd thought. Unless, of course, my employer was on the preferred list.

"Mellow Yellow Taxi?" I asked dubiously. "No, uh, I don't think we have any taxi drivers here," she confirmed with a smile. I put it on a credit card, had my photo taken, and headed to the lockers.

There it became clear that this was not a place where people came to reduce—everyone was already reduced. Around me were a lot of supermen: blond guys, many of them middle-aged, with small waists and big muscles and all their hair. Down the bench from me a trim fellow with graying hair and teenage son in tow donned a pair of pink Lycra leggings. In my bag was a pair of old-style sweat pants, which I'd brought in case it was cold on the basketball court. I stuffed them way down to the bottom and hoped nobody would notice.

I changed into a T-shirt, shorts, and cross-trainers and followed the man's directions to the room with the electronic exercise machines. All were situated so that everyone was facing the same direction, the side of the room where the door was—this allowed everyone to plug headsets into their machines and watch a bank of large TV monitors overhead. It also allowed them to monitor new arrivals. I pulled my stomach in, mounted a StairMaster, and joined their ranks. These were the fabled hardbodies, the abdominal snowmen and snowwomen, people for whom exercise is like a drug. A woman I'd met while skiing one day told me she was headed here after the lifts closed, for "some upper body work." Jane Fonda, it was said, worked out in this room when she was in town; so did Schwarzenegger. Here exercised the upper ranks of the fitness culture, the committed, the obsessed, the body Nazis. The fitness ethic was enshrined at the Aspen Club: Here was where you worshiped.

Like the locker room, this exercise room was a hall of mirrors, and they were heavily used. Though people would look up and dab away the sweat when someone new walked into the room, most would then return to their exercise and their mirrors. There was an air of competition in the room, but my self-consciousness faded some as I noticed that my fellow members seemed less interested in sizing each other up than in admiring themselves. The solemn narcissism, if nothing else, took some of the pressure off.

Having burned 538 calories, I decided I'd earned a rest and went exploring through more of the club. The racquets courts were beautiful and, at 5:30 P.M., only about half filled. One of them caught my eye as I passed—through its Plexiglas wall I could see numerous paintings hung on the wall, and below them, a series of identical machines upon which several women were performing slow exercises. A brochure on a table nearby explained that the machine was a Pilate (pi-LA-tee). Shaped like a wooden cot arched slightly upward in the middle, it had a small platform which slid upon it from end to end along a track. Large rubber bands pulled on the platform from either end: The further the platform was pushed from the middle, the greater the tension forcing it back. The women stood on the platform and pushed back and forth; some of the routines involved ropes and stirrups. Pink paper placed over the ceiling lights cast a warm glow over this scene. Presiding over it all, gently helping his women onto the Pilates, coaching, touching, demonstrating, was a single, striking-looking, forty-something man whom the brochure identified only as . . . Stephan.

With his craggy features and gray-brown hair, parted in the middle and falling wispily to his shoulders, Stephan bore an uncanny resemblance to Mother Teresa. His physique, though, attested to the apparently wondrous powers of the machine. Nothing said men couldn't try it, so when Stephan appeared to have a free moment I signed up and climbed aboard.

Though not especially interested in talking about himself, Stephan answered my questions as he put me through the slow but torturous motions. He was Austrian. He was an artist; these were his paintings. So many of his clients were moving to Aspen from California that he had felt he should, too. He had been a graduate student in politics at Tufts University's Fletcher School, he said. "Do you feel it? Does it hurt? It should not hurt, it should make you tired." Among his California clients had been Joan Collins and Daryl Hannah, Diana Ross and Henry Winkler. Over Christmas, many of them returned for sessions: Kate Jackson, Priscilla Presley, Cher, Jessica Lange, Bianca Jagger. Back in Beverly Hills, he would go to their houses. No, not many of his clients were men. Frankly, he said, he did not like men. He called the racquetball court his studio, and as he left it to talk with a client, I hobbled around it on my cab-driver legs.

The works of art—mostly in acrylic and chalk—all sold for over a thousand dollars, and most were simply of the form of a cello or cello-as-woman's-body or both; this seemed to be Stephan's *idée fixe*. One was a single brushstroke. A framed newspaper feature about him had the headline MAKING STARS SLIM FOR FAT PROFITS; his own literature said he had been featured in *Vogue, Parade, Mademoiselle, Self,* and other magazines. A photo had him posing next to a hard-bodied client with a hammer and chisel pointed at her thigh. Stephan was a strange item of imported Californiana, the émigré fitness guru/artiste/entrepreneur. But in a way I liked hanging out in his studio—he was so weird I didn't feel out of place.

I had to leave to start my shift, so I showered, changed, and limped from the Aspen Club out to my car. As it warmed up, I read from the promotional literature I had been given: "The Aspen Club—the name does not do it justice. . . . The Aspen Club is more of a philosophy that focuses on the integration of mind and body, a vital union whether involved in professional sports or simply the trials of everyday life."

Well, for me it would be the trials of everyday life. But with my already sore body, I was for once looking forward to sitting in the cab. In my wallet was a membership card to the Aspen Club. No one had to recommend you for entrance to this club, but there seemed to me a self-selection involved: If you weren't one of Them, you didn't feel quite right. I wasn't one of them, and I couldn't remember any other experience that had made me feel quite so sympathetic to the overweight: To visit the Aspen Club as a fat person would require true courage. For all its emphasis on health, something about the Aspen Club struck me as bruising.

"K-ninety-one, special request for a delivery, you free?"

"Ten-four."

"Okay, K-91, go to Clark's Market and buy some two percent milk and chocolate-chip cookie dough. You know, the kind in the tube. Turn on your meter as soon as you get there. Then take it to the Gant, C-207."

"Howard, right?"

"That's correct."

I had met Howard, a property developer from Padre Island, two days before at the airport. His companion was a "new girlfriend," he confided as I dropped him off, and he wanted help in making sure everything went smoothly during their stay. Would I be available during the next few days for "this and that?"

"Absolutely," I confirmed. Like drivers in the third world, Aspen cabbies tried hard to make a repeat customer out of you. If the driver didn't print up his own cards, with name and cab number (and I could never bring myself to do this), the company provided him with generic Mellow Yellow cards that could be filled in. The dispatch system allowed special requests, and with many tourists wanting the personal connection to an "insider" they liked, special requests could be lucrative for a driver.

Howard had wanted a regular driver for his trips to dinner and Snowmass, and the day before, I had picked up a large bag of purchases from Aspen Eel, the all-eelskin-product boutique, that he and his paramour had not wanted to carry home. The next day there would be a drop-off and pickup of some dry cleaning. I was quick becoming Howard's manservant. But this evening, at II P.M., Howard was hungry.

Thinking she would be amused, I told the grocery checkout girl about my errand. She yawned.

Howard answered the door in a silk bathrobe. "Ted, it's darned good to see ya!" he exclaimed, looking not at me but at my package. He yelled back to Carol, in the bedroom, "Okay, honey, get to work!"

He grinned broadly and slapped me on the shoulder. Howard, I could tell, was an expert at the art of vacations, and he earned my respect for knowing his desires. He also tipped well. "There's nothin' I wanted more than chocolate chip cookies. What do I owe ya?"

Other deliveries practically constituted hazardous duty. I was first up, midnight of the next day, when the call went out for a delivery to Bobbi Barker's.

"You ever done this before, K-91?" asked Susan, a certain smile in her voice.

No, but I had heard. "Virgin," I replied. Somebody else broke in on our conversation.

"You won't be, time you get out of there," he advised me.

"Whatcha wanna do is wait till she's wobblin' a little, then poke her," counseled another lecher.

There was raucous laughter over the airwaves.

"Stop it!" Susan commanded. "Now what you want to do, K-91,

is to go to City Market, start the meter, buy a package of Salem Menthol 100's, then take them to 518 S. Hunter, number 4, with the receipt."

"Aw, he won't need that if he does it right," came the comment.

"Hush! Then let me know when you're finished, 91." She sounded like a mother, wanting me to wake her up when I came in late on a weekend.

"Ten-four." I wondered, How dangerous was this Bobbi Barker? How true were the stories you always heard? How did I feel about this sort of endeavor?

"You're new," she noted, fixing on my eyes, when she found me at her door. I held out the bag of cigarettes. "That was $1.85, plus $7.00 on the met—"

She stopped me in midsentence, and took me by the elbow. "Here, come on in for a sec," she said. This time her purr was more of a slur. She was holding a lowball glass, and it was low. "What can I fix you?" She was fortyish, bleached blonde, with a cigarette perched between two straight fingers, palm thrown back in the offhand way of certain women of the generation for whom smoking was almost de rigueur. She was Mrs. Robinson, in velour robe and fuzzy slippers.

"Uh, seltzer," I said. *Research, this was research.*

"Seltzer and what?"

"Oh, seltzer and a little, uh, seltzer."

"Sure," she said, and mixed in a jigger of Scotch.

We talked about something dumb while I wondered exactly what she was used to getting from the drivers—the downvalley degenerates, as they called themselves. The thought was not appealing. The apartment felt like a cocktail lounge. I sipped at the drink, apologized for the busy night that summoned me back and, as I made her porch, sighed a deep, cold breath of relief that hung in the air under the porch light as I skipped to the cab.

"Fifteen minutes—a new world record!" cried Susan as I logged back on.

Hazardous duty took different forms. One afternoon when I was in the Mellow Yellow office, Steve Clark hung up the phone, waved a dispatch chit in the air, and yelled out, "Hunter Thompson, liquor delivery!" A cry went out from various corners of the office, whoops of glee. Alex came in to handle it personally. "Half the drivers we send on this job never come back," he remarked bemusedly, mostly to himself. He looked around. "Send Ted," said Alex.

The first stop was the pickup at Airport Liquors. "He wants what?" said the clerk, looking at my list. It read, "4 750 ml Chivas, 5 green chartoos." He went around gathering the bottles, placing them in a carton, and shaking his head as he wrote out the charge slip.

"What's wrong? Are you worried he won't pay up?" I asked. The bill was for about $215.

"No, no, not that," said the man. "It's just that yesterday, we delivered five Chivas to him, and two days before that, four more. In fact, I can't give you all the green chartreuse, because we only have three left. He bought all the others."

I was to deliver them to the Woody Creek Tavern, but a figure who could be no one but the gonzo journalist was just climbing into his Jeep Cherokee as I arrived in the Suburban. "Hunter!" I yelled. But, along with his knee socks, shorts, and baseball cap (all these in frigid weather), the Duke was wearing a Walkman and did not even hear me. He drove away quickly and left me feeling I'd missed a brush with a certain sort of greatness.

I took my delivery inside the bar. The waitress nodded when I explained the situation. She didn't know where he'd gone, she said, but she knew he'd be back. We placed the carton in a rear storeroom, and though Thompson had no official connection with the Tavern, she paid the meter charge from the cash register.

The true temptations were the pizza deliveries. O'Leary's Pub, which had no delivery service, made the best pizza, and Mellow Yellow was often called to deliver it. The temptation proved too much for some drivers.

"Hey, this pizza's missing a piece!" a guy called in to Susan one night.

"How do you know?" she demanded back. Another driver, she said, had been known to remove a thinly cut slice and adjust the others in hopes the customers wouldn't notice. But they usually did.

Driving, I gradually learned, was a hustle. With a little alacrity you could also profit by, say, an ability to produce a six-pack of beer when the stores were closed. I had heard enough veiled requests for this service over the late-night radio that I bought a couple of extra sixes the next time I did my weekly shopping. The meter charges would include the trip home to pick one up, and then deliver it to the customer. Twenty bucks seemed to me a fair price for the contraband, and the whole affair would easily run the customer over thirty-five. But these people were evidently thirsty—hot tubs will do it to you—and on an expensive vacation, it probably seemed a small splurge.

But this was the small time. I was sitting in the cab of another driver one night when acquaintances of his, in an outlying town, called in and asked him to drive over. They would pay him "a C-note and a half," they said. He would think about it, he answered. He sat quietly after the call, doing some mental calculations. "That's more than I'd make the rest of the night sitting here," he concluded.

"Sounds like a lot of money for a short drive," I offered.

"Oh, it's not the drive they want," he said, and smiled. He stepped out of the cab for a moment to make a call, and it all dawned on me. He was calling his supplier; he didn't have a gram in stock himself. The hundred dollars would be the price of a gram of coke, and the fifty a tip for delivery. Of course, he would also be making a profit on the gram, maybe twenty-five bucks, which wasn't bad for a quick errand.

The special functions of Aspen cabbies extended beyond valet, delivery boy, or customer's favorite local. In a town with seventy-one places to get a drink, somebody had to be responsible for drunks. As the night grew late and they stumbled into the taxis, that person was usually the driver.

There were drunken customers all evening, of course, but their numbers peaked at around the 2 A.M. bar-closing time. Propelling them into cabs was Aspen's fairly strict DUI enforcement, coupled with a community chest program called Tipsy Taxi. With Tipsy Taxi, if you'd had a few too many, the bartender could sign a voucher worth cash to a cab driver, who would get you home free.

Warden of the tipsy was, needless to say, a job with both rewards and hassles, a constant chance to assess the proposition that when drunk, a person's real nature came out. For the bellicose worker, there was the chance to pick the fight she had been wanting to have with a tourist or boss all day. For the tourist, there was a chance to explore the general idea that Aspen was ripping him off by questioning whether you were taking the most direct route home. For other passengers, talking to the disembodied voice on the other side of the front seat was like talking to a shrink: No one sat in judgment; you could tell the truth. I heard from a man out late with his mistress who was headed home to his wife. I listened to a woman wondering out loud whether to despise her boyfriend because he wanted to sleep with her sister.

And there were adventures. Many of them seemed to emanate from a bar, called Shooter's, with an especially high number of closing-time calls. Shooter's was a basement country-Western bar with a dance floor and barbecue menu. Hoover, who ran it, attracted all the cowboys, hicks, and cowboy wannabe's in the area. She had a famous trick, of spitting a mouthful of 151 rum into the air and igniting it with her cigarette lighter. "She's the only person in town who sleeps less than I do," Susan the dispatcher told me—about three hours a night, according to Hoover. Shooter's had a higher percentage of locals than most bars. My favorite was a thin guy with droopy eyes, boots, and slow, lugubrious voice who was trying to kiss Hoover good night one evening when I arrived to pick him up. She held him off, but affectionately told him to be careful, she'd see him in the morning. Then, apparently out of Tipsy Taxi forms, she slipped a twenty-dollar bill into my hand to pay for his fare. His head kept nodding forward as I drove him to his trailer. He was really drunk. The insignia on the front of his cap read, CHEYENNE, WYO.—WILD HORSE RACE—1987.

I stopped the cab. "Have a nice evening," I said.

Slowly, he lifted his head. "Did Hoover pay you?" he asked. I nodded. He got this hangdog look in his eye. "She's my best friend," he confessed. "I don't know why she loves me—I'm useless. Did Hoover pay you? I love her so." He lifted the door handle and, almost in slow motion, fell out onto the ground as the door yielded to his weight. Then he picked himself up and walked into the night.

Another time at Shooter's, at around midnight, I drove a man who initially did not seem very drunk. Another cowboy type, he identified himself by name—Todd McEwen—as he climbed in, said he lived at the T-Lazy-7 Dude Ranch, and asked my name. "Ted, would you mind just backin' up a few feet? I'd like to have a word with those folks on the corner there."

"Sure," I said, shifting into reverse and stopping next to two couples, each of them in matching, gutter-length fur coats. Todd McEwen rolled down his window.

"Excuse me, you people there in the fur coats?" he began. They looked up. "Well, I just want you to know YOU CAN SUCK MY DICK!"

I quickly shifted back into drive and stepped on the gas. Todd McEwen, now dropping the pretense of sobriety, leaned back in his seat and howled with laughter. "You ain't mad, are ya?" he asked me as we waited to turn onto Main Street.

"Nah," I said. "That was pretty funny."

"Give you five dollars to go around the block so I can do it again."

"You want me to lose my job?"

"Ten."

"No way."

"Twenty, then."

I shook my head.

"Well, piss on it."

On the way up to the ranch, Todd told me he was in charge of customer relations at the dude ranch, which made a kind of sense. He also mentioned he was snowmobile champion of the T-Lazy-7. I was only listening with half an ear, but the information came rushing back to me as I headed down Maroon Creek Road after dropping him off at the ranch. There was a single light behind me, and it was jiggling. I was being followed by a snowmobile.

I could safely do about 35 MPH on the well-sanded road and felt sure that would be enough to lose the crazy cowboy. He wasn't wearing gloves or a hat, after all, and it was a cold night. But the bastard stayed right on my tail. I crossed a bridge, upon which the snow had melted—that would stop him. But he cruised right over it. Finally, on the next sharp turn, I suddenly lost him. A quarter mile further down I stopped, and waited: no light. I began to worry that he had cruised straight off the road. I turned the car around, backtracked, and checked the likely crash spots for someone lying bleeding in the woods. But no one had gone off the road. He had probably just been sobered up by the chill and headed home.

Another night, I got sent by Susan to the Hunter Creek condominiums. "You're looking for a slightly high Marilyn," she said. I had been waiting nearly ten minutes outside the building, listening to a KSNO radio ad for Ferraris, when she appeared in the headlights. The road was icy, so at first I wasn't sure whether her motor skills or the slippery footing was responsible for the way she staggered right up between the headlights and leaned both hands on the hood, making her way, hand over hand, around to the front passenger door. But as she pushed her hair back and tried to focus on me, I knew it was more than the ice.

"You're not high," I said when we'd greeted each other. "You're drunk."

"Wasted. Smashed," she agreed in a light Texas accent. "Take me to Andre's."

On our way to the three-story disco/restaurant/folk café, she told me her story.

"Andre's," she said. "I've got to go there before I leave. I wanted the other girls to go, but they're too drunk, so I'm going to do it myself.

"I just graduated. Four years, it means nothing to me. Now I'm supposed to go to get my MBA. That doesn't mean anything, either. I don't care."

Her friends were ten and twenty years older. "They've got lots of connections, I guess, at the bank and Mason & Morse [a large real estate brokerage]. They told me to get a job as a receptionist or something, but I don't know . . . I just graduated. Four years, I feel hopelessly under—, or I mean, overqualified or something. I don't know, it might be kind of fun for a year."

She wanted me to come into Andre's with her for an hour because she was nervous about going in alone. As she sat there vacillating, she confessed, "I don't know, I just don't trust them. They know so many people because they sleep around all the time. And I don't mind that . . . I enjoy doing that . . . but, they're not honest people, I don't trust them. Won't you come in with me?"

Like too many cab stories, it ended because I couldn't go in. But I wanted to; I sympathized greatly with her. I felt like her priest. I felt she wanted me to tell her what to do.

I started feeling gritty and streetwise after two or three months on the job. I saw sad and funny and frightening things and began to entertain the notion that nothing could surprise me anymore. I was wrong. It was about 2:20 A.M., a bit later than normal after closing time to get a call. "K-ninety-one, Romeo, at the Paradise."

That sounded interesting.

Snow was falling heavily, blanketing everything dark and encouraging the belief that tomorrow would truly bring a fresh start. When Romeo didn't appear immediately, I didn't mind: The snow was beautiful. But town was quickly becoming deserted, and it was going on fifteen minutes when I finally put on my parka and climbed out of the cab. "Romeo, wherefore art thou?" I mumbled, heading toward the entrance to the Paradise club.

I almost stepped on him. Really: I nearly planted my waffle-stomper squarely on his chest. The man was spread out on the pavers, dead drunk. I brushed the snow off him, to make sure he was alive. He was. He even had the Tipsy Taxi form clenched in his fist. I pulled it out to make certain he was my man. "Romeo," it read. Fortunately, they'd also filled in the destination. Only half an hour ago Romeo had been lucid, so I reasoned he was rousable. I opened the back door, sat him up, and finally, after much encouraging, got him to his feet. His knees buckled just as he reached the door, but I got him in, face down on the seat, head positioned over the rubber floormats, in case.

You could act like a kid up here, I mused as I deposited Romeo in his front hall (the house keys were in his coat pocket), and people would take care of you. That was the meaning of an Aspen vacation: You got to act silly, irresponsible. Part of our job as drivers was to indulge the drunks, help them into the car, put up with them. It was kind of interesting at first, but dealing with inebriates was ultimately wearing on the sober.

Outside, the snow continued to pile up, ethereal and weightless. Borne on air from the deserts to the west, it was bone-dry, the lightest snow in the States. I wouldn't be the first one up the lifts, but if I settled for five hours' sleep, I might get in an afternoon . . .

Even Aspen slept. The bar-closing rush led to a gradual dwindling that qualified as a definite calm by 3:00 or 3:30 A.M. This period brought the least reward to the becalmed taxis, only two to four of which were likely to remain on duty. But it was my favorite time, because the sudden decompression—the absence of people, of traffic, of noise—left a sense of calm and, if fleetingly, of ownership. Cabbies like me didn't even own our wheels, but when everyone else cleared out, we were like the janitors in the museum, lords of our domain.

The people you would see at that hour formed a thin procession of Aspen's marginal. About every other night at around 3 A.M., a young Mexican would hop into my car. Four or five condo units around town—the cabbies all knew which—seemed to house the Mexicans who had found places in town (many, many more lived downvalley and were altogether indispensable in the running of restaurants and hotels). My passenger, Rafael, from Veracruz, was the last to go at one expensive restaurant every night and the first to arrive at another, smaller place every morning. From Crossroads Drug, the other downtown cab stand, it was only seven blocks home, at one and a half the normal fare, but after the double shift, he seemed to feel he'd earned the ride.

Others you would see at that hour included the hated car-boot man, who attached the disabling devices to vehicles left on the street near the commercial area after 2 A.M. This was to allow for nightly plowing and sanding: City government kept the streets scraped clean. In the core area of downtown other cars would be towed away, and there was a certain interest, behind the taxi windshield, in viewing each night the poor, forgotten vehicles that fell victim to the vulturelike tow trucks. (The only way to get yours back without paying the fine was to present the Tipsy Taxi receipt from the ride that got you home.)

At that hour of the night, it was nice to have company. A driver I liked, Kenny, from Connecticut, often parked his cab next to mine at Crossroads Drug. Often one of us would join the other in his cab and tell tales of the night's fares or else just stretch out, one in a front seat and one in the rear, until a call came or a fare walked up. One such night, I vaguely realized there was a man peering through Kenny's windows at the two of us. He knocked on the window closest to me and asked for a ride home. I climbed into the Suburban and obliged.

"Like some toot?" he asked, scooping out with a dollar bill a small pile from a Baggie filled with cocaine. I said no; normally, it was only offered as a tip. He asked about me, I asked about him, in the usual friendly Aspen manner. He worked at a clothing store on the mall. He invited me in for a beer when we got to his place. That actually sounded better than twiddling my thumbs back at the Beach, so I went in. He turned on the television, got me a beer, and sat down on the couch. Too close.

"Uh, not what I thought you had in mind," I said.

"No? What's that?" he said.

"Contact."

"Oh well, I'm sorry . . ."

We parted then, I a little wiser. Aspen had a small gay alliance but no gay bar, and when groups like the National Gay Ski Club came to town, you could sense an antigay streak in some of the locals. My fare had been cruising, I supposed, at one of the few times of the day when he could probably get away with it.

There was a 6 A.M. reservation for a ride to the airport from Starwood, so at about 5:15 A.M. I headed over to Aspen's most exclusive subdivision. Starwood, home at least part-time to the likes of Rupert Murdoch, Jill St. John, and John Denver, had been made famous (probably to the chagrin of its other wealthy inhabitants) by Denver's song "Starwood in Aspen." No sign announced the Starwood turnoff on McLain Flats Road; you had to know it was the first right past the bicycle sign.

A steep, winding road led uphill to a bright red stop light, a guard house, and a boom across the road. Rex, the night guard, seeing it was a taxi, raised the boom. He recognized me as I rolled down the window. "Six A.M. ressie, Rex, for Coonts."

"You're a little early—want to stop in?"

I parked the Suburban next to Rex's decrepit Subaru wagon, behind the guard house, as he lowered the boom back down. "I'm cookin' a little macaroni if you want some," he offered as I squeezed into the small space. Rex had set up a little hotplate in the second room, near the chemical toilet. But I could barely reach either of them, given all the boxes addressed to Starwood residents that were stacked everywhere. "Christmas presents," Rex explained. "Some of these people haven't picked 'em up yet." It was three weeks past Christmas.

Rex was in his late thirties, I guessed, a bit portly, and always eager for a chat ("It's lonely up here at night," he told me). His employer was Westec, the California-based security company. On my last visit, he had explained the exotic chemical toilet, which he was afraid to use because someone might suddenly arrive and want to be let in. This time, as I ate my plate of lukewarm macaroni-and-cheese and scanned the famous names on the mailbox labels, we thought we heard an owl.

There were plenty out there, Rex confirmed. Because Starwood residents "want it to be like Disneyland," there was no predator control. As a result, he often saw or got reports of fox, ermine, owl, and coyote—even a bear, once. The coyotes, he said, were particularly incompatible with the cats and tiny dogs residents brought along. When someone called up to say, "My Fifi's missing!" explained Rex, the first question he would ask was, "How big is it?" He was, in other words, sizing up the odds that Fifi had been eaten, snatched off the redwood deck in the prime of its little life.

One night, just down the road toward the Starwood tennis court, he had heard a terrible squealing and screeching. Turning on a powerful flashlight, he saw a pack of coyotes crowded around something small and thought, One less little dog.

Rex handed me the photocopied Starwood Courtesy Map as the sky began to brighten in the east and circled house number 79, my destination. "Wait a minute, I know that one," I told Rex. I had pulled Kenny out of the snow there one night, I explained, after the nefarious bachelor who lived above had insisted it was safe for him to take his Checker up the steep driveway. He had gotten stuck. Cursing Kenny for his "stupidity," the man had abandoned him near the foot of the drive and escorted his pretty date up to the house.

"The worst part," I told Rex, "was that the date had been telling him how she had to get back to town after a cup of coffee. She wanted Kenny to wait. After that, though, she stayed." Cabs without four-wheel-drive seldom made it up that drive, Rex confided to me. I was ready to act cold to the man this time, but he wasn't the one who needed the cab; it was a woman. I kept my mouth shut as I drove her to the airport.

With a slow hour remaining before I had to pass the cab back to Herb, I returned to the Beach and stretched out again in Kenny's backseat. He asked me about my other jobs and I asked about his. He had worked on a tobacco farm and in a warehouse for UPS. In Aspen he had held a lot of different jobs, from snow shoveler to short-order cook, "mostly real dull," but it was worth it, because of "all the partyin'," the good times to be had in Aspen.

"That's why I'm here, in a word. What else is there to life, anyway?" Maybe if I stayed long enough, I thought, Aspen could help me with an answer to that.

. . .

Finding affordable housing in Aspen was a nightmare, but I had chanced upon a dream situation: house-sitter. Every morning as my shift ended, I returned not to an overcrowded condo with four people in two bedrooms, not to a trailer an hour downvalley, but to a six-bedroom glass-and-stone house with a view of Aspen Highlands.

This good fortune was due to the generosity of an artist, Johanna, whom I had met the previous summer. Johanna's Aspen-raised sons were off at college and her husband was away most of the time, working on a big deal in Los Angeles; she was thinking of going there, too. When I called her in the fall to ask if she'd heard of any apartments, Johanna had just landed a great job designing playground equipment on the West Coast. Could I attend to household chores, forward messages, and make myself scarce on weekends when the family was around, she asked? If so, the house was mine indefinitely.

I remember the first time I saw it. It was a huge house, a lovely house. It was set into the side of a hill, with the driveway above; the other side, the side with the view, was even bigger. It was two stories, flat-roofed, and subtly landscaped with aspen and willow to look as though it had been there forever. Johanna wasn't back yet, but she had left a note on the door telling me to make myself at home.

This meant, of course, that the door was open—the house, certainly worth upward of a couple million dollars, had been left unlocked. And indeed, as Johanna later explained, I would really need no key because the house was hardly ever locked.

Alone, I began to explore. I poked my head into the kids' rooms, guest room, work room, TV room, the master bedroom sauna, mud room, home office, and three-car garage, with its snow blower, snowmobile, and dirt bikes. Tinted floor-to-ceiling windows all along the valley side of the house afforded a view of nature as through large, expensive sunglasses. I took off my shoes and, barefoot, crossed a bear-skin rug in the living room, the cool milled-stone slabs of the dining room floor, and then the sun-warmed redwood deck to get a better look. Below, fifty feet away, shimmered a stand of aspen trees, their limber white trunks bending in the fall breeze that carried their golden leaves out of sight. Beyond that, hung with clouds that let the sun shine through like spotlights, the broad lower valley.

At the foot of the road, I would soon discover, were four public tennis courts, seldom fully occupied, and a twenty-five-yard public swimming pool, as well kept as one at a private club, where the entry fee of two dollars, most hours of the day, would get you your own lane.

Until then the inhabitant of a cramped, hot apartment in Denver, I couldn't believe my luck. The price seemed so small. I had to invest some time in learning the art of hot-tub maintenance—turned out it was like a huge aquarium that needed its pH adjusted every few days. In addition, there were chemicals like Anti-Sudser and Scum-B-Gon to rid the water of things that hot-tub users leave behind, like traces of moisturizer, sunblock, hair conditioner, and cosmetics. And, of course, the bacteria that love the warm hot-tub stew and could cause "hot-tub rash" in a horizontal line across the neck or chest of hot-tubbers—where the water level was. But as chief hot-tub maintainer, I was also the chief hot-tub tester, and there was no better ending to a long shift in the taxi than climbing into the tub to watch the dawn.

Of course I felt a little guilty sometimes, as the other drivers returned downvalley; I tried not to let them know my arrangement.

My paradise, alas, was short-lived. Johanna's new life didn't suit her as expected, and she resumed spending a lot of time in Aspen. She said I could stay—with me working the night shift, we hardly saw each other anyway, and I decided to give it a try. At first it was all right: When we crossed paths in the kitchen, I would tell her weird tales of the road and she, more guardedly (for I had told her about my project), would recount stories from her years in Aspen. But after a while, when we shared a cup of tea or sat around the roaring fire that Johanna loved to make in the evenings, our former ease with each other felt strained. I noticed she had been reading my books, but I didn't think much about it. Then one Saturday morning, when her husband was due to arrive for the weekend and I was on my way out the door, she asked how work had been the night before. I mentioned something about a rude passenger and about a hard-working Mexican I was getting to know. She asked about a fancy country club out of state that had paid me to talk about my researches; hadn't I mentioned that Mexicans had served the meals while I gave the talk?

"Yes. It was very strange," I said.

"It must feel strange to be critical of your hosts," she replied. The strangeness was more a matter of role reversals, I began to say, but then noticed how hard Johanna was staring at me. Slowly I began to understand what she was getting at.

It was a few days later when Johanna, putting down my book, remarked that with me in the house, "I feel like I have the soup kitchen upstairs, a little eyeball resting on my shoulder"—as though the house now had a "big conscience" resident, she said. Others I met would take me as a writer interested in Aspen and never give a thought to what I had written, but Johanna was smarter than that. Though I had tried to hide it, she could sense my ill intent, and I didn't like the way it felt.

We sat down and talked. I was not judging her, I promised—she was my friend. In fact, the challenge for me lay in trying to keep life at the house from influencing my general attitude toward Aspen: It was truly pleasant there. She did feel a little guilty sometimes, she offered in response, "burning a big fire, sending all that energy up the chimney, just for me." She was not entirely sure about living alone in the huge house, with so much unused room. The conscience, I could see, was not mine alone.

"But I think when the big judge up there looks at me, he'll be asking, 'Did she make good use of it?' " Her husband had done well in real estate, and the crime, in her eyes, would be having all of this and not enjoying it; she believed that was her role, even her responsibility.

"I mean, hey, I went to P.S. 168 in Brooklyn, you know what I mean?" she asked. And I tried: It wasn't like this life was preordained for her, like she was born into the oppressor class of American society. Would it be stupidity for her to live in a house less gracious? That was a dilemma of the Aspen "have's"—or at least those with a conscience—and one I hadn't figured out yet.

Our discussion had to end at about 4 P.M. so that I could get ready for work. By 5 P.M., I was back on the road in the Chevy Suburban. The insights about Johanna's background were a revelation to me, and I thought about them while negotiating traffic. I knew I would have to find another place to live.

My second call was for the Aspen Country School. As I arrived, the parking lot outside the beautiful school, with its tasteful buildings and woodland setting, was jammed with Saabs, Volvos, and Jeep Cherokees in which mothers waited to pick up their children. The kids all looked about ages seven to ten and just down from the after-school ski program: They were wearing brightly colored ski suits, skittering across the icy lot in tiny Nordica boots, juggling armloads of miniature skis and poles. The little girls' knitted hats had blond braids falling from the back; two little boys with fancy padded racer-style stretch pants and gloves were tossing fluffy snowballs at each other. I was supposed to drive one of these kids home; the dispatcher had given me a description: green hat, green boots.

"Hey, Billy Mallery, is that you?" I called out the window. The kid looked up and dropped his snowball. He said " 'Bye" to his adversary and lugged his pint-size skis to the car. "Can I turn on the meter?" he asked, hoisting himself into the front seat with me. "Sure," I said.

"The slopes were awesome today," declared Billy Mallery. "I caught some air on Thunderbowl, and I'm working on my helicopter. We ran gates. Michael can already do a helicopter. He's my brother."

I tried to listen to more of Billy's stories on the drive home. My mind kept drifting, though, to thoughts of P.S. 168, what it would be like to attend a school whose name was a number, trying to imagine a tough Brooklyn neighborhood, a playground. The children of immigrants had been trying to leave Brooklyn for years, my Dutch ancestors among them. What parents wouldn't prefer their kids to grow up like Billy Mallery?

I glanced over at him, his blond hair, his face raccoon-tan from daily skiing with goggles. He was a spoiled kid and wouldn't last a second in most parts of Brooklyn, I thought. But then, why should he have to? He looked familiar to me, and when I remembered who he looked like, I didn't want to admit it. Billy Mallery reminded me of myself.

Chapter II

In the Temple of the Silly Gods

According to Johanna, the night made sense if you thought of my new Sorels. Sorel boots are the Aspen winter shoe. Imported from Canada, they have a deep tread, a rubberized, calf-height shell, and a thick felt lining. White fleece rims the top. A foot slides easily in, and a tug on the two long laces closes the sides snugly, warmly, around it. An indulgence is to wear no socks: No shoe will ever have felt this good. With Sorels, you actually look forward to stepping out into the cold.

They last almost forever but do change appearance as they're worn. The sparkling white fleece around the top gradually grays. The shiny black rubber around the foot proper gets scuffed and loses its gleam. As a pair of Sorels achieves that truly beat-up, utilitarian look, it enters the realm of old Aspen status symbols that help people in their seniority calculations: a 925 telephone prefix (newer numbers begin with 920); a ZG license plate (new ones all start with VC). But if your Sorels still shine, odds are you're new in town, at best—or worse, a *tourist.*

"K-ninety-one, to Poppies bar."

"Ten-four," I answered the dispatcher.

I had been on the job only two weeks, but as I pulled up to Poppies Bistro Café, I felt the call was unusual. Poppies, an elegant nouvelle cuisine restaurant in a restored Victorian house, stopped seating diners around 10 P.M. and was normally closed by midnight. It was now 1:30 A.M., late even for the chefs. I clomped into the entry hall, knocked the snow off my new Sorels, and proceeded to the bar.

The last time I'd been in here, a week before, Teddy Kennedy was seated at the bar, a blonde on his lap. This night, a group of about twelve were pressed around the bar, drinking and singing. I recognized a couple of them as waiters; the others looked richer, like customers, but young. One, wearing cowboy boots and a blazer, with long, stylish blond hair, turned to greet me.

"You're from the taxi company?" He was Australian.

"Mellow Yellow," I said.

"Well, look, mate, we're going to go pick up Stevie Nicks, but we're not quite ready—can you hold on a few moments? Here, have a beer."

I took off my parka, accepted the drink, and turned to a tall, pale man standing alone on my left. Bald on top, he had black hair falling thinly from the sides of his head down over his shoulders. He looked like some sort of Victorian undertaker, except that he, too, was wearing new Sorels. The face looked vaguely familiar: I had seen it on a record album and in the papers.

"Mick Fleetwood?" I finally asked.

"And the band," he replied, bowing.

Fleetwood was the founder of and drummer for Fleetwood Mac. He and Stevie Nicks, a singer in Fleetwood Mac, now performed mostly separately, with their own bands, but they were performing together again in two nights, on New Year's Eve, at the High Altitude Paradise, Aspen's premier nightclub. Tickets, priced at $150, had sold out instantly. I wracked my brain for something Fleetwood and I might have in common.

"How do you like your boots?" I finally asked.

Fleetwood went on and on about his Sorels, which he had purchased in Aspen that day, "on sale," for $119, "a really good price, I think," he said. I had gotten mine in Denver, on sale, for $75, but didn't mention it. He was extremely happy with them. Growing up in Scotland, the gangly musician had suffered from chronically cold feet and hands. "But with these, I'm in heaven," he concluded.

As Dennis, the Australian, opened a new bottle of wine, I ducked out to turn off the taxi engine—I'd left it running in front, and it looked like it might be a while yet. So cold was it outside that a cloud of the car's exhaust obscured most of its angles. Since Poppies was on a narrow stretch of the main drag through town, I turned on the emergency blinkers.

Inside, I chatted with a sullen raven-haired woman named Gina who was the girlfriend of Dennis. Dennis, she explained, once a drummer himself, was the manager of Fleetwood's band, Zoo. She was furious with him. He had promised her that for once, Zoo and its retinue would not be out to watch the dawn break, but here he was, pouring more wine all around. She refused a glass when he came by. I glanced at the others in the room. Poppies' waiters and bartender were having a blast; the members of Zoo looked surly, short, and wasted; their girlfriends appeared passive and oblivious.

An hour had passed when someone put Guy Lombardo's Christmas tape on the stereo. Within minutes Fleetwood, who had been looking logy, migrated to the back of the bar, picked up spoons, and began playing the liqueur bottles. Quickly, he came alive, somehow memorizing the sounds of the different bottles, and then performing a wonderful percussive accompaniment to Lombardo's songs. Fleetwood, clearly, lived to drum. Dennis joined him on the adjoining liquor bottles, and soon the two virtuosos had an impromptu duet going. A joint was passed around. It was nearing 4 A.M.

Gina finally wrestled Dennis into his overcoat, and the others started gathering their things to leave. I led the procession to the cab and helped pack the nine of them into the Suburban's three seats. The cab was icy-cold. I turned the key in the ignition . . . nothing. I turned off the blinkers and tried again. Again nothing. Shit, I thought, a cab full of multimillion-dollar band and I can't even get it to turn over. Fortunately, there was enough juice left in the frigid, drained battery to reach the nighttime shift leader on the radio. I explained what happened.

"Okay. I'll be by," he said.

"Great. When?" I asked. "I have nine passengers, and we're freezing."

"Uh, pretty soon."

We waited and waited and waited. The inside windows frosted over completely with everyone's breath. On the radio, I heard the shift leader answer a query from the only other driver still on duty, and I called in again: "Hey, you still coming over here?" But there was no reply. I tried again, and still nothing. Finally, it dawned on me what was happening. The shift leader, I realized, was one of the old-time, year-round drivers who resented the appearance of seasonal drivers such as myself. During the big crunches, the company would have sunk without us, but nights when it was slower and they had to share the wealth, resentment crept out. He didn't like me because I was new, and an outsider. He didn't like me, in other words, because of my new Sorels.

But I wasn't going to hang there and twist in the wind. It was too cold. Every cab had jumper cables; I reassured the band they would be taken care of in a moment (besotted, they were remarkably patient) and got out to flag somebody down. I was grateful that the first car on that deserted road was not a rental, which might have zoomed right by, but an ancient pickup truck containing a farmer from downvalley. He nosed up to my hood, illuminating the engine with his headlights, and gave me a jump. As the cab's interior gradually thawed, we cruised to the Paradise club, but Stevie Nicks had gone. Next it was back to their hotel, the Grand Aspen, where Gina, the only sober one, undertook to pay me.

"Look, I know we messed up your whole night," she said. "How much would you have made if we hadn't tied you up?"

Messed up my night? I'd had a ball. "Look, don't worry about it. If you just pay the meter fare . . ."

"No, no, I insist. How much would it be? A hundred? Two hundred?" She wanted the band to *pay*. I couldn't deprive her of her revenge.

"Well, probably about $250." It was high season, after all.

"Fine." She pulled thirteen twenties from her pocketbook, and asked for a receipt.

I called in a 10-5, that I was free, and thought the shift leader sounded a bit surprised to hear my voice. It was around 5 A.M. I steered the Suburban over icy streets to the Beach, yawned, and listened to the idling of the engine.

It was a funny thing, meeting Mick Fleetwood. I had spent literally hours listening to the songs of Fleetwood Mac while growing up—there was even a song, "Sentimental Lady," I associated with an early trip to Aspen to meet a teenage sweetheart. His photo from the cover of the *Rumours* album was permanently etched in my mind. That was the reason I'd found it hard not to stare at him, to endlessly compare the "real" Fleetwood with the one in the photo—a celebrity's face is oddly transfixing, no matter how many of them you've met. He was one of the creators of the popular culture I felt in many ways a product of; to talk to him was sort of the pop equivalent of coming upon the words, "A horse! a horse! my kingdom for a horse!" in Shakespeare's *Richard the III* for the first time, or the line "A thing of beauty is a joy forever" in a collection of Keats poetry and thinking, Oh, so that's where it comes from. I had found the source, and it was curiously satisfying.

At the same time, the encounter reminded me of the first time in my life I'd ever met a celebrity. That had been in Aspen, too, on a ski trip to Snowmass with my family. My sisters noticed that the man in the condo next door was Lloyd Haynes, an actor who played a high school American history teacher on television's *Room 222*. Mustering all my courage, I asked the amused Haynes if I could interview him for my paper, the Hill Junior High School *Torch*. The interview, and a photo of me standing next to Haynes—my hard evidence—appeared on the front page and made *me* briefly famous.

"What was he like? How did you meet him?" they asked me around school. I acted like it was nothing at all, but the secret I kept was that that was the truth: It took years to admit, but the fact was that meeting Lloyd Haynes had given me the fan's first experience of disillusionment. Haynes the actor wasn't as impressive as the wise, sympathetic teacher he portrayed on TV. He didn't seem as smart, as kind, or as decent—and who could be? The point is, he was a real person.

Mick Fleetwood, it appeared, was just a guy, too. He could be stuck in a cold cab as easily as the next person. His group of party-weary dissolutes depressed me as I thought of them stretched out on the beds in their nice rooms, probably snoring away.

I stretched, rearranged myself on the seat, and while waiting for the next call tried to picture the life *I'd* lead as a rock-and-roll star. . . .

Don Johnson was having a party, a *big* party. People had been talking about it for months; it was going to be the celebrity event of the season, a social who's who of the Aspen Christmastime crowd. The star of *Miami Vice*, an actor who appeared to have succeeded on the strength of his looks and ideas of not shaving or wearing socks, was cohosting the event with Don Simpson, a producer of films like *Top Gun, Beverly Hills Cop,* and *Flashdance,* and Tony Yerkovich, a screenwriter and the creator of *Miami Vice.* (Johnson and Yerkovich owned houses in Woody Creek, and Simpson was a longtime visitor; often, they came and went from Aspen in a Paramount studios jet.) Though many Aspen old-timers liked to try and ignore the party, pretend it didn't even happen, most people knew about it and some seemed to talk of nothing else. I heard about people involved in its planning—like Lizzie, doing the flowers, or Louise, doing the catering, for months before. But only a fraction of those who knew about it, of course, would be at the party. The number of guests was limited to 150, which meant the party was—as it had to be—exclusive. It would be fair to say that not only on that night, but for that week, and possibly weeks on either side, it would be the highest-profile social event in about a thousand-mile radius.

I had to get in.

The other problem was that I was not invited. I had it on good authority, however, that many of those who *were* invited did not know Don Johnson, either. Certainly, most of the locals did not— since Don was in town only occasionally, he did not know many locals. He knew a handful, among them Dick Butera, the guy who ran the Hotel Jerome, in whose ballroom the party would be held. Dick Butera, it seemed, did most of the local recruiting for Don Johnson.

I decided to try and leapfrog over Butera: a magazine editor of mine in New York knew Don Johnson's publicist, and publicists seem to run the social lives of most movie stars. The publicist would probably decide who was coming among those just visiting Aspen, we agreed—not Dick Butera's hip local people, in other words, but the famous national people. The editor said he would call the publicist.

I waited and waited.

"Sorry, no dice," he finally reported. "She said, 'No press.' They're being very strict on this one. Absolutely no press." I didn't quite believe this—why would a publicist be running a party if there truly was a desire for no press? And who said I was press, anyway?

But the challenge was growing, and my appetite had been whetted. There had to be a way in to Don Johnson's Christmas party.

I had a couple of other lines on how to do it. One was Lizzie, whose flower store had been hired to supply the party with Christmas trees, bouquets, and wreaths. I caught up with her the afternoon of the party, fretting over how to get electricity to the wreaths on the walls. The wiring was proving impossibly complicated, so Lizzie had decided to hide some alkaline D cells inside each wreath and pray they'd last. I offered to help her for free, but she saw through me and said no thanks. She wouldn't want to risk losing a client like Don Johnson.

Another possibility was Bettina. I knew she'd be invited and thought that maybe she needed a date. But when I reached her in the tub on her cordless phone, she told me she was already committed to an actor from *All My Children*. "Do you know any other locals who have been invited?" I asked her. She mentioned a couple of names.

I wasn't in yet, but I had to try. The night of the party, December 26, I got dressed up and went over to the Hotel Jerome.

My suit was black, the trendiest I owned; my shirt was white with black embroidery on the placard, and buttoned to the collar; my hair was slicked back. Given the lack of a plan I knew that success in this attempt could depend greatly on attitude, and I tried to wear one as I strode through the doors of the Hotel Jerome, indifferently checked my coat, and wended my way through the throng in the Victorian lobby. They were gawkers, and the less I looked at them, I was feeling, the more they looked at me—precisely as it should be. The way to the ballroom was a bit complicated, but I had done it many times, so I walked directly back, through the Jacob's Corner bar, past the large black marble Jacuzzi outside, the antique brass door handles, the Victorian furniture, the framed sepia prints of old Aspen lining the halls.

Right before the Antler Bar, which led into the ballroom, the way was blocked by three thugs in tuxedos. Each had a list on a clipboard, and as I paused to tie my shoes, I noticed they each would check a name off the list when an invitee approached and gave his name. Besides those entering legitimately, a crowd of would-be partygoers besieged the thugs, insisting their names should be on the list: *There must be some mistake, I came all the way from L.A. for this*

party, when Don hears I didn't get in, he's going to be very unhappy.
It looked like a crowd outside a trendy Manhattan club, turned
mean and aggressive.

I backtracked to Jacob's Corner to have a drink and consider my
strategy. A kitchen, I knew from earlier reconnaissance, sat between
Jacob's and the ballroom and probably provided a passageway in. I
tipped the waiter who brought me a drink a few bucks and asked
how clear was the coast.

"They've caught three people trying that already," he said sympathetically. "They're saying they're going to prosecute them."

"I see." I glanced at the kitchen door. Beside it stood a guy I knew
as a bouncer from the Paragon, dressed in a gray suit with a red
carnation. "Is he security?" The waiter nodded. The bouncer would
know me and seemed a nice guy, from the times he'd handed
passengers over. There was one possibility.

A well-dressed couple was seated at the table to my left, and I
struck up a conversation.

"How long have you been here?" I asked.

"Two hours," they said. "That's when the buffet dinner started.
After the dinner is when the party is supposed to really get going."

"And that's when you're going in?"

They looked at me with confusion. "No, we're not invited," said
the woman. "We're here just to watch. This is the way people will
leave." They glanced at each other and a light bulb seemed to go
on. "Are you invited?" she asked me hopefully.

"Um, not exactly."

It wasn't long before a few of the early-night people exited right
by us. There were Donald and Ivana Trump, Michael and Diandra
Douglas, Sally Field. It was like bird-watching, with *People* magazine the field guide.

My discomfort grew as I felt a few of the good ones were getting
away. I had to get in there. I picked one of the two names of local
men Bettina had told me had been invited, pulled myself together
in the men's room, and strode back down the hall.

"Are you going in?" a woman asked eagerly from a banquette
along the wall, en route. I looked at her. "Can I go with you?" She
smiled flirtatiously. I shook my head. No baggage. I was stream-
lined.

With what I hoped looked like aristocratic disdain, I elbowed my way through the crowd of supplicants besieging the thugs and looked one of them straight in the eye.

"You are?" he asked.

"Monte Melitty," I said. This was the name of a soon-to-be-convicted drug dealer.

He scanned his list. "Sorry, Mr. Melitty, you've already gone in," he barked. "I see," I said, nodding and flushing a bit. A miss. I beat a hasty retreat, not wanting them to recognize me when I tried again.

It was about fifteen minutes later. A different thug raised his eyebrows expectantly as I approached. "Tom Cleaver," I intoned.

He went down the list with a pencil, stopping at the name. "Yes sir, Mr. Cleaver, go right in," he said, stepping aside.

"Thank you," I said, not looking at him. A giddy sensation washed over me. I was in.

My admittance seemed to me a promotion, and walking through the Antler Bar, I immediately felt more important. I walked straight toward the ballroom, the inner sanctum. I was headed for the pantheon of the gods, even if they were silly gods.

The room was cavernous and elegant. Heavy draperies framed the outsize windows that lined three sides of the room. Carved wainscoting lined all the walls; above it, textured wallpaper matched the thick carpet underfoot. There were Lizzie's wreaths, hanging between all the windows; numerous lighted Christmas trees, and indirect lighting in red and purple and pure white. A band was setting up next to a dance floor at one end of the room, while in the center, round tables had been cleared of dishes and drinks were being served. Along the room's edges, serving tables had desserts and coffee going. It struck me that nearly as many people must be serving the party as attending it, for every table had one or two neatly uniformed waiters to itself, and no sooner were you looking for something than somebody offered it to you.

I searched for familiar faces. Somehow I was even more nervous than before I got in. Part of it was the rather irrational fear that I might still be spotted and dragged out. But the bigger part was the sudden realization that I didn't know my role here. My identity during the preceding weeks had been that of cab driver, and as a cabbie I knew what to do and, basically, how to act. But now what was I—a voyeur? How could you play the veteran partygoer if you didn't know anyone?

With relief I spied Bettina, and her date. After a moment's surprise at seeing me, she smiled mischievously and ask me to join them and Ed Bradley, the CBS *60 Minutes* host, at a round table. "How'd you do it?" she whispered. "Just call me Tom Cleaver," I whispered back. I sat back to sip a drink and for the first time looked around the table.

It's strange when the familiar faces you see aren't people you *know:* Next to Bradley sat Don Henley, the rock star, in a white shirt something like mine, dark hair falling over his shoulders. Two blond women were next, and then there was Kurt Russell, wearing glasses and looking quite handsome. Finally, I turned to look at the person whom, because of the tight seating around the table, I had inadvertently been leaning against—it was Goldie Hawn. She wore leather boots that rose to her knees, tight jeans under those, and a black top that left her waist exposed. I was so surprised, I did a double take. "Hi!" I blurted—the dead giveaway of a person used to *knowing* his familiar faces. She looked at me, smiled, and looked away.

It was no surprise so many had gathered with each other at this table: Just by being famous, they had a lot in common. But what were my lines? I chatted with Bettina, had a few words with Ed Bradley, and gave up. I wasn't going to talk to Goldie Hawn about ski conditions or tell her I loved her in *Private Benjamin,* the last movie of hers I was sure I had seen. If only she'd been wearing Sorels, I thought . . .

Bettina touched my arm. "Ted, I'd like you to meet a friend of mine, Tom Cleaver," she said, smiling archly. I looked into the face of the man I'd impersonated—evidently, with no ill effects for him, but did he know?—and shook his hand. Unfortunately, he pulled up a chair next to mine. "Um, excuse me," I said, rising. The band had started to play. I borrowed Bettina for one turn around the floor and then sallied forth to other tables. At this point, truly on my own, I felt like I was on the prowl at some elegant club. Here, though, the eligible women far outnumbered the men. Almost all, it seemed, wore fashionable heels, dark hose, and miniskirts and had bountiful blond hair. For another thing, when I asked one to dance, she almost leaped to her feet. It was another of the perquisites of being one of the elect, of the anonymous exclusivity I had purloined: Not knowing who you are, people at the party were eager *not* to rule out the possibility that you could be someone important, powerful, glamorous. And indeed, that's exactly how I felt.

On returning to the floor with a third partner, I noticed that the band was playing yet *another* Jimmy Buffett song. With a little relief, I made a mental note of the flaw—the local band they'd found had a limited repertoire. Then I looked beyond my partner's hair and took a more careful look: *The singer was Jimmy Buffett.* Oh my. This was his band. This was Jimmy Buffett and his band. I danced harder, felt I was entering a new realm of social understanding. Some people had Jimmy Buffett play at their *party.*

Needing a breather, I sat at an empty table with John Colson, a reporter for *The Aspen Times* I had once met briefly. Colson? A waiter descended on us with cappuccino and chocolate gateau topped with fresh raspberries.

"So, what brings you here?" asked Colson, beating me to the punch.

"Oh, you know, friends," I replied by way of not answering. "How about you?" A friend of Colson's was sitting down, and he introduced me: "Stu's staying at my place while he's here. He invited me."

I recognized Stu from the dance floor, where he seemed to be having the same kind of luck I was. It felt good to move around, he said, after such a long drive.

"Where'd you drive from?"

"Oh, L.A. The Paramount prop lot. I drove a big truck of furniture out from there."

"What for?"

He extended a hand and his gaze swept the room. "Voilà," he said. "Victorian couches, side tables, everything. Don Simpson ordered it. He wanted everything to look perfect." An invitation to the party, and a thousand dollars, had comprised the compensation package.

Again I looked around. In the low light it was hard to notice, but the furniture was beautiful. I then realized this was more than a party. This was a movie set. The organizers had re-created the environment in which the actors were most at home. It cast a different light on everything. Suddenly, I didn't feel so funny impersonating a guest at the party—everyone else was acting out a role, too. More than ever, then, I felt as though the inner sanctum *was* a movie—I had climbed up into the silver screen, entered the 3-D world of actors' real lives.

Bettina introduced me to Don Johnson and Melanie Griffith on her way out. We shook hands; what was there to say? "Great party," were my words, which sounded singularly inane. Nearby was Tony Yerkovich, the co-host; I happened to know his sister from college, which kept us talking for all of three or four minutes. From my mental bird-watcher's list I was able to check off Jane Fonda and Tom Hayden, Cher, and George Hamilton before heading for the door.

The star watchers were still sitting in Jacob's Corner as I walked by, looking tired and probably aloof. They waved at me. Asking the concierge to get me a cab—I made a special request for Herb—I stepped through the front doors of the Jerome into the bracing air.

Wait till Herb sees me here, I thought, feeling the real pleasure of the party—the telling about it—was only beginning. But the instant Herb pulled up to the curb, as if on cue, a bevy of photographers backed out of the double hotel doors, strobes blazing around the object of their interest, a short, rather plain looking woman I did not recognize. A doorman rushed to the cab's back door, they bundled her in, and Herb, perhaps panicked, stepped on the gas. "Hey, that's my cab!" I shouted after him. Nobody paid any attention, because another hubbub was brewing inside. "Who was that, by the way?" I asked a woman standing next to me in a big parka.

"That was *Sheena Easton,*" she said, staring as though I were the class dope.

"Oh," I said. "Really?" The name had a vaguely familiar ring to it.

The doors burst open again, and flashes lit the faces of Ryan O'Neal and Farrah Fawcett. They climbed into a waiting limousine. Finally, Don Johnson and Melanie Griffith exited, lingering just a moment so the photographers could get some good shots. According to later reports in the press, the party had been in honor of their engagement, or rather, re-engagement—they were first married in 1976. Actually, the engagement idea was more likely a last-minute addition: The party had been planned for months. Given its status as a known press magnet, though, and the recent success of Griffith's movie *Working Girl,* organizing the party around the engagement must have proved irresistible, a publicist's dream. Of course, they were being "very strict" about press inside the ballroom, but that did not prevent the photos from reaching the cover of *People* magazine the next week or a story from somehow being written about the affair.

A REKINDLED LOVE PROVES ENGAGING FOR DON & MELANIE, read the headline. Below, "Even by the ever-rising standards of Rocky Mountain high society, the Don Johnson–Melanie Griffith engagement party the night after Christmas represented some sort of peak . . . Life has so few happy endings, it's no wonder *le tout* Aspen turned out for a party in their honor at the Hotel Jerome . . ."

"*Le tout* Aspen?" Was that what we were? How pretentious! And yet, as I had seen first hand, the moments spent pretending could be surprisingly fun. Pretending, in fact, was what the whole thing was about. As down-to-earth Herb returned and drove me home, I realized that the world of taxis was perhaps a bit too unpretentious to serve as the best window into Aspen life. Aspen was an upstairs-downstairs kind of place, with a lot of the pretensions going on up the steps. I would have to find more ways to climb them.

In the celebrity culture that is late twentieth-century America, Aspen is not only a celebrity watering hole, it is a celebrity *itself.* Visited continually by correspondents for the glossy magazines and film crews for TV shows like *Entertainment Tonight* and *Lifestyles of the Rich and Famous,* its celebrity has elevated the status of everyone who lives there. Tell the person next to you on the plane that you live in Aspen, and you're likely to be in for a half hour of questioning. Though there are degrees, living in Aspen makes you an instant insider. You don't need to go to the movies to see Schwarzenegger; he's on the street. You don't need to turn on *Oprah*—she's on the slopes. Probably no place has so many famous people per capita as Aspen in high season, and the rest of the year there are a lot of them, too. They are one of the factors behind life in Aspen seeming so surreal much of the time, behind the observation that, even outside Don Johnson's party, no place on earth is so much like TV.

The famous have been drawn to Aspen nearly since its inception, as a silver-mining town. Jerome P. Wheeler, co-owner of Macy's Department Store in New York and a principal mine owner and town benefactor, built the eponymous and still-operating Hotel Jerome and Wheeler Opera House, which late in the nineteenth century attracted such famous "silver-circuit" acts as Madame Modjeska, Shakespearean actor James O'Neill (father of playwright Eugene), and Conreid's English Comic Opera. Aspen slept from 1893, when the price of silver collapsed on world markets and the U.S. Congress quit its silver price supports, until around 1949, when Chicago industrialist Walter Paepcke kicked off his plan to revitalize the town by celebrating the 200th birthday of the German humanist poet and writer Johann Wolfgang von Goethe. Though residents of the near-ghost town found the idea odd, Paepcke's event attracted leading arts figures of the time. His choice today seems prescient: Goethe was, in the words of poet W. H. Auden, "so far as I know . . . the first writer or artist to become a Public Celebrity."

More recent celebrities tend not to have been the high-minded cultural figures Paepcke was thinking of to people his paradise. The appeal for Hollywood seems to have begun in the late forties, with the arrival, for a fishing holiday, of Gary Cooper. Kim Novak and Lana Turner are remembered from the fifties. Others who arrived in the sixties and early seventies—now regarded as "pioneer celebrities"—include John Denver (still perhaps the celebrity most closely identified with Aspen), Jill St. John, Jimmy Buffett, George Hamilton, Jack Nicholson, Dr. Hunter S. Thompson, Goldie Hawn and Kurt Russell, Robert Wagner, Claudine Longet, and Sally Field. Hollywood appeal mushroomed after 1978, with the purchase of most of the Aspen Skiing Corporation by Twentieth-Century Fox. The Fox studio, and *its* new owner as of 1981, oilman Marvin Davis, made Aspen look more important to Hollywood and encouraged film stars to visit—work continued in the late eighties by such figures as Marshall Field's department store heir Ted Field, a producer of movies like *Three Men and a Baby*. Regular visitors of recent years have come to include Arnold Schwarzenegger and Maria Shriver, Cher, Paul Simon, Oprah Winfrey, Kris Kristoffersen, Michael Douglas, Don and Melanie, Don Henley, Martina Navratilova, Chris Evert, Barbara Walters, and many others. Among the nonentertainer bigwigs are: publisher Rupert Murdoch, Teddy Kennedy, Donald Trump, Leslie Wexner (owner of The Limited stores), Disney head Michael Eisner, and Columbia Pictures chief Peter Guber.

Originally, celebrities appear to have been attracted (like everyone else) to skiing and the beauty of the place. Another quality, as well, made Aspen particularly congenial: Those who came to Aspen came by choice and tended to be unusual, exceptional in their own ways. It is somehow not surprising that Harold Ross, the famous editor of *The New Yorker*, grew up there. The town's idea of itself as special meant that its residents weren't going to be overly impressed with celebrities, like people in any other "normal" place. Aspen's elitism made it possible for the "pioneer celebrities" to take a vacation, from fame and everything else. My longtime waitress friend Lanette tells a story of a local named Pete, who walked into his favorite bar one evening, pulled up his sagging Levi's, took his customary stool, and noticed a friend named Vodka George chatting away with Jill St. John and Jack Nicholson. "Say," he asked the bartender, raising his glass of whiskey. "Who're those people with George?"

Longtime locals like that tale because it puts celebrities in their place. But the idea of a local identity strong enough to deny the significance of celebrities is now dated. The celebrity presence has achieved a critical mass, and the hype that attends it is now a main fact of life. A reporter is mistaken by Don Johnson for a parking-lot attendant. ("Go get my car, will ya?" Johnson demands.) Herb, who drives the cab days, is stiffed by Ethel Kennedy. (She had a charge account with High Mountain and felt it wasn't her fault she'd climbed into a Mellow Yellow.) Lanette can't take a Sunday bicycle ride because she's working security at John Denver's wedding.

Once a simple getaway, Aspen is now a place for stars to be seen. Celebrities' press agents call local papers and the wire services to let them know their clients' vacation plans, and Hollywood figures in Aspen, especially around Christmastime, regularly hold parties to which they invite a lot of the same people they would be inviting in Hollywood. From the perspective of many old-timers, these people are not part of the community in the manner of earlier celebrities. Rather, they come in order to be associated with the name and to enlarge their own profiles. In so doing, it is felt, they exploit and undermine the community.

After his party, I called producer Don Simpson—who regularly throws celebrity parties—and asked how much publicity figured into his trips to Aspen. "We don't go to Aspen to get publicity," he said hotly. "We never have and never will. We don't go to Aspen to work. We don't talk business. We don't hang around with people who want to talk business . . . I ran into Schwarzenegger in the street, and we never talked about movies. It was, like, how's your skiing, how's your weightlifting and playing tennis—we talked like *civilians* talk." According to Simpson, Aspen is actually a Hollywood antidote: "At our party I noticed moments between Jane Fonda and Farrah Fawcett, who've never gotten along, and they were having the greatest time. And Farrah Fawcett said to me later that was the case. You take people out of this high-pressured Los Angeles environment and what we do for a living. You put them up there in God's country for two weeks and they got a couple of drinks and they're relaxed. And they become . . . they become what they really are, what we really all are, we're nice people." That all this might also help showbiz types who *do* talk business seems, of course, undeniable.

Even among "nice" celebrities, as among other visitors, there remains a strong desire to become an insider, meaning: to have friends who are locals. Friends who are locals are indispensable in finding out which restaurants are hot, where the good parties are, and who's cute and available. And local friends, used in conjunction with a personal track record ("I've been coming to Aspen for ten years, way before it was like this"), are good for deflecting the suspicion that a celebrity "uses" Aspen. Some locals seem to specialize in this job of "pet local." The relationship may seem unnatural, but in fact it's a perfect commensalism: The ski instructor (or other service-economy employee) gains the prestige of high-profile clients and companions and adds excitement to what's basically a dead-end job, and the celebrity gets some local credibility and a feeling that he or she is part of the scene.

The locals have their own code. They don't ask for autographs. They don't look impressed. Not only are people blasé about passing Jane Fonda or Julie Andrews on the street, they're *intentionally* blasé. In a cosmopolitan town, it would reveal a lack of sophistication to *notice*. You don't want to look like some shopping-mall person from Denver. "*What, you've never seen a movie star before?*" In Aspen, being cool is part of the pact.

Discretion is an aspect of this, and many move beyond it to protectiveness. Waiters at Abetone, for example, where Jack Nicholson enjoys an occasional meal by himself, are famous for the lengths to which they'll go to protect his privacy—sometimes physically blocking the way of other diners eager to introduce themselves. A waitress friend recounted a night when former Oakland Raiders quarterback Ken Stabler was seated at the bar of another restaurant. A patron who was drunk came over and began to hassle Stabler about a fumble that had cost the guy money in a bet he had made on the game. The bartender, as a matter of course, had the man escorted out.

The longer I was there, the more I found that attitude becoming my own. As a resident, I found myself unconsciously taking the side of the celebrity when confronted with questions about the manners of fans. That first summer, a local liquor store began selling maps to the homes of the stars; I agreed with the general outcry which persuaded them to stop. And I remember the feeling of anger that welled in me unexpectedly upon seeing a teenager holler, "Hey, Ed!" when he saw Ed Bradley walking down the sidewalk across the street. When the TV journalist looked over and stopped, expecting to see a friend, the kids just laughed. Under the Aspen ethic, celebrity locals such as Bradley become sort of adopted, like mascots that need looking after.

The *Daily News* may engage in it, but Aspen's paper of record, the weekly *Aspen Times*, tends to look askance at celebrity news. It is probably no coincidence that the editor of the *Times*, Mary Eshbaugh Hayes, has lived in Aspen for nearly forty years. "Who cares?" she interjected with irritation when a staffer mentioned that Senator Teddy Kennedy was back in town with ski celebrity Suzy Chaffee. "We don't cover it." This was a matter of warring images, warring self-perceptions. Hayes was concerned to convey an impression of Aspen as she knew it (and as it still is for some), an Aspen that was not simply a playground for the rich and famous but was a real community. To cover that sort of news, Hayes seemed to be saying, would be to acknowledge that it defined Aspen in some way, that it was important to the life of the town. And that was something that her Aspen ethic, forged in a precelebrity era, strongly resisted. Celebrity coverage was corrosive of the ideal of community.

Longer-established Aspenites were those least in celebrity's thrall. From them I learned the pleasures of critiquing celebrity manners. For his wedding, for example, Don Johnson hired security men to stop any cars ascending Little Woody Creek Road and keep out gawkers. One of those who fell into this net was Jessica Catto, publisher, developer, and wife of the U.S. ambassador to Great Britain. "What do you mean I can't go up there!" she demanded of the rent-a-cop before stepping on the gas. "I *live* up there!" And Johanna, coming home one night from dinner in town, had been infuriated by the shabby way Barbara Walters, seated at the table next to them, treated the waiter. " 'Get me this, get me that,' was all she said the whole meal," according to Johanna. It was fun, feeling superior to Barbara Walters.

Though too many celebrities may ruin the atmosphere, they do bring an affirmation: You live where they do. You share the rooms, the food, the sidewalks. Johanna's story was enjoyable to hear (as, indeed, these pages are enjoyable to write) exactly because of the words she didn't have to say: "There I was, eating dinner next to Barbara Walters."

My next visit to the Hotel Jerome was to see a celebrity I never would have imagined in Aspen: the Reverend Jesse Jackson. Don Johnson's bouncers had been replaced by Secret Service agents, who looked me up and down but let me pass. I watched the ballroom fill with Aspenites. The beginning of the rally coincided with the closing of the ski lifts, so many wore their brightly colored ski suits and even ski boots. Outside, the scene was chaotic as attendees squeezed between television news trucks, their satellite dishes raised, police cars, and official-looking vans. Inside, television cameras, microphones, and lights surrounded a table on a raised platform. Over a sound system, to a disco beat, the voice of Lou Rawls sang "Run, Jesse, Run," the candidate's campaign theme song. Rawls would sing out the name of a city, and a chorus in the background of the recording would answer him. "Detroit!" sang Lou Rawls.

"Run, Jesse, run!"

"Chicago!"

"Run, Jesse, run!"

"Cleveland!"

"Run, Jesse, run!"

"Aspen!" cried some wag in the room. A few people laughed.

Four-term mayor Bill Stirling, a delegate for Jackson at the Democratic National Convention, introduced the presidential candidate.

Silver-haired, fortyish Stirling was the only mayor in Colorado to announce his support for Jackson. (He was also the only one to have appeared naked on a calendar, the only one to support a ban on the sale of furs, and the only one to keep his dog on a strictly vegetarian diet.)

"People ask, 'Why should he come to Aspen?' " said Stirling. "It's too lily-white, too middle-class." He was interrupted by laughter. But, he continued, Aspen and Jackson had a number of common concerns, and he introduced Jackson to talk about them.

Jackson's passionate oratory was not dampened by the plush surroundings. He preached on civil rights, the liberation of women and gays, the needs of the urban poor. "We must revive the sense of the noble that distinguishes us in this world of turmoil," he said, and his audience listened raptly. Those who might have come just to view a presidential candidate got a little more: Many were weeping at the end of the speech, and there was loud applause.

But "why should he come to Aspen?" The real answer became clear over the next few days. At a private reception before his speech, Jackson had gotten to meet locals like Ed Bradley, activist Tom Hayden, Golden Hawn, and Hunter Thompson—people whose support could mean a lot to the campaign. Also, Jesse Jackson, in a few hours in Aspen, had raised $15–20,000, more than in any other stop in the Rockies. Jesse and Aspen were a perfect fit.

George Hamilton was sitting at the front table at Mezzaluna, the table reserved for a customer with good face recognition. I understood George Hamilton was an actor, but what he was famous for was his tan. No matter what, when, or where, George Hamilton had a suntan, a dark one that set off his white, white teeth. Were he to be hospitalized for six weeks in the dead of winter (and if he keeps doing that to his skin, he is likely to be), George Hamilton would walk out sporting a tan so deep and dark it's like a fetish.

George Hamilton, I noticed, was not really looking at the woman seated across the table from him. She was no one I recognized, and perhaps, I thought, that was why. His eyes darted up every time someone came in through the front door, they dodged to the left to size up the action at the bar, they glanced out the window at what was happening on the street. Occasionally, he seemed to be staring at simply a wall. This didn't make any sense until, on my way back from the bathroom, coming up behind him and in alignment with his gaze, I realized that on that patch of the wall was a mirror: George Hamilton was staring at himself.

Aspen is a great celebrity laboratory. You get to see the three-dimensional person, compare it to the two-dimensional image, and in so doing begin to see the ways celebrity is mistaken for accomplishment, and noise for wisdom. The achievement of many of those who come to Aspen appears to be 1) keeping their looks, and 2) succeeding in staying in the public eye for years and years. Certainly, there are exceptionally talented actors and musicians in Aspen, people whose fame rests justly on their art. But after seeing the others, close up and from a distance, you start to feel you've seen the emperor, he's not wearing any clothes, so why not say so?

Why not?

I was at a wedding reception and, with mixed emotions, found myself chatting with an attractive blonde, a longtime Aspenite, who from a past encounter I knew was suspicious of me. "What exactly is your book going to be about?" she had asked at our previous meeting. "What are your conclusions?" In a way that she might have imagined she could pass off as friendly, she had bid me goodbye with the words, "Better be careful what you write!"

Or what? I had thought—the goons are going to get me? The resort-association hit squad?

But if not guileless and sweet, Brooke had had the presence of mind to realize that a writer might mess with her myths, might question some of her self-understandings. And sure enough.

At our second meeting, we had both been drinking champagne, and Brooke elaborated on why she was worried about my book. My responsibility, she told me, was to portray Aspen the way it used to be, to write about the Real Aspen.

"And how did it used to be?" I asked, wondering which of the hundred standard Paradise Lost litanies she was about to recite.

But she was talking about something more personal than that. "I don't know, I'm just thinking about the times we'd hang out at Galena Street East, you know, with Glenn and Bernie and Don—"

"Henley?" I interrupted. She was naming members of the rock band the Eagles. She nodded, and carried on, about her life.

". . . and then Jimmy would come in, and Jann Wenner would be there . . ."

Jann Wenner, the publisher of *Rolling Stone* magazine, and singer Jimmy Buffett. Her svelte friend Nikki sidled up. "Remember those days?" Brooke asked.

"What, with all those guys?" Nikki had had a couple of drinks too. "Yeah, I remember. I remember when you could walk into the bar at the Mother Lode, say hi to all the guys—not on a weekend, okay, but maybe a Tuesday—and say to yourself, 'I've fucked every one of you!'"

Brooke smiled and laughed, and I imagined that back then, she too was a pretty hot little number. But now she was married, with two children, and her memories of the times when she partied with nationally known musicians . . . well, clearly, those were the days. Among other things, she could tell everyone back home, wherever she came from, that she was in Aspen, hanging out with, not the Eagles, but Glenn and Bernie and Don. She herself, by the Lloyd Haynes effect, would then become a minor celebrity.

But I wanted to ask Brooke: Beyond the name-dropping value, what was it like to know Glenn and Bernie and Don? Beyond their fame, how were they interesting? On what level did you click? Behind the image, were these people you could count as *friends?*

But we were at a party, a wedding reception. We were there to have fun, and everyone in Aspen, I sometimes thought, had helped sew the emperor's clothes.

The ski season had ended, and with it my employment as a taxi driver. I was not too sad about that, as I felt overly familiar with the view from behind the wheel, but I did miss the income. I had become friendly, however, with the proprietor of Lauretta's, a Mexican food restaurant where I frequently ate, and when Lauretta offered me work helping out on her catering dates, I took her up on it.

My first mission was to help cater a Saturday brunch for the members of the Roaring Fork Hounds, or the Hunt Club, as it was also known. These were people who, in the fashion of *Town & Country* magazine, donned their riding caps, black boots, and red jackets and galloped off on the trail of their baying hounds. The only difference I could discern between this event and the authentic English one was that in lieu of the fox, the hounds were on the trail of a coyote—a concession to the American West.

The others on the crew were Sandy, a bartender at Andre's who wore his white hair slicked back and had an earring; Whit, a precocious fifteen-year-old from downvalley who idolized Sandy; Harry, a low-key condominium manager; the robust Lauretta; and three Salvadoran women, Clara and Josefa, two sisters, and Joaquina, their cousin. Everyone on the crew, in their other lives, worked hard and a lot: the Salvadorans put in twelve or fourteen hour days for Lauretta six or seven days a week, Whit was a full-time student, and Sandy had been up till 3 A.M. the night before, bartending. When we had stopped outside Sandy's apartment in Lauretta's van to pick him up, it had taken Harry several minutes to rouse him.

"Three women," said Harry as he returned to the van with the bartender. "It seems such a shame."

"Do you remember their names?" asked Whit.

The Salvadoran women, as usual, were almost silent. Lauretta told me they had immigrated only two years before and were excellent cooks and the most tireless workers she'd ever seen. In addition to everything else, they had sweet dispositions. I didn't inquire after their immigration status; anyone who had made it out of El Salvador, I figured, deserved to be congratulated. They lived in a trailer, with their husbands, at the KOA Kampground near Basalt, and so had a forty-five minute commute twice daily in addition to their restaurant duties. Lauretta said they sent most of their earnings back home, to relatives. Though Aspen's worker corps had once been comprised mainly of ski bums, the cost of living and new immigration restrictions had reconfigured the laboring class: There were fewer Americans, far fewer European illegals, and many more Hispanics, who worked mainly back-room jobs.

The brunch was at the sprawling ranchhouse that presided over the fields where the ride would take place. As we pulled into the driveway, the riders were saddling up in the stables. A tennis-ball shooter by the garage was aimed at us like a cannon; poodles swarmed out, barking. Harry had been here before. "This is the part I hate," he said. " 'Good morning, Meredith. Yes, you *have* lost weight.' " It was a matter of debate whether she was on her fourth or fifth husband, and the extent of her plastic surgery. Through it all, the Salvadoran women said nothing, not even to each other.

Inside, though, they sprang into action. While we rolled up silverware settings in cloth napkins, sliced fruit for a large display, swept the deck, and lit Sterno under the "chafers," they placed aprons over their long cotton dresses and started preparing the more difficult food: *chilaquiles, chiles rellenos,* fat *quesadillas.* Meredith breezed through the kitchen, ignoring us and issuing orders to Lauretta.

Sandy, setting up the bar, began to feel the effects of his lack of sleep. He rubbed his temples, kept saying things like, "I've got an attitude. They better be ready for an attitude." I brought him lemons and limes and caught him staring out the picture window at some early-arriving guests on the deck. "Look at those Texan bitches," he said rather viciously. "Those big round glasses they wear, all that makeup. 'I think, uh, I think I'll have, uh, uh, club soda with grapefruit juice.' You bitch!" He continued to glare and then brought a hand to his forehead. "Oh, it kills, it kills." I said I'd try to get him something.

Our hostess was unavailable, the other guys had nothing, but Joaquina, when I inquired in Spanish, produced a big green tablet from her handbag. "*Esta buena,*" she said. "*Es fuerte.*" Andy appeared in the doorway and weighed it in his hand. "What the fuck is this?" he demanded skeptically. Clara and Josefa gestured at him to put it in his mouth, but still Sandy hesitated. "What is it, Demerol? Percodan? Percoset?" Josefa handed him a glass of water, and he tossed it down. Shortly thereafter, he underwent a miraculous transformation, sweet, happy, smiling at the Texan women.

I placed serving utensils on a pewter plate of the sort that usually read, "A loaf of bread, a jug of wine, and thou" or "*Salud, amor, y dinero.*" This one read, "Love Me, Love My Dog." With some time on our hands till the beaglers appeared, I stepped outside and picked up a stick to toss for the big poodle. As I cocked my arm back, however, he jumped the gun, leaping up to grab the thing out of my hand and in the process mangling two of my fingers. "Bastard!" I yelled at him. Trying to keep the blood off my white shirt, I went into the kitchen.

"*Ay, que te pasó?*" asked Clara, the first to notice my wounds. She put down her mixing spoon, washed her hands, and then ran water over mine. Clara clipped off a little stray skin using sewing scissors from her bag, and then Josefa dressed the wound. In moments I was back in action. I asked Lauretta if I could work in the kitchen.

The equestrians began to appear and soon were swarming over the generous spread of food we had laid out. Instead of the fifty people Meredith had told Lauretta to prepare for, it soon became clear there were more like seventy-five. The pace in the kitchen reintensified, letting up only when Lauretta told her cooks they should stop for a moment and see how the guests were dressed. They came back, looking amused. Clara said something very quietly to Lauretta, and later I asked what it was. "She said she thinks many American women would look better in pointier bras," Lauretta reported.

Besides our hostess, who I was told was in her sixties though she wore tight black jeans, black cowboy boots that reflected a coppery color in the sunlight, and a rhinestone-encrusted black sweatshirt to offset her bleached blond bouffant hair, there was one other standout character in the crowd. Instead of muddy riding gear, he was wearing a white linen shirt, unbuttoned way down, expensive European loafers, and a close-fitting dark suit. Also unusual for the crowd was his jewelry: rings, a bracelet, a small necklace. After the meal when he popped his head in the kitchen to ask, *"No hay cafecito?"* ("Is there a little coffee?"), there was sudden silence. Our cooks just stared at him, until Clara recovered and scurried over to pour him a cup. *"Muy amable,"* he said, exiting, and the women erupted in a babble of excitement. Lauretta came and confirmed their suspicion: *"Es el cantante Fernando Allende,"* she said—it was Fernando Allende, the international Latin singing sensation and part-time Aspen resident. I knew his music from my travels through Mexico, but when I mentioned him to the other guys catering, no one had ever heard of him. He had given a special concert at the Wheeler Opera House, which I'd heard was sparsely attended. It must be hard for him to come to Aspen and in effect leave his celebrity behind, I thought, though perhaps it carried weight in the south to be known for vacationing in a gringo glamour capital. I watched him move around the room: He was charming and gracious and seemed known by several people. Maybe it wasn't so tough, I thought; maybe it was a relief.

Back in the kitchen, they couldn't get over it. *Fernando Allende, in the next room! And Clara served him coffee!* Would it be improper to ask for an autograph? they asked Lauretta; she said she'd look into it. Wait till cousin Amanda heard they'd met the famous heartthrob, they were saying. *Don't you have his LP* Aunque Muero de Ganas *("Though I Die of Longing")?* The reverie was momentarily interrupted when a guest came in who had been konked on the head by the heavy kinetic sculpture on the deck: The women were gaining a reputation as first-aid dispensers. Joaquina dabbed his wound and sent him away with a green pill. But then they were back at it, constructing *chilaquiles* and even giggling—quite the change for the taciturn trio.

El cantante Fernando Allende, then kept repeating, as if unable to believe it. Jack Nicholson? Jill St. John? Who cared? *Fernando Allende. Fernando Allende!*

Though it was past 2 P.M., the lunchtime crowd at Bonnie's Restaurant showed no sign of abandoning the sundeck. "There are more people here than on the slopes," commented Tracey, a Denver friend as we clomped onto the deck in our ski boots. After a windy, icy-cold morning, people were thawing out, working on their tans. So brilliant was everyone's ski clothing, with colors not found in nature or, really, in most any other quarter of the human world, that you imagined a flock of birds comprised only of the males, a selection of the most dazzling.

The feel of the place told you it was an in-crowd—there was a sense of confidence and ownership in the easy way ski equipment was scattered across the picnic tables and benches, in the slightly out of place feeling you got as a newcomer; something in the air said, "We belong." The crowd was more middle-aged than fit the popular image of Aspen and had an L.A. look. The one-piece ski suits, covering all the women and most of the men, had come unzipped; and I felt our look, of separate ski pants, sweaters, and windbreakers, was dated. Clothing white, black and iridescent was belted and scarved in silver and gold. Among the jewelry were big diamond earrings, Rolexes, flashy rings; Walkman cords were the most common necklace. The older women had been face-lifted; the younger women were with older men. A well-maintained man was wearing a Warner Brothers ("WB") sweater, with the Bugs Bunny logo on the chest. Somebody had bought a bottle of Sarah's Vineyard chardonnay and was filling plastic cups all around. There was blond hair everywhere.

Inside, we stood in line to buy what would prove to be the best ski-area restaurant food we'd ever eaten, as well as the most expensive. Bonnie's served meals far superior to the average ski-area fare of cheeseburgers and chili: We got grilled ahi steak on French bread with pineapple salsa, caesar salad, a spinach burger, and apple strudel with freshly whipped cream. There was a wine list with twenty-four kinds of chardonnay, high-end champagnes, or reds like the fifty-dollar Banfi Brunello di Montalcino—but we got seltzer. The wall we stood next to as we waited was covered with photos of beloved locals and celebrities on skis. Five people ahead of us stood Martina Navratilova and another very fit woman; we followed her brown-eyed gaze to a photo of . . . herself, shooting off a mogul, backlit. Martina stared at this photo for rather a long time.

Trays loaded, we walked clumsily out the door, trying not to be too distracted by the beautiful crowd or the beautiful view: You didn't want to fall. Two thirds of the way up Aspen Mountain, Bonnie's was perched on the edge of Tourtelotte Park ski run, commanding a view of most of upper Aspen Mountain, with the Silver Queen gondola in the far background. Two months earlier, Donald Trump had stormed down this staircase, eager to escape Ivana, who had become enraged inside over the attentions her soon-to-be-broke billionaire husband was lavishing on a fledgling starlet named Marla Maples. We scooted onto the end of one of the crowded tables and took off our jackets.

A few months earlier, I remembered, I would have felt intimidated here. All these perfect people, all the beautiful smiles and taut bodies and right clothes: It could really wear on you, the kind of pressure the place exerted. But Tracey had helped me become less self-conscious. We grew up in Colorado, she reminded me. It's our place, we've been at it since we were kids. The fashions were superficial; these people would come and go, but we would last. It was the only snobbery available to us, the underdogs.

Tracey nudged me and murmured in my ear. Across the table, at the far end, was Jack Nicholson. He was standing up to go and looking rather shorter and pudgier than I expected. Still, he had the face, those eyes . . . it was kind of exciting, and we tried not to stare. Two women were with him, both attractive, as well as a young male ski instructor. Most celebrities in Aspen hire instructors to ski with them all day, whether they want a lesson or not: With them, they can cut lines, avoiding both the wait and the possible encounters with fans. By the weight of Nicholson's clothing, I could see he had started the day early, when it was still so cold: He had mittens, not gloves, a heavy knit hat, goggles, and a black half-face mask. He was kind of sweating, his forehead. Trying not to be too blatant, we stared at Nicholson as he and the entourage trudged off.

We reapplied factor-twelve sunblock to our faces, hoping to avoid the premature wrinkling you see on longtime Aspenites. We leaned back in the sun, enjoying the high altitude, the cold breezes, the occasional visits from big Gray's Jays—"camp robbers," as they're known—swooping in to boldly lay claim to lunch scraps. After a while I sat up and put my sunglasses back on—the sun was too bright without them at this altitude, with the white slopes reflecting light back at us from every direction. Ajax is the local nickname for Aspen Mountain—it comes from an old mine claim nearby, but the Homeric resonances seem fitting.

Suddenly, I noticed something left at the other end of the table—it was Jack Nicholson's face protector. Made of a thin, foam-rubbery fabric, like that of a wetsuit, it was cut to fit over the nose, cheeks, and chin, with tiny holes punched out for breathing and a Velcro closure to secure it behind the neck. It was for keeping cold wind from burning your face. It was quite damp, probably from being breathed in.

"Tracey, look."

We discussed going after him to give it back, but he had been gone several minutes—it would be hard to find him, though fun if we did. I decided to keep it with me, in case we saw the entourage on the slopes.

We shook off lethargy and returned to our skis. We rode the number 3 high-speed quad lift to the summit and tightened our boots. It was cold up there at eleven thousand feet, so I zipped up my jacket and put on my hat. Then, reaching into my pocket, I pulled out Jack Nicholson's face protector. Smiling at Tracey, I put it around my face. It seemed like a good fit. As we leaned on our poles and started an easy glide down toward Gentleman's Ridge, I filled my lungs. The air was passing through Jack Nicholson's face protector. His face had just been there; I could feel the moisture of his breath. It was like being pressed against his face. We were on top of Gentleman's Ridge, with a view across the summits of all the other peaks. Earth was meeting sky here. This was Ajax Mountain, pantheon of the gods, and I was breathing Jack Nicholson's air.

Chapter III

His Rocky Mountain Highness

*For years I listened
to the incomparable John Denver
Singing of stratospheres
and Rocky Mountain splendor
But I never knew the meaning
of Rocky Mountain High
Till I boarded a plane for Aspen
and took off through the Western skies . . .*

*Nobody's fat in Aspen, everybody eats brie cheese
Disco-dances at Tippler's all night,
in the daylight strap on skis
You can see them sliding down Snowmass Mountain
Drinking at Little Nell's
Nobody's fat in Aspen, everybody's so damn . . .
healthy.*

—CHRISTINE LAVIN,
"NOBODY'S FAT IN ASPEN"

I got a job working as an extra on the filming of *John Denver's Christmas in Aspen*, a TV special. Paul Andersen, a friend I'd made during my short time in Aspen, had snagged us the tickets through a connection at *The Aspen Times*, where he was a reporter. Also along was Devon "Devo" Meyers, a *Times* photographer with a crazy streak.

Much of the special had already been filmed around town—a duet with singer Anne Murray in the lobby of the Hotel Jerome, scenes of John Denver and his new wife riding horseback in Starwood, shots of madrigals in front of the Sardy House, and a distant aerial picture of a couple of hundred motion-picture hopefuls holding candles at night on the Hyman Avenue mall. But this was the prime opportunity: We got to be part of an "intimate" audience watching John Denver sing "around the campfire" with the Nitty Gritty Dirt Band. The night was clear and cold; the invite said to dress warmly in "Western ski wear." With our down parkas, Sorels, and long underwear under our blue jeans, we drove up Maroon Creek Road, toward the Bells.

John Denver seemed to do these specials almost every year; since his career fell off, back in the late seventies, it was his best public exposure. It was a popular combination—John Denver, Aspen, and Christmas: family-style entertainment in a storied mountain setting, with songs that by now evoke a nostalgic glow. Also, Christmas is a sentimental holiday, and John Denver has never been embarrassed by sentiment.

Who could be against John Denver at Christmastime? His proposal this year to close some streets during filming had caused a stir; some on the city council objected to the inconvenience, the commotion. But as is often the case with John Denver, it was hard to know if they were really against the street closings or against John Denver himself. Councilman Michael Gassman, in an attempt, one felt, to not get personal, said that Christmas in Aspen—the high season— was popular enough already. Representatives of the resort association countered that it was a free promotional bonanza. And they won.

There was a free feed first, at the T-Lazy-7 dude ranch—burgers and beans, beer and wine. We were served by T-Lazy's "wranglers," who in winter had mostly snowmobile duty at the ranch's rental center. I recognized one guy called Big Sky, as in Montana, from nights in the cab—he sat at the reins of T-Lazy's stagecoach-taxi, behind horses equipped with diapers so that their manure wouldn't foul the streets. He and a couple of others did a good job looking like cowboys, and I asked Paul and Devo if they thought they really were.

"Shit, man, this is a dude ranch," replied Devo. "They ain't cowboys. They're hicks."

Aspen, I kept forgetting, was about pretending. We shared a table with part of the film crew, who were visiting from Los Angeles. They didn't like the cold, didn't like to work at night. "Have you met John Denver?" I asked the worker next to me, a soundman. It was a serious question, but he thought I was joking. He rolled his eyes. In much of the country, I recalled, John Denver was unfashionable. John Denver was beneath serious discussion.

At around 10 P.M., the wranglers rose to shepherd forty of us up a snowpacked, moonlit trail in the woods to the snowy clearing where filming would take place. Paul and Devo dropped into conversation behind me, so I struck up an acquaintance with Julie, a teenager from Oklahoma. Recently arrived in Aspen, she was working as a maid at Aspen Highlands. Julie told me she was a big fan of John Denver's and that this was possibly the most exciting night of her life.

"He's the main reason I thought of coming to Aspen," she told me. "You know, he's from here."

"Well, he lives here, but he's not actually from here," I said.

"He's not?"

I explained what most Coloradoans know, that Denver (born Henry J. Deutschendorf, Jr., on New Year's Eve of 1943), was actually from various other places, including her state, Oklahoma, and moved to Aspen in 1970, at age twenty-seven.

"He did?" As we neared the brightly lit clearing, I could see her eyes, and the look in them made me feel like the Grinch. The clearing was surrounded with production-company trailers and the noise of generators. We entered it squinting, ducked under a camera on a boom, and all took our frigid seats on bales of hay.

Half an hour passed, and the chill that set in made it easier to empathize with the stoical group of square dancers, dressed in skirts and shirtsleeves, who staged a brief performance for the cameras inside a log pavilion at the clearing's edge. We waited some more, and Julie began to shiver: Being an extra was harder work than we'd expected. It was about 11 P.M. Finally, someone poured gasoline on a pyramid of logs to our left—this must have been the campfire. But no one complained about the size of the blaze. In fact, many abandoned seats far away from it in hopes of thawing, but they were told to return—the show was about to begin.

John Denver appeared, and we applauded. Julie perked up, wide-eyed. He was garbed in jeans, boots, sweater, scarf, and guitar and standing with the woods behind him. Amidst the trees had been placed a chuckwagon and a banner reading CHRISTMAS IN ASPEN. Though it had been years since he scrapped his granny glasses for contacts and a more up-to-date look, to me he still looked funny without them.

John Denver tested the microphone, and reminded us of our job: "Remember, when they introduce me, I'm your favorite guy." Moments later a production assistant, standing off camera and clapping his hands emphatically, let us know that now was the time. John Denver smiled and launched right into his signature ballad. *"He was born in the summer of his twenty-seventh year . . ."* It was kind of thrilling to be just a few feet away. When I was younger, this was a song I believed in. In the freezing cold air, warm breath left his mouth as steam.

To our surprise, a voice over a loudspeaker interrupted him half-way through the second verse. "Okay, we got it," it crackled. But even more startling, as the performer put down his guitar and turned away, was that the song continued on for several seconds, as though John Denver were still singing—prerecorded! At this point I decided that Denver was also a good actor. Evidently noting our dismay, he turned back to the mike and explained, "I'm going to have to lip-synch tonight—you know, like they do in the big cities." In the big cities? I figured Julie, even if she never left the side of her television in Lexington, Oklahoma, would know what lip-synching was—where did he think we were from? Or, more to the point, where did he want us to think *he* was from?

Julie still wanted an autograph, though, and asked me what I thought the protocol was. "Maybe between songs," I suggested, "when he doesn't look too busy." We listened and watched and clapped dutifully as John Denver mouthed the words to the start of "Rocky Mountain High" four or five more times. "Now?" Julie kept asking me. Finally, between takes, she approached him. Sorry, he said, she'd have to wait until after all the filming was done. Returning to the bale, she was sheepish and apologetic.

"I'm not really this immature," she explained, "but nobody famous lives in Oklahoma." In fact, I couldn't think of anybody—it was an interesting point. "But a friend of mine met James Garner at the Marriott," she added, in Oklahoma's defense, "and someone else I know saw Tom Cruise at the airport."

Reading from cue cards held up behind us, John Denver introduced the Nitty Gritty Dirt Band, which frequently doubled, these days, as his backup band. Looking surprisingly clean-cut and blow-dried, they stepped up to four microphones and sang along with "Country Roads," the other big hit that Denver was doomed to repeat ad infinitum to oldies fans. We spent quite a few minutes, Paul, Julie, Devo, and I, debating whether this one was lip-synched too, and decided that with all the instruments now backing him up, it probably was not.

A wrangler threw another log on the fire, almost slipping on the smooth sole of his cowboy boot, and answering my question about real cowboys. Real cowboys would not be wearing cowboy boots on packed snow. Devo confirmed this judgment, saying he preferred not to be flat on his ass when he was shooting a story. What was going on up there, at the dude ranch, was ersatz cowboy, Westernalia, cowboy style but not cowboy substance. That was fine, of course, but why was I suddenly lonesome for the real thing?

"Hey, he's wearing blush!" added Julie, becoming infected by our undercurrents of skepticism. On the third take, they cranked up a fog machine that in the cold air worked shockingly well, threatening to obscure the entertainers entirely. "It smells like medicine," she observed, finally concluding it was "kind of gaudy." By the end of the evening, with frozen toes and fingers but still without an autograph, she muttered to herself, "I must've been crazy to come up here for a stupid autograph." I was surprised by such a sudden change in a die-hard fan but was sort of getting to like Julie.

The voice over the loudspeaker returned, this time speaking to us. "No videos or cassette recordings," he warned. "This show is copyright."

"Yeah," John Denver chimed in jokingly. "I'll sell it to you—for ten million dollars!" This was interesting because ten million was the sum the Soviets wanted from Denver as fare for a space-shuttle ride. The papers had reported that he refused to pay it. The papers also reported that some of Denver's detractors were trying to raise enough money for half of that sum—for a one-way ticket. And in fact, after he flubbed the next several takes by misreading a cue card ("Rats!" he cursed), someone did yell out, "How about five million?"

"Far out!" hollered someone else. John Denver knew when he was being heckled. He did not respond.

The celebrity most closely identified with Aspen over the years must be John Denver. He also may be the celebrity who most closely identifies *himself* with Aspen. From "Rocky Mountain High" to his hit "Starwood in Aspen," from the city he chose as a surname to the town he chose as a home and a headquarters, things alpine and outdoorsy are his image and his passion.

"Doonesbury" cartoonist Garry Trudeau wrote several series of comic strips featuring his profligate character "Duke," a Hunter S. Thompson takeoff, reacting with outrage (and rifle blasts) to the strains of "Rocky Mountain High" drifting over his fence from a neighbor's house. Though Thompson and Denver actually live a couple of miles from each other as the crow flies, each is a perfect foil for the personality of the other. As surely as Hunter S. Thompson represents to outsiders the profane Aspen, worldly and sinful, John Denver is the clean Aspen, natural and innocent and upright.

When he first went there from Minnesota with his wife Annie, "in the summer of his twenty-seventh year," he was in transition, deciding what to do following the dissolution of the Chad Mitchell Trio. Aspen offered him beauty, inspiration—and acceptance. He played to admiring audiences at the Leather Jug in Snowmass and the Wheeler Opera House, sang a benefit concert for the Visiting Nurses Association. He remembers his decision to settle there in tones suggesting a revelation. A reception had been given in his honor at a home in Starwood, and the day after, he told me, he returned to take a second look at some land he had seen there. "I'll never forget, I had Annie in my hand, I looked out there, and I said, 'We'll take it.' I didn't know what it cost, didn't know anything. But I knew I was home."

If the presence of Hunter Thompson was an unpaid advertisement for bohemian Aspen, a call for freaks and rebels, the presence of John Denver seemed to pave the way for seekers, for nature lovers, for spiritualists, for flower children. His supporters, some of them now New Agers of the nineties, viewed him as a champion of honesty and of children; to them "Rocky Mountain High" was never Muzak but heraldic, a sort of spiritual call to action.

Apart from his recording work and promotion of Werner Erhard's est seminars, in Aspen he is known mainly for his efforts on behalf of the Windstar Foundation, a group he helped start in 1976, to "inspire and bring forth ideas and models that contribute to a world that works through research, demonstration and education," according to its literature. His main partner in the project was Tom Crum, a local expert in the martial art of aikido and author of a book about it, *The Magic of Conflict*. (Crum, who still teaches aikido classes at the Aspen Club, is one of those amazing middle-aged men, of which there are many in Aspen, with the muscular, well-defined bodies of teenage athletes.) With $3 million of Denver's money they founded Windstar, involving R. Buckminster Fuller in the building of its geodesic dome greenhouses, various "futurists" in its annual "Choices" symposium, and scores of Aspenites in its environmental education programs, Earthkeepers children's program, educational exchanges, and audio and video productions. The Windstar Foundation has evolved from an entity devoted to fighting nuclear power and promoting "appropriate" energy technologies into one devoted to "personal transformation" and "planetary consciousness."

More than most figures of popular culture, John Denver has always inspired polarized responses. Fans, though their numbers have dwindled, still see him as the embodiment of positive values like love, home, friendship, and a pure environment. Detractors, more than a few of whom might be found to have one or two of his albums in the basement, consider John Denver the Hallmark card of contemporary music. (A *Newsweek* cover portrayed him as a human sunflower.) They disdain his Pollyannishness, his Mr. Good Guy attitude and, in Aspen, his trumpeting the virtues of their secret paradise (and, in the same stroke, the promotion of his own career). The press has seldom been his friend—"a cross between Johnny Appleseed and the Singing Nun," wrote one reviewer— and newspapers have reveled in stories that were less than admiring.

In Colorado, and Aspen in particular, John Denver has a special meaning. He's a sort of living embodiment of the profound local ambivalence toward tourist promotion. On the one hand, people are glad to have someone talented singing about their home, extolling their way of life, and attracting the visitors, who, to anyone involved in most local business, mean a good financial future. And on the other hand, fearing the growth and change associated with too many new arrivals, people wish he would just shut up.

Though it's often been national news, in Aspen what John Denver does is local news as well, and it was with more than a little interest that citizens read about what has probably been John Denver's biggest public relations fiasco. While Colorado was suffering from a gasoline shortage in 1979 and rationing was being imposed, it was revealed that the singer had installed on his property a four thousand-gallon underground gas tank to prevent any personal shortages. "His Rocky Mountain Highness" crowed one local headline. Denver's protests that he needed a sure supply to make all his concert dates sounded feeble ("Hey guys, hey guys, I got no gas," he told reporters at his house), and finally, disgraced, he removed the tank.

Then there was the time the singer shot a neighbor's young dog with a BB gun. The BB lodged in the dog's shoulder, and the neighbor complained. Her dog had been "giving my little dog a hard time," Denver explained, in apology. From a low-key headline in *The Aspen Times* ("Starwoodite 'Fesses Up to Dog Shooting"), the story quickly made its way to the wire services, fueled again by the implicit comment on the singer's "good guy" image.

Detractors' mouths watered again during his divorce from Annie, his first wife, who still lives in Aspen and is widely known there. Annie, the woman to whom he dedicated "Annie's Song," seemed to become a John Denver hater herself during their marital troubles in the late seventies, and while he was away on one of his many protracted absences, she had a tree company cut down some scrub oak her husband left in front of the house. Furious, John returned brandishing a chainsaw and proceeded to cut a kitchen counter in half. Annie left it there on display for a while, showing it to those interested. I actually like the story, because it showed John Denver to be capable of some of those less-nice emotions he had so thoroughly excised from his public persona—vindictiveness, violence, anger.

I kind of grew up with John Denver; it was hard not to. During my high school and junior high years, when his career was peaking, it was the done thing among my friends and me to try and *look* like

John Denver: jeans, hiking boots, flannel shirts, granny glasses, longish blond hair, big smile. Everyone who learned how to play the guitar would sooner or later sing "Sunshine on My Shoulders" and "Leaving on a Jet Plane" (which Denver wrote).

We Coloradans, lacking our own strong regional identity, are susceptible to outside influences. Country music is popular here, but it originated in Texas and the South. Cuisine we adopted from everywhere—especially Mexico, of late. Beef, though an important industry, is prepared in ways invented elsewhere. The oldest residents are Native Americans, but they're scattered around a few reservations, culturally insignificant except, perhaps, for takeoffs on their art; and the next oldest are Spanish-Americans, descendants of early explorers, who are concentrated in the southwestern part of the state. Much more than Denver, Santa Fe and Albuquerque are their cultural capitals. Hard rock miners—prospectors seeking silver and gold—were something of an indigenous population, but their day, too, has passed. There are plenty of farmers on the plains of eastern Colorado, but culturally they are more a part of the Kansas and Nebraska plains of which their land is a natural extension. When people think Colorado, they think mountains. But the settlement in these mountains is new. Here in Colorado, we lack hillbillies, Appalachians—indigenous culture. What we have instead is John Denver.

John Denver filled a void. In school in Denver, we grew up singing some pretty peculiar songs that someone cooked up so we could have Colorado pride. Everyone I know here winces to remember our song-festival recitations of "If I Had a Wagon."

> If I had a wagon I would
> go to Colorado
> go to Colorado
> go to Colorado!
> If I had a wagon I would
> go to the state
> Where a man can walk a mile high!

Verses proceed according to different vehicles and how they would get you to Colorado ("*If I had an airplane I would* fly *to Colorado*"; "*If I had a Chevy I would* drive *to Colorado*"; and finally,

"If I had a spaceship I would land *in Colorado").* At least this song catches the spirit of the place by alluding to arrival: in a state barely a hundred years old, nobody's been here very long.

Perhaps then it is not hard to see how John Denver made inroads into our local culture. We always felt that growing up near the mountains and learning to appreciate the outdoors made us special, and his lyrics and popularity confirmed it. Whether it was because the sixties weren't long gone or because junior high was a time for that, John Denver's seeming sincerity, directness, and praise of the environment spoke directly to us. My sisters wrote him fan letters, and he sent back photos of himself, long-haired, smiling, in a floppy hat, signed, "Peace, John."

Denver still records and his voice sounds better than ever, but radio stations rarely play the songs and almost nobody buys the records. Though it's available, *Rhymes and Reasons* is somehow not the sort of LP one imagines being re-released as a CD. The thought of being caught playing his old records is a little embarrassing.

When, in Aspen, I walked into a record store to buy a tape of John Denver's 1988 album *Higher Ground,* the store clerk sort of laughed under his breath. He had hated Denver, he said, ever since his junior high school chorus in Colorado Springs had had to sing "Rocky Mountain High."

Hate seemed a little broad, I suggested; could he pinpoint his objections? After some thought the clerk said, "You know what it is? *The guy has no scar tissue."*

I believe the clerk hit upon the right metaphor. Though he's approaching fifty, there remains something annoyingly peace-and-flowers about John Denver. His image is too innocent, like the supposed qualities of Aspen he promulgates: untrammeled beauty, unspoiled nature, goodwill ("Skiers are the friendliest people in the world," he once told a reporter). Despite unsavory episodes in his life and his times, he insists on optimism. It seems a zealot's optimism, on a level with the *Up with People* show ("Up, up with people/They're the best kind of folks we know!"), one difficult for the average person to share. On most of us, as we get older, can be seen some evidence of tracks where the world ran us over. John Denver, by his own telling, had a tough childhood in certain respects. An Air Force brat, he was constantly being uprooted. He didn't have many friends. Life wasn't so great. But for so long, the greatness of life was all he could talk about.

It's one of the many contradictions about the man. He frequently counters questions about his sincerity by remarking, "I'm very much like I have seemed all of these years." It's said with a tone of humility but in fact seems intended to discourage further inquiry. John Denver probably *is* just what he has seemed—except for the parts of him that come off as uncomplicated or unsophisticated. It takes a complicated person to simplify things the way John Denver does. It takes more than just a nice guy to get to the top of the recording industry. Another paradox, as one critic noted, you notice from your earliest observations of the singer from up close: John Denver is innocent; John Denver is tough. "The great Middle Class that produced him teaches, ardently, that tough people aren't innocent and innocent people aren't tough."

Maybe this is what happens when you get ahead of your image. While John Denver the singer had to be canny and single-minded to succeed, John Denver the celebrity had to remain sweet and oblivious to maintain his appeal. I think the John Denver who sang so ecstatically of nature and the passing of time, of friendship around campfires and "how right it is to care," really meant those things. The lyrics to "Poems, Prayers, and Promises" (which I have known by heart since age thirteen) constitute nothing less than a raw manifesto for being in love with life.

Writing songs like that, in these cynical times, is risky: You have to stick your neck out. Belief is not trendy; and bald declaration can get you hung. But there was a moment when for millions of people his songs did not cloy but affirmed, when his positive outlook evoked the spiritual attainments of a Jonathan Livingston Seagull. At its best, the work of John Denver suggested that maybe you didn't have to give in to the dark side, maybe you could walk away from collisions with the Big Truck of life.

To see his present-day moodiness is to sense the collapse of a grand edifice of positive thinking. If people don't believe him now, perhaps it's because he could never understand the ironies other people sensed in his career, because, in his boundless sincerity, he couldn't laugh at himself. The possibility seems doubly unfair for one who, in essence, may be a simple man: Amidst the hipness, the knowingness, the overwhelming irony of contemporary times, John Denver, God bless him, doesn't get the joke.

Even in Aspen, $6 million buys a lot of house. It was a rectilinear mass of glass and stone, with four floors that sort of stepped down the steep mountainside and full-length balconies overlooking the valley on at least two of them. The house, at the end of a dark dirt road, was brilliantly lit; the wide, long front drive looked like a short airport runway. Walking down it, Paul, Devo, and I passed a three-car garage with all doors open, revealing a Range Rover, a Bentley, and a small American luxury car. We had just left Paul's rusty old Volvo in the hands of a parking valet; that, and the sight of this mansion at the end of a country dirt road, gave me the feeling it was going to be another one of those nights. One of the two massive front doors was open, and we stepped in onto the marble floor of the foyer.

Our host, Ritz-Carlton developer Mohammed Hadid, was there to shake our hands. He was throwing this summertime bash to celebrate the impending marriage of his neighbor, John Denver, to an Australian singer named Cassandra Delaney. We were there because friends of ours were friends of Cassie's, and they needed more boys at the party. The friends, Abby and Jennifer, introduced us around. It was hard to pay attention to the people, though, with the house making such a big impression. We had entered on the third floor; the wall on the side of the valley was practically all glass, and lights glittered below. Above us, at foyer's edge, a long indoor balcony overlooked the foyer from the fourth floor. To the left were a living room, with a sofa unit big enough to sleep about five people ("That wouldn't even come close to fitting in my apartment," said Devo), a bar area, black, with a mirrored ceiling and formally dressed bartenders, and a gleaming black pool table.

We got drinks, and Devo fantasized on the seeming likelihood that someone would burst through the front door and kidnap or murder the mysterious Hadid in a rain of bullets, shattering the many mirrors. Something about the opulence of the place seemed to invite, or be associated with, that sort of thing. Hadid interrupted these unworthy thoughts by showing us the food, and then we met more guests, including a number of female Australians (aggressive, good dancers), Hadid's lieutenants, a pretentious sculptor, a slinky, serpentine blonde named Amy who met each of us by standing too close and staring deep into our eyes, the lovely Cassandra Delaney, and even John Denver's future mother-in-law, a somewhat rambunctious woman with leathery skin and a broad accent. Everyone except John Denver.

Hadid's wife, a decorator, had evidently tried to soften the look with some tapestries, Impressionist-style paintings, and wooden furniture. But a certain hardness still prevailed, enforced by all the glass, the many gold-plated fixtures and, especially, the marble floor. A creamy alabaster shade, it extended the length of the ground floor and was polished to a high luster. So solid and expansive was that floor that one could imagine it a natural outcropping from the mountain, responsible for the siting of the house, which had been blasted, chipped, planed, and polished down to its present perfect horizontal flatness.

Onto this surface, occasionally that night, some hapless guest or caterer would fumble a crystal champagne glass, and the instant the delicate vessel connected with the marble, it shattered like a star, sending tiny glittering fragments sliding to the walls. With the impact also came a delicate but sharp report, and by the third time you heard it you knew without looking that the floor, like a windshield speeding toward tiny insects at 60 miles per hour, had claimed another victim.

Though he was most of the reason for the party, I was still surprised to see John Denver come through the door. What was he doing in a place like this? Was it silly to think he'd be out camping or sitting in a cabin somewhere? And the developer Hadid—what could possibly bring them together as friends? Dressed in jeans and a western-style snap-front shirt, John Denver shook hands and touched the shoulder of Hadid, briefly said hi to us and the many people in the room who must have adored him, and then retreated to a corner and spent most of his time talking to a guy named Roger, who was both caretaker of his house and his massage therapist.

Installed on the marble floor, next to a fountain and not far from sumptuous spreads maintained by the many caterers, was a country band. The members of the band, dressed in country clothes—jeans, boots, plaid shirts, and cowboy hats—served as a quaint backdrop to the elegant surroundings. But they were good, and the vigorous dancing taking place on the expanse of marble in front of them made them seem more a part of the place. I danced with Abby, but having expected the ideal surface—no bumps, perfectly uniform—I was chagrined to find my feet wouldn't slide. Something about the polish made the marble want to bond with the soles of your shoes. To move them, you had to lift them, and the dancing was hard work.

The band's fiddler led a dance line across the floor and into the foyer. With my hands on the waist of Hadid's slender wife and someone else's hands on mine, I noticed that between the small pair of hands clasping the fiddler's ample waist a transmitter had been belted to the small of his back. This allowed the fiddler's music to keep coming out of the band's speakers, since he—stepping around like the pied piper—couldn't possibly be attached. It was the new country music.

Then John Denver stood up. Suddenly, he was all smiles, all charisma. He strode to the microphone, cowboy boots wobbly on the marble and, accompanied by the band, sang a song entitled, "Homegrown Tomatoes." It was an upbeat tune, and I noticed some of the people from Australia slapping their thighs or tapping their toes. But something wasn't quite right; the country-boy thing didn't go over in that mansion. John Denver singing that hokey song made me want to get out of there.

Paul and I snuck into the glass-walled elevator and went down to the bottom level. Besides two guest bedrooms, there were an indoor-outdoor swimming pool, a large bathroom with gold-plated fixtures, and a very fancy workout room. There was a deck overlooking the darkened valley and a big Jacuzzi. We stood out on the deck, like kings surveying our realm. A commuter plane, climbing out of the valley from Sardy Field, passed close overhead, illuminating us starkly with its headlights and momentarily drowning out our conversation. What did John Denver really know about homegrown tomatoes, which didn't grow well in Aspen anyway? I asked Paul. Scrub oak covered the hills beneath us. Paul guessed there might be guards out there somewhere, patrolling the perimeter. It was strange to think—this was John Denver's neighborhood.

My friend Gary is from New York. He was in town for a couple of weeks, writing a piece for *Esquire* on the Aspen Physics Institute.

So far, he was enjoying the welcome: Always eager for the right press, members of the local publicity corps were making him comfortable. Caroline Bishop, for example, of Bishop & Bishop Marketing Communications, got him a two-week pass to the Aspen Club, gratis. Gary told me he liked working out over there but felt a little out of his element. "Everyone's so nice, everyone's so attractive," he told me suspiciously.

I wanted him to meet some locals, get a taste of the "real Aspen," so when I heard Alison was having a little get-together and John Denver was expected, I invited Gary along. About eight people were there when we arrived, lounging around the living room of Alison's log cabin, drinking beer, smoking dope, talking, and giving massages. John Denver hadn't shown up, but his Australian mother-in-law had, and she was enthusiastically sharing in the spirit of the thing. Specifically, when my friend Suzy offered to rub my feet, John Denver's mother-in-law offered to rub Gary's.

He looked panicked. We looked down at his feet: He was a tall guy and they were big feet, in penny loafers, with no socks. "I-I'm not sure you want to do that," he suggested, unstretching his legs and curling them up close beneath him.

"Don't be silly!" protested the vigorous Australian, grabbing Gary by the calf and unsheathing the left foot. It didn't smell too good—I could tell that from my seat across the room—but she didn't blink an eye. Soon she was pouring Alison's scented oil between the toes as she kneaded them. Though foot massages were heaven to me, Gary was squirming, glancing up at me for sympathy or a rescue. But I had no thought of intervening. Gary's right foot was next. But no sooner had his benefactor removed one hand to reach for her beer than Gary wrestled free, sprang to his large feet, and excused himself to the bathroom.

Beer and massage calmed everyone else to the point of somnolence, and we were revived only when Suzy lifted her guitar from the case and sang some country songs. She then passed the guitar to Paul. As a singer and, especially, satirical songwriter, Paul was a minor celebrity in the valley: His "Downvalley Shuffle," about the plight of Aspen's commuting class, was a hit on local radio, as was his "Ghost Bikers in the Sky," a paean to mountain-bike culture. Most people in the room also knew Paul sang some parodies of John

Denver songs. Inevitably, somebody requested one. It might have been me.

Paul laughed, reddened, and sang a different song. With the mother-in-law present, it was a bit awkward. But a short time later, out of Paul's mouth came this version of John Denver's greatest hit:

> He was bored in the summer
> of his twenty-seventh year
> Bought a condo in a place he'd never been before
> He left poverty behind him
> But soon he was bored again
> Now he's buyin' up the key to every door.
>
> When he first came from the city,
> He didn't really see
> All the money that was waiting to be made
> But then his eyes were opened
> To the values that are real
> Real estate, that is,
> His brand new stock in trade.
>
> And it's Colorado Rocky Mountain Bu-u-y!
> You can see those dollars rainin' from the sky
> You know he'd be a poorer man
> If he didn't buy low, sell high
> Rocky Mountain buy! ("in Co-lo-ra-do . . .")

We were all laughing except one. John Denver's mother-in-law seemed to have lost a bit of her ruddiness. But I could have sworn I saw the hint of a smile. She had, I was thinking, remarkable self-control. Two songs later, a guy named Fred who'd had several beers took Paul's guitar in hand for this version of "Country Roads":

> Grunt and moan
> Make me come
> Use your mouth
> Use your tongue
> Wet vagina
> Mountain mama
> Grunt and moan
> Make me come

As a full smile broke out, this time she deserted the circle for the refuge of the bathroom. We were a tough crowd. Fortunately, Gary was out by then.

"Why don't you go see how she's doing, offer to rub her feet?" I asked.

"Fuck you," said Gary.

At 10 A.M., I was John Denver's first appointment of the day, and I wasn't a minute late: The interview had taken seven months to arrange. The door had been left unlocked; I let myself in. It was the guest house next to the big house Denver owns in Starwood, at the bottom of a steep dirt road with several switchbacks. One wall of the room was a long floor-to-ceiling window affording a panoramic view across the Roaring Fork Valley and the Elk Mountains, including snowy Pyramid Peak and 13,200-foot Mount Daly. Alone, I stared at the view for about fifteen minutes, wondering how I would ever get any work done with such a thing to gaze at. Finally, John Denver, hair blow-dried but still slightly wet from the shower, arrived with a brown Labrador retriever at his heels. He shook my hand. He wore a purple Windstar sweatshirt, embroidered cowboy boots, designer jeans, and a lot of gold: gold Rolex, gold chain around his neck, big gold rings with stones encrusted—I even wondered whether his glasses frames, now more aviator- than granny-style, weren't gold. The expensive accessories and his often preachy style of rhetoric came to remind me of Oral Roberts. A New Age Oral Roberts. He was, however, earnest and attentive and sat on an ottoman while I took a chair. The Labrador, Bear, rested between us.

We talked for two hours. He was fairly articulate and spoke in long thoughts, not changing subject frequently. Having read several interviews with him that had been done over the years, I knew the new ground I wanted to cover. He, though, continually turned our conversation back to the old ground: After years in the public eye, he had a firm understanding of what he would reveal and what he would not. (He did not want to show me his house, for example.)

We both had recently visited Australia, and that was my opener. There remained a strong demand for his music down under, he said, and he liked the country: "It seems very innocent to me." I noted he liked it so much he had found a new wife there. Cassandra was in the main house, he said, still sleeping.

He told me of his love for Aspen, about arriving there nearly twenty years before.

We talked of contradictions. I wanted in particular to understand how his promotion of Aspen could square with his environmentalist, no-growth stance regarding change in Aspen. On my flight from Sydney to Los Angeles, I said, they had shown a film promoting Aspen and the Rockies that featured him as the narrator. He said that his promotion of Aspen (his "support of Aspen," he called it, using the language of est) was not tourism-hype—"I'm not in the tourism business"—but simply singing about his home. "I think that's the kind of person I am—I would've been that way wherever I had lived, and this is where I happen to live." When I answered that regardless of his intention, productions like his television specials served the purposes of promotion, he took a different tack, downplaying his importance. "There were things that are . . . going to happen to this place irregardless of what someone like myself does. . . . The world is getting too small, we know about places like here, and like Telluride, and we know that more and more, there are people from all over the world who can afford to come to a resort like Aspen, Colorado. And whether it's Aspen or Key West or whether it's the Bahamas or whether it's the Indies or whether it's the Whitsunday Islands in Australia, they're all going to be dealing with the same problem." In other words, it was the land developer's rationale: Somebody's going to do it, so it might as well be me.

The United States may be unique among nations in that here, not only can an entertainer become wealthy enough to found an institution designed to change the world, he will do it. So it is with John Denver and Windstar. We talked about the genesis of Windstar, and he gave me the same reminiscence I had read elsewhere. Even though I knew the material, I was mesmerized by the rhythmic way he told it and fascinated, when I typed it out, to see how much it nearly resembled a passage from the Bible. The simple declarations, repetitive structure, and prophetic tone made me think every sentence deserved its own tiny verse number, as in the Book of John (Denver), 3:14:

"You know," he said, "I take this back to when I was twelve years old. This is in Tucson, Arizona. And I used to spend a lot of time by myself. I wasn't a real popular kid, didn't have a lot of friends, and I'd go out in the desert. Or across the street. There was a neighbor, caddy-corner across the street, that had these three tall eucalyptus trees. I used to climb up in the top of those trees, and sit and daydream and fantasize.

"I always knew that I was someday going to have a place in the mountains, that people would come to from all over the world. And these people would be friends of mine. And I would be the catalyst for their coming to this place. And whether I was there or not, they would have places they could stay. And they'd meet other people, and there would be great relationships that would come out of this, great friendships. People would come out of this place, and they'd sort of be strengthened. They would get what I get out of sitting up in the tree or being out in the desert or being in the mountains. Or what people in the city get out of walking in Central Park. And they would be able to go back to the world where they live stronger, nurtured, a little bit wiser through the people they'd met, and also knowing that they weren't alone in the world. And part of it was I felt kind of alone in the world when I was young. So I can take that back to when I was twelve years old.

"So it was amazing to me that this vivid picture in my mind was always there, and that when I finally found this place here and got to spend time in Aspen, that it was everything I ever dreamed my home would be and what the mountains were to me. And then I started meeting people—there were other activities going on here that made it a pretty interesting community, and met people who had the same kind of feelings that I did. And then all of a sudden—I was being *very* successful and making lots of money and what was all of that for, you know? And here was this idea."

And he said something that helped me understand how he is different among recording artists. His sunshiny image, he pointed out, "wasn't the kind of thing that really created success and interest in the general terms then and now in the music business. If you look back at it, most of the big stuff that happened in music over the period of years started getting really hot over here in New York or L.A. or Europe and then it would sweep the country. You know? I started in the Midwest. And I spread out the other way. And I'll bet you I'm darned near the only recording artist that has had the kind of success that I've had that has done that."

At this point in the conversation, I made the mistake of steering us onto the subject of John Denver in space. It was a rut that would, a tiring hour later, lead to the end of the conversation, a track I couldn't get out of.

His efforts to get himself up on the space shuttle had lasted nearly eight years and stemmed from the need, he explained to me, "to really communicate the space experience and what it offers people, not only our people but the world at large. And I think the way to do that is to fly a private citizen, someone who can communicate, and I volunteer." A broadcast of songs from an orbit around the earth was part of his plan.

It was a good fit in some ways—John Denver, the son of a pilot, was a licensed jet pilot himself, with a public commitment to the sort of global thinking that people associate with space exploration. He made headway with the NASA bureaucracy but never seemed able to convince politicians or the American public. Too many, probably, just couldn't get past the idea that apart from being a selfless act for the planet, it smelled a lot like a mammoth effort at self-promotion.

When the *Challenger* explosion put the kabosh on the idea of any more civilians in space, John Denver approached the only airline that was still flying: the Soviet Union. (It was around this time, significantly, that the Windstar Foundation began inviting Soviet journalists, politicians, and aerospace officials to Aspen; one of them, Yevgeny Velikhov, a politburo member and top science adviser, was bestowed $10,000 and the Windstar Award in 1988 "for contributing to the creation of a sustainable, peaceful future while advocating and promoting ways for all of us to participate.") After much cogitation, the Soviets decided that the best they could offer was the $10 million round-trip ticket. An erroneous newspaper report that Denver was willing to pay that sum, coupled with a factual, simultaneous story that the astronauts were against him ("John Denver, You're No Christa McAuliffe" read the headline), caused an uproar and the second public relations crisis of his career. At a news conference at the 1988 Windstar "Choices" symposium in Aspen, he officially took himself off the trail.

"I have no plans now to pursue it," John Denver told me. "Everything is on the back burner till way after that baby is born." The impending birth of his first child, and his recent marriage, had supplied a way to save face.

Though he said he had given up, I couldn't get John Denver off the subject of space. He seemed obsessed, and filled another side of a cassette tape with details of his abortive search for this Holy Grail. You could see he had invested a great deal of emotional energy, probably even pegging all hopes for resuscitation of his career on a space flight. As he spoke, it slipped out that he had written only one song in the past year.

His joyousness had been a major theme of interviews from early in John Denver's career, something the interviewers would remark upon. Now, though he tried to be upbeat, the singer seemed more preoccupied than joyous. John Denver suffered that malady, endemic to Aspen, of being rich and washed up at a fairly young age. Though he had had a longer run than most, he was typical of many pop stars in that his work spoke to people for a strictly limited period of time. Mick Jagger and Paul McCartney could keep drawing large audiences well into their middle age, but not many others could. There was a twist to John Denver's malaise, though: He refused to accept it.

Throughout the conversation, both of us had occasionally glanced out the window, and once John Denver remarked on it: "I think that view right there is the most beautiful view that I have ever seen." So striking was the view that it had almost seemed like a participant in the conversation. I thought of the quote from Oliver Wendell Holmes, Jr.: "Fresh air and innocence are good if you don't take too much of them—but I always remember that most of the achievements and pleasures of life are in bad air." It seemed too much to suggest to John Denver that maybe he come down off the mountain, take a change of scenery, muck it up with the riffraff for a while. More than the contact lenses, it might suggest to the world that there was something more to John Denver, something important we didn't know about yet.

Chapter IV

Changing Times

My job was to report on the doings of Stefan Albouy, and it wasn't easy. All day long Margaret Albouy, mother of the controversial young miner, had been telling me she didn't know where Stefan was. At around 2 P.M., though, I learned that Albouy had made his move: The county had granted him special permission to drive big trucks up to his marble claim in the Maroon Bells-Snowmass Wilderness. By 3 P.M. I was changing into hiking boots at the trailhead and grumbling to myself about his mother: Stefan, as it turned out, had departed her house for his claim at 4:30 A.M., accompanied by five armed Forest Service personnel. I had been tricked and now had to make up for it.

I set off at a slow jog. I was worried about the advanced hour—I didn't want to arrive or have to return in the dark—and also I was worried about the competition. This was my first big assignment for *The Aspen Times,* my new employer, and with the weekly paper due out the next day, we had a good chance to pull off a rare scoop of the *Aspen Daily News.* But only if I got there first and only if he'd talk: Stefan Albouy, twenty-eight, seemed mad at the world, indeed at the twentieth century. The press had probably helped fan the flames of hostility against him and he had no reason to be well disposed toward me, an uninvited stranger.

The Conundrum Valley looked as pristine on that warm August afternoon as it did any other summer day—verdant evergreen slopes rising up to snowy peaks in the distance, an environmentalist's paradise—except for the deep, muddy tracks impressed on the soft grass alongside the footpath. Only hikers had been allowed since the valley was designated a national wilderness area in 1980, and the road had begun to disappear. Wilderness, with its prohibition on machines of any sort (including bikes), livestock grazing (permitted on other federal lands), and campfires (except by permit), was the most protected category of public land—wilderness was practically sacrosanct. Albouy's truck tracks, as I stepped over them, seemed a rude defilement, an environmentalist's nightmare. And that's what the whole thing was about: Albouy's mineral rights to the patented claim superseded the Forest Service's surface rights. But in heavily "green" Aspen, people were furious.

After an hour and a half's hike, I could see the tracks of Albouy's caravan veer uphill off the track at a steep pitch and I followed. The way was blocked almost immediately by a fluorescent ribbon strung between two pines and hung with a sign saying DO NOT CROSS. KEEP OUT. I stopped to catch my breath, but my heart kept pounding with nervousness. If the rangers that morning had been armed, Albouy probably was too, because he expected trouble: Recently spray-painted on a block of the marble he wanted to take out were the words *In Memoriam, Stefan Albouy*. A newsletter from the extremist Earth First! group had been found in a truck parked at the Conundrum trailhead lot earlier. And according to Albouy, radical environmentalists had phoned in a threat to a Denver television station, saying he would be physically prevented from removing any marble from his claim.

"Hello! Anybody there? Stefan!" I stood at the tape and shouted loudly. Minutes went by and there was no response; I wished I had worn a bulletproof vest. I held up my reporter's notebook, the closest thing I had to a Red Cross armband. "Stefan!"

Three figures appeared in the dark space between the trees ahead; I saw the silhouette of a long gun. Stefan Albouy, whom I had seen only in pictures, entered the clearing in front of me, followed by two men holding pistols. He carried a sawed-off shotgun. Stocky, serious, and short-haired, Albouy approached slowly, stopping at about fifty feet.

"What do you want?" he asked in a surprisingly deep voice.

"*Aspen Times!*" I called out, in a higher one. I explained my mission: to talk to him about the quarrying, to hear *his* side of things. He interrupted by waving me in, looking annoyed. The trio turned to walk back up the trail as I caught up with them and introduced myself.

Dusk was falling when we arrived at their camp. Hidden amidst a grove of blue spruce, it was set up in the manner of covered-wagon trains in hostile Indian territory, the four vehicles—a six-wheel-drive military truck, small bulldozer, and two pickups—parked in a protective semicircle. Two horses were tied to trees, and I could also see an old sheepdog on the periphery, nuzzling for scraps. In the middle was a fire, and seated around it were two more men and two women. Stefan told them who I was but didn't introduce me. The gray-haired woman cackled when I asked if she was Mrs. Albouy—she'd been on her way out the door the last time I called, she laughed, and Stefan had been here all day! I tried to manage a smile. The others were younger—friends of Stefan's, it turned out, mostly contemporaries from Aspen High School who worked blue-collar jobs and helped him with mining when they could. They wore caps, denim jackets, and work boots. The young woman, pretty but not glamorous, was his girlfriend.

Mrs. Albouy, showing no hard feelings, offered to feed me along with the rest of them—dinner for the troops was fried chicken, corn on the cob, and mashed potatoes. I conducted the interview as we ate, Stefan answering all the questions and no one adding to or questioning a word he spoke: He was in charge. And he had some definite feelings. I asked why he had started work so furtively at 4:30 A.M.—did all the negative reaction make him feel criminal?

"I did it in an effort to avoid useless confrontation with would-be idiots," Stefan asserted. He was referring to environmentalists, especially the radical kind that would practice civil disobedience or break other laws to make a point. It was ironic that the press portrayed him as a renegade and troublemaker, he said, when it was extremists like Earth First! that "don't respect the law."

He pointed out that the deal he'd made with the county allowed him only to retrieve certain blocks of previously cut marble and that he had to "revegetate" the road when he was finished. His goal was simply to "prepare slabs" of the marble and test the market. Ultimately, of course, he dreamed of reopening a quarry operation on the site; but this, I knew, would provoke howls of outrage from environmentalists as well as the owners of the houses built near the trailhead, who had probably never seen anything more industrial than an old Volvo rumble by.

"Of course," chimed in Mrs. Albouy, "recreation causes more damage than miners do." "Conundrum," her son explained, "was a nice, quiet valley" when he was growing up in Aspen, "but once it was turned into a wilderness and advertised and everything, it turned into a cesspool." Vastly more disruptive than a few miners, he argued, were the "legions of weirdo backpackers who come through here with their hideously colored backpacks." One "hypocrisy of the environmental movement," he claimed, was that far-ranging recreational backpackers scared away much more wildlife than did operations his size. "There's almost no real wildlife left around here anymore."

I wondered out loud if the original mining boom of a hundred years before hadn't been the pivotal crisis for the environment: Aspen then, with smelters spewing smoke, with raw sewage, large-scale deforestation, toxic tailing piles, and hungry prospectors fanning out to work any conceivable mineral deposit, had been an environmental disaster area. Stefan shot back that a return to those days was barely conceivable and that it was just the sort of sensationalistic scenario his opponents cooked up to discredit him. Arguing, I realized, would only put Stefan more on the defensive, and that wasn't what I was interested in. I wanted to get him off the soapbox for a while and learn how he came to occupy the position he was in—one man against a town, a new rider on such an old horse. So I threw some wood on the fire, sat back, and listened.

Stefan went back to chatting with his friends. They seemed to have known each other most of their lives. They were guys who drove pickup trucks, worked with their hands, enjoyed country music. Work with Stefan was sporadic, since he couldn't pay much, but it was a role they liked: renegade miners, transplants from a different economy and a bygone era. As the fire crackled they rolled their own cigarettes and told tales of rappeling in the dark, inside mountains. It was clear they cared for the mountains as much as their enemies did, but in a different way. Swearing, Stefan had once told a reporter, "The ski company can take a D-9 [bulldozer] and hack the top of a mountain off [e.g., to build a gondola station] and there is not a squawk. It's not like the mines are raping the country." As a miner in Aspen in the 1990s, it seemed Stefan spent more time in court than in the mines, and the frustration was palpable: They were trying to do hard work, traditional work, work that was a calling, and everyone was in their way.

I slept briefly at home, then drove into the office early to write my story by the 11 A.M. deadline. Frank Martin, the staff photographer, planned to shoot the group at work that morning and rush his film down: We had a front-page story. By the time I'd put in a couple of hours at the aging computer terminal, it was 9 A.M. and the *Times* was humming.

I first became intrigued by the *Times* because, in a town changing as fast as Aspen is, permanence is interesting. *The Aspen Times*, published continuously for 109 years, is a piece of the soul of old Aspen. Located on Main Street between two other local institutions, the Hotel Jerome and Carl's Pharmacy, its very soulfulness makes one sense it must be threatened. And yet every Thursday, in delivery trucks and in the shoulder bags of boy vendors who try hard to keep the change from your dollar, out it comes.

It was my friend Paul Anderson, a reporter and columnist for the *Times*, who had helped me land the summer job. Paul, thirty-eight, was a refugee from suburban Chicago who came to Colorado for college, became the editor of the Crested Butte *Chronicle*, and moved to Aspen when life in the smaller resort began to seem claustrophobic ("It's too much to keep doing the same story three or four times, interviewing the same people, writing the same features"). He was a fitness buff, not of the health club but of the gearhead (mountain biker) and three-pinner (cross-country skier) variety, finishing work as soon as possible in order to do one or the other daily. Never married but often dating, he was an adherent of bluegrass music, puns, and recycling. On the bumper of his old Volvo, which out of principle he drove as little as possible, was a sticker that read HONK IF YOU'RE JESUS.

I liked Paul immediately, and when I told him of my mission, he said that working at the *Times* would be a natural for me and that in fact there might soon be an opening due to a reporter's maternity leave. I interviewed with the editor, Mary Eshbaugh Hayes, who said I "seemed okay," and in April I began as a reporter, making $350 a week.

Like the skiing company or the Hotel Jerome or Aspen Mountain itself, *The Aspen Times* is one of those fixtures of town life—repositories of local culture—that change over the years but not fundamentally. Its graphic design and multisection format have been the same for years, its tone is familiar, and its adherence to the rules of journalism is perennially flexible. If *Times* reporters are aggressive, it is mainly in their drive to be comprehensive. The editorials are liberal, and the lively letters and op-ed pages offer a forum equaled only by public meetings for citizens to let off steam. In a typical week, the paper will feature an editorial against a proposed development or the use of short skis (they create small moguls, which the classical, longer skis find hard to negotiate), a column about dogs or housing or world affairs, and the standard photo sent in by readers who had their picture taken reading the *Times* while visiting Tibet or Madagascar or the Mariana Trench. (Five thousand of the twelve thousand subscribers live outside Colorado.)

The most popular feature is probably Mary Hayes's "Around Aspen" column. Neither a society nor a gossip column, Hayes's listing of Aspen people and their recent doings is basically a chatty chronicle that spreads over two pages. The elfin Hayes, who with her straight-cut bangs, shoulder-length brown hair, lively eyes, and huge glasses somehow looks girlish at sixty-two, is pictured at the top. She tries to attend the major functions with her camera—and is often pressured by big-city press agents to put their clients' names in the column, but she refuses to play social arbiter: John Denver's name may or may not come before that of the town clerk. The column follows locals and part-timers to New York, Hawaii, and Patagonia: "Aspenites have had a summer full of memorable moments. **Phil Weir** has bought a scuba-diving resort in Honduras . . . giving a going-away party for him last weekend were **Lilly Garfield**, **Jimmy Lynn**, **Johnnie Walker**, and members of Mountain Rescue. In Aspen Phil sold real estate and also . . . appeared in cigarette ads in national magazines. Blacksmith **Francis Whitaker**, who now lives in Carbondale, has returned from a six-week jaunt around the country. First he went to Salinas, Calif., where he gave a talk about writer **John Steinbeck**, whom he had known in the early years before Steinbeck became famous . . ." The column always ends with Mary's "Undercurrent," which may be a paragraph's meditation on the state of the world or simply a sentence noting that "the sugar-daddies are back in town with their sugar-babies . . . must be winter." Over the years, Mary has also summoned popular locals on to the pages of *Aspen Potpourri*, a cookbook featuring her black-and-white portaits and the person's favorite recipe. The book—not the sort of thing you still expect to find in Aspen—has sold 10,000 copies.

The office is as deceptively simple as Aspen itself: A single-story storefront presents itself to passersby, who enter the old wood-and-glass door to find an L-shaped counter and a bench for resting. But beyond the reception room matters get complicated. I discovered this the first day, when I was sent to find the photo editor "in the back room." The warrenlike *Times* office has many back rooms. The one I ended up in, three turns and two changes of level from the front office, was a cul-de-sac that had an entire wall with rocks set into it. A typesetter in an adjoining room informed me it had been modified by *Climbing* magazine, whose staffers would occasionally be moved to get up from their typewriters and do a little practicing. ("Now it's for the rest of us when we get to climbing the walls!" she quipped.) The apparent end of another route was a room reserved partly for back issues but more prominently for ski and bicycle maintenance and repair. A dozen pairs of old skis of various descriptions rested in the corners, and there was a long workbench covered with the residues of hot ski waxing and bike part lubrication. The room also functioned as an indoor garage for fancy mountain bikes owned by employees who didn't want to park them out front.

One such employee left with his bike as I stood there, befuddled, and slammed the door behind him; from overhead came a shout of rage: *"Don't slam, goddamnit!"* A woman appeared at the top of a short set of stairs and glared at me. "Never slam that door! Our computers crash!"

"It wasn't me!" I insisted. "Are you the photo department?"

"No, *Climbing* magazine," she said, disappearing back into her garret. I stood. Another door opened.

"Photo department?"

"Sorry. *Aspen Free Flyer,*" said a portly fellow, emerging from another dead-end room. "Photo's over there." He disappeared behind another door, which I saw was the bathroom, and I looked at the only remaining door. "Anybody home?" I said, knocking and opening it.

"*Shut the door, we're developing!*" hollered Frank, the photo editor. Bingo.

The last dead-end was the line of six plywood stalls, overflowing with phones, computer terminals, and papers, known as Reporters' Row. "I hope the fire inspector never comes in here," mused reporter Madeleine Osberger one day, echoing my concerns if not my exact wishes: Seated toward the very end, I had an interest in hoping one would. The stalls were so small and so close together that virtually anybody's conversation could be heard by anyone else down the row; and speaking *sotto voce* to one's paramour or secret source over the phone was likely to provoke a protest from a neighbor that he or she couldn't overhear you. Among the constant sounds one had to deal with was the noise of the police scanner, which the police reporter left on twenty-four hours a day, in hopes of getting early notice of the latest drug bust or car wreck.

In the large central room stood the illuminated layout tables, a curtained-off camera room for producing enlargements and half-tones, and the kitchen area, dominated by a huge old white porcelain sink. More than the front-office switchboard, the sink often seemed to be the information center of *The Aspen Times*. Vacationing or departed staffers wrote to old friends care of the sink ("Dear Sink," began a dozen postcards affixed above it), and current staffers posted invitations to parties there. A bit further along the wall sat the photocopy machine, decorated one morning with an image of one reporter's pressed-to-glass face, the next with someone's buttocks, and yet another with a woman's flattened breasts and the notice FREE MAMMOGRAMS.

The Times was a place where, as my friend Claudia told me upon taking a job as receptionist, the want ad for her job included the stipulation "must like dogs." Someone called repeatedly, her first day on the job, to ask if Hershey was back yet. "Hershey, call on line one," she paged repeatedly until someone informed her that, um, Hershey was a brown Labrador who had decided to take a little walk.

Hershey had lots of friends; their names, Claudia explained to me, kept coming up on the front-office wall calendar, where someone had noted all their birthdays. Sugar, an ancient and practically blind black dog of unsteady bearing lay under his owner's desk and trembled during thunderstorms; Sparky, a visiting Boston terrier, could run a fair distance up walls; Dante, a big smelly mutt, belonged to the window washer, who was suspected of "mistakenly" leaving him behind when he had jobs to attend to in less congenial environments. I met a Golden named Molson and a retriever named Skylab. Because the corridors were narrow and busy, major disruptions could be caused by pitching a tennis ball for Hershey or by the meeting of two dogs that didn't like each other. Hershey, unfortunately, took an instant dislike to me, growling and even barking when I came into whatever room he happened to be reclining in. I developed a commensurate dislike, which lasted about three weeks, after which both of us just forgot about it.

If the atmosphere was a reflection of Aspen outside it, it was also a reflection of the *Times'* longtime publisher, Bil Dunaway. The robust, gray-haired man, who occupied a tiny, crowded carrel situated between Reporters' Row and the advertising offices—right where a publisher should be—*was* the *Times* in many ways. He had bought the nearly moribund paper from a printer in 1956, a few days after being fired as editor of *Skiing* magazine in Denver and a few years after serving in nearby Leadville with the army's Tenth Mountain Division. Dunaway (as he was known by all) had been there so long that by the time I arrived, the paper, guided by tradition, seemed almost to run itself. This allowed Dunaway to keep a relatively low profile. Yes, occasionally he would have to fire someone or "have a little chat," but his decisions were never capricious or personal and they seemed, in most cases, long overdue. From his little carrel he ran something of a corporate empire, including radio stations, downvalley newspapers, and property holdings all over town. Success for the low-key Dunaway had come from cunning and perseverance and had resulted in stability, for which I was grateful: Had Dunaway not owned the *Times* building, surely it would have been renovated and let out as a big Gucci store.

At his flagship *Aspen Times,* Dunaway concerned himself mainly with writing editorials and editing the letters; in addition, he covered meetings of the city council. Dunaway was such a fixture at council meetings, seated inevitably in the first row, that members frequently consulted him on points of information: "Bil, was it '78 or '79 we first took up that option on the Gerbaz property?"

On Dunaway's cluttered wall hung a black-and-white photograph of one steep face of a snowy peak; Dunaway had made the first descent of Mont Blanc on downhill skis. Though that had been some thirty-five years before, he was still in top condition. "He was a handsome cuss back then, when he still had hair," said editor Mary Hayes, "a real ladies' man." My most indelible image of Dunaway came from the day when, returning from lunch and in a hurry to get to the phone down Reporters' Row, I had been blocked in the narrow corridor by a man in cycle gear struggling to get a sweaty woolen jersey off his body. It was stuck somewhere around his head, and arms pointed up, unable to see, he was bumping his white-haired torso around, creating a commotion, causing the more excitable dogs to bark. "Excuse me," I said impatiently, moments before my boss finally succeeded in freeing his head.

"Dunaway!" I choked. He pulled on a chamois shirt and reached for trousers he'd left across his desk. His lunch break had been a twelve-mile bike workout. If you were unlucky, he'd nab you for a hike on the weekend—"just a quick one"—up 14,265-foot Castle Peak or up a long circuit off Independence Pass.

Dunaway made no bones about his liberal orientation, and his reporters—like many Aspenites—tended to share it. "Hayduke Lives!" proclaimed stickers affixed to several surfaces around the offices—a reference to the radical environmentalist hero of Edward Abbey's *The Monkey Wrench Gang*. As I sat down to write my Stefan Albouy piece, I was glad Albouy hadn't been by lately to notice.

In such a rarefied town, the beats were strange to match: Among mine were tennis and polo; others had such territory as the *Food & Wine* Classic, "churches and cults," and drugs and alcohol. These were, however, the spice: They added flavor to what was, to my surprise, a mostly ordinary menu of small-town journalism. Most of my time was spent on obligatory sorts of subjects like weekly church news, new nurses at the hospital, high school sports (all the teams were "the Aspen Skiers") and summertime softball league results, the boring yet reassuring trivia that filled small-town papers everywhere. The Elks Club *did* still meet, even if most Elks lived downvalley. There were the features on the advent of tick season, the Carbondale arts fair, summer hockey camp at the municipal skating rink, and audition calls for the Aspen Community Theater production of *Harvey*.

As drama critic, it was my job both to publicize *Harvey*, through a feature on its preparations, and then to review it, on opening night. "Just summarize it, say the things you liked," my predecessor advised me when I asked her for tips on the review process. But I wrote what I actually thought. Sadly, I opined, despite some winning moments, the performance was deeply flawed.

It was a big mistake. From that day on, for two or three weeks, I couldn't walk down the sidewalk without passing one of the actors or backstage people who had devoted weeks of unpaid time to making *Harvey* a reality. None spit on me, but I felt like a heel; I realized that apart from its sophistications, Aspen was a small place and the community theater was aptly named.

A second realization was that the big story in Aspen, the subtext to almost all news of interest, was growth, resistance to it, and the strains it brought and choices it created. Stefan Albouy was just one example. In the four months I worked at the *Times*, we covered the controversy over the building of the Ritz Carlton Hotel, which would be the largest structure in town; the possible development of the Aspen Meadows, a plot of sacred land near the music tent; the shortage of affordable housing, which threatened the summer festivals; teardowns of historic structures; and the proposed widening of Highway 82. Every new strain and every reaction was news; the paper was perhaps the main public way Aspen tried to keep track of its identity and deal with what was happening to it.

Sometimes it was from the "extracurricular" assignments that you could learn the most.

Mary Hayes and I got along well, and a consequence was that when her husband was disinclined, I got to escort her to the society events she covered for her "Around Aspen" column. First there was the Ballet/Aspen auction buffet at the home of an enormously wealthy arts patron named Christine Aubale-Gerschel, where guests bid on items from a humble Gore-Tex windbreaker (sold to me, for $50) all the way up to a week at Goldie Hawn's Malibu beach house ($5,000) or at another couple's Palm Springs condo, with round trip via their private jet ($12,500). We went to a ball and to an art museum benefit. And there was the soiree outside at Floyd Watkins's Beaver Run Ranch, catered by Les Dames d'Aspen.

This was an event I particularly looked forward to, given the host's horrifying reputation. Since cashing out of his bill-collecting business in Miami and moving himself to Aspen, he had been setting the town—and in particular Woody Creek, his new home—on its ear. First there was the matter of his behavior as a person. According to lore, he had insisted on paying for his first three drinks at the down-home Woody Creek Tavern with hundred-dollar bills. At a Ducks Unlimited dinner, he was said to have stood up and told the conservation-minded hunters of a place in Mexico where in a single day you could shoot more than a hundred ducks. During another day of shooting on a private hunting ranch, Watkins's shotgun apparently misfired, striking, of all things, a prize AKC golden retriever named Pennygold of Aspen. Pennygold's owner tearfully scooped her up in his arms and ran her to the vet, where she died within hours. In a dispute with his wife, Janelle, Floyd pleaded guilty in court to having dragged her by the wrist behind a Kawasaki motorcycle. Not long after, Janelle called police twice one morning, first to say Floyd was threatening her, and then to say she was afraid she'd shot him through a locked bathroom door. He told her he'd been hit, Floyd later explained to deputies, to trick her into stopping her shooting.

But as far as folks in Woody Creek went, that wasn't even the bad stuff. I was reminded of the rest of the controversy as we turned onto the dirt Woody Creek Road and soon found ourselves eating the dust of a pickup truck with an eleven-foot fiberglass trout in the back of it. "That must be for Floyd's pond," commented Mary, and I nodded: Alongside bucolic Woody Creek, last stronghold of funk-iness and authenticity in Pitkin County, Floyd was building a giant trout pond. And a giant house, with a giant stone wall. But it was the pond that had raised local hackles the most. To build it, Floyd had basically bulldozed Woody Creek—illegally changed its course, using bulldozers, graders, and front-end loaders. The resulting dis-ruption and silt had caused the death of fish downstream, and the county had filed a criminal-misdemeanor charge against him, to which he pleaded no contest.

A group calling itself the Woody Creek Running Beavers took

defensive measures. First they defaced the RUNNING BEAVER RANCH, 6 MILES sign Floyd had posted at the bottom of the road, covering it with one that read, FAT FLOYD'S TACKY BEAVER RUN RANCH. PUBLIC FISHING WELCOME, 6 MILES. Later, they sawed it down completely. Floyd had also been harassed by the attempted poisoning of his dog, rifle shots that had knocked out his bright nighttime "security lights," and the inscribing of his massive, freshly poured concrete driveway with the words, *Fuck you, prick.* Late on the night of that final offense, hidden near his gate in a four-wheel-drive truck, Watkins awaited other tormentors. When he was awoken by what he described as five shotgun blasts, twenty rounds of automatic weapons fire, and six shots from a pistol, Watkins gave chase to the Jeep from which they came. Confronting its occupants in the driveway of another nearby ranch, Floyd came face-to-face with a young woman and . . . Hunter S. Thompson. According to Floyd, Thompson said, "You have been given a warning: There is to be no trout operation or any more concrete poured in Woody Creek." Instead of murdering him, Watkins filed a complaint with the police.

"I was attacked by a giant porcupine" was Thompson's alternative version, delivered to the papers the next day in his defense. "I was going up there and saw this huge porcupine. I stopped to look at it. It swung at me and attacked me. And I blasted it.

"Hey, don't laugh," he added. "Look at Jimmy Carter. Jimmy Carter was attacked by a killer swamp rabbit. He had to beat it off with his oar." The authorities claimed to have no hard evidence that Thompson had done the shooting, and he was never charged.

Property in Woody Creek had never been marked by anything more permanent than a three-strand barbed-wire fence, but Floyd changed that. Into a valley of rustic log cabins he had imported the amenities of posh suburbia. We followed the eleven-foot trout through an opening in a Little Wall of China that protected Floyd's property from dirt Woody Creek Road. Inset in entrance towers along the five-foot-high rock-and-mortar wall were heavy brass plaques that announced not a country club or a bank, but FLOYD & JANELLE WATKINS and BEAVER RUN RANCH. From the side of each tower sprang a brass lantern-style coachlight such as one might find on a driveway in Beverly Hills. Once inside, we saw spread out before us the infamous pond, surrounded by lawn, and some of Floyd's herd of prize mules, penned off to the side. A wide drive took us down a hill, past the foundation of what Floyd planned as a 15,000-square-foot house and around the wooded edge of the pond to where a gazebo and wooden deck had been installed to overlook it. Near here, approached by parking valets, we got out of my car.

Mary's heels immediately sank deep into the mud. "Oooh, the same thing happened to me!" said one of my favorite Dames d'Aspen, Jan Fox, coming up to greet us. Two hours earlier, she said, we would have been witness to a small army of Mexican workers, laying "about an acre" of sod around the banks of the pond in preparation for the party. They had wetted it down, as must be done with sod, with all-too-obvious results.

Standing near the bar, Jan and Mary chatted about how the party had come to be. Les Dames d'Aspen, at a spring charity auction for the arts, had offered to throw a party, catered by them, for the highest bidder. To their dismay, Floyd, apparently aiming for the respect of his neighbors, had gone for it and won. Les Dames was a sort of hip Junior League; among its members were social doyenne Lita Heller, daughter of one of the original Warner Brothers founders, Indy car driver Janet Guthrie, and the titian-haired and aptly named Jan Fox, who snapped photos for the society pages of *Aspen Magazine*.

As Buddy Hackett swept by and, with a cackle I knew from the movies, commandeered an hors d'oeuvres tray from a Dame, Jan asked if we wanted to see the stable. It was sitting nearby, the only real structure on the property; with the circular drive in front, I had mistaken it for an eight-car garage. The stalls, "as big as my last apartment," according to Jan, and filled with fresh cedar chips, were not for thoroughbreds but for Watkins's mules. (Future residents of the stable would include a pair of tigers, one of which would make headlines by biting off the fingertip of a woman who was watching it eat.) Upstairs, from the outside, it looked like hay storage, but Jan explained that Floyd actually had built apartments into it. Floyd, evidently a big game hunter, had covered one wall with a zebra skin; elsewhere were wall-mounted trophies of big-headed mammals with horns, photos of Floyd and a young man, perhaps his son, on safari, and a statuette of a kneeling, half-nude, buxom Pocahontas. We moved on to an item of fanciful taxidermy, a beaver in running shoes, fishing pole slung over its shoulder—the totem for Floyd's Beaver Run Ranch. Also examining it was a stout, middle-aged woman dressed all in white—silver-studded white jacket, white jeans, and little white cowgirl boots. "Floyd likes them big beavers, don't he?" she mused.

Waiting for the bathroom, I stood next to a framed studio photo of Floyd, dressed in a business suit, one foot up on a stool, arm resting on his knee: FLOYD E. WATKINS, it read, FOUNDER, TRANS-WORLD SYSTEMS. Then, below that, inscribed in brass, WORLD'S GREATEST SALESMAN.

But Floyd was evidently done with sales, done with dunning deadbeats, done with pleasing clients and anyone but himself. He was now into the middle-aged fantasy stage of life, a big bad boy enjoying the abundant fruits of his labors. Back by the pond, Jan asked me if I was now ready to meet "one of Aspen's truly bad men," and I said yes. Floyd was a tall man wearing snakeskin boots, with a belt to match, balding, with a big belly. It seemed only fair to say I was with the *Times*, which for a guy like Floyd was like reading him his Miranda rights. As his smile melted, he looked at me through narrowed eyes and offered brief answers to my questions about the prize trout, fat yellow things that could be seen just under the surface of the cold waters behind him. They were circling an automatic feeder painted with alpine scenes in the middle of the lake. The fiberglass fish statue had just been erected nearby, and as we spoke, Mary, to my surprise, asked Floyd if he would scoot over a little so she could snap a photo of him with the trout in the background.

She would put the photo in her column, I knew, and this was unusual: Mary, a sweet and even-tempered person, wasn't usually so arch. With Jim, her silversmith husband (known for his aspen-leaf belt buckles), she had lived in Aspen for thirty-eight years and raised five children; she was accepting of peoples' differences. But on the drive up, as we had passed the foundations ready for building, trees cut down from a scenic bluff, and newly cut driveways, I had seen how her world was being shaken up.

"They're all so big, these places!" she marveled. "I tell you, the rich are coming out of the closet, like gays. At lunch today, [one of the wealthy, high-ranking dames] was telling me that the wealth of the new people coming in makes them look poor. Giving $45,000 to the musical festival is one thing—she says the new people are the type to give a million, the type to back a whole performing-arts center!

"And it changes people who lived here so many years, and we didn't know how much money they had. They were like anybody else. But now they're showing it, with all these other people coming." The arrival of the superrich exerted new pressures on the more-established Aspen rich, and ostentation was on the rise.

One would have thought that in the spirit of the Old West, Woody Creekers would have conceded a grudging admiration to an ornery old guy committed to doing exactly what he wanted to do, neighborhood opinion be damned. After all, there was really no surprise in Floyd Watkins; indeed, for Hunter Thompson, who had written at length on the "rich are monsters" theme, the advent of Floyd must have been a vindication, a proof of his thesis. But Woody Creek, like Aspen, was a place threatened, its residents of the "last stand" mentality, and patience was wearing thin.

I covered county commissioners and politics; I listened to the arguments of constituencies. I wrote about tennis star Jaime Fillol at the Grand Champions Club and did a feature on a promoter of polo. I responded dutifully to press releases from Windstar, Dance/Aspen, the Music Associates of Aspen, the Aspen Chamber Resort Association, and the Aspen Substance Awareness Project (there are nearly 150 registered nonprofits in Pitkin County), and then I heard something through the grapevine that really got my attention: The Jehovah's Witnesses were about to build a Kingdom Temple—in Aspen, on the highway just outside the town center. And what's more, they were going to do it over a single weekend.

At first I had been surprised by the existence of Witnesses in Aspen—it did not seem at all a congenial turf for their conservative Christian doomsaying. It went deeper than trendy *vs.* square: Where Aspen reached for every chance to celebrate anything, the Jehovahs were doctrinally against celebration, including Christmas and Easter. Alas, they seemed the only people in town who knew of the existence of the tiny A-frame I'd moved into after my talk with Johanna and my retirement from Mellow Yellow. Practically every Sunday there they were, coming down my driveway and spying me through the sliding glass doors before I had a chance to hide in the bathroom.

The Kingdom Temple—not church—was designed by a member of the congregation who was a local architect, and early in the week they poured its foundation. Construction aboveground began on a Thursday, with the volunteers peaking at between five and six hundred on Sunday. Sunday evening, the first meeting was held ("We didn't want to get behind on our Bible discussion," I was told), and by Monday a sprinkler system was watering the new trees and sod and the main activity seemed to be cleanup.

Why the rush? "We do it this way because we have more important things to do, and that's preaching the good news," said Terry Badger, a member of the building committee. Badger was one of the town's most highly visible Witnesses, since he for years had run Aspen's premier health food store, Nature's Storehouse. Seventy-five percent of the laborers came from the valley, he said, but the craftsmen volunteered from everywhere: "The framers came from Denver, the drywallers from Buena Vista, the painters from Idaho Springs, the cooks from Brighton, and the electricians from all over the place, even outside Colorado."

No individual was in charge of the project; the building committee directed all efforts from a trailer on the site, right next to a first-aid trailer. Planning had been going on for a year, but Badger insisted to me that the 3,000-square-foot building benefited from other help: "We really feel we had Jehovah's spirit with us."

No one I asked in town could ever remember so many people having gathered purely out of a spirit of voluntarism in Aspen. Certainly, the music festival and design conference had scores of volunteers, but they were rewarded with free passes to the pricey events. It was impressive, there was no denying it. Equally impressive to me was the Witnesses's perseverance in a place whose dominant ethos rejected everything they stood for. Why live in Sodom? Terry sat me down to explain that one.

"Ted," he said. "Let's say you're a ski patrolman. And let's say that in the course of your patrolling, you notice that a family has built a house at the bottom of an avalanche chute. Now, given what you know, wouldn't you do everything in your power to convince them to move?"

I stared back at Badger. "And if they didn't move, if they refused?" I asked.

"Wouldn't you go back, again and again? As long as there was a glimmer of hope they could be saved, wouldn't you go back and talk to them?"

Mary Hayes was unhappy. In her hands, Mary was holding a copy of the latest issue of *Life* magazine.

"World Class Snow! Unbridled Pretension! Awesome Mountain Vistas! Shameless Commercialization!" it said in large-point type on the first page of its article. "300 Days of Sunshine! Drop-Dead Snobbery! Heavenly Ski Runs! Surreal Real Estate Values! WELCOME TO ASPEN."

"Have you seen this?" she asked everyone. "I can't believe it." Heads were shaking. Aspen was frequently covered by the national press, and occasionally slammed, but by *Life*? *Life* magazine had no ax to grind. *Life* didn't make gratuitous insults. "I'm just sort of shocked," she said.

Mary got on the phone and called *Life*'s reporter, who was based in Denver. "What's going on?" she asked him. One glaring problem, to Mary's eyes, were the many quotes by Billy Kidd, known in Colorado as a PR flak for Steamboat Springs, about the quality of the local snow ("Perfect—the best in the world," Kidd had said. "You want to sink so deep into the champagne powder that you can't breathe without a snorkel."). Kidd's "champagne powder and snorkel" remarks were so widely quoted they had become a Colorado cliché—but why had they been used in regard to Aspen? Mary wanted to know. And why focus on all the glitz?

Mary reported on her conversation in a first-page story in the arts-and-entertainment section, entitled "*Life* in Aspen?" The reporter had evidently backed down, defending himself on the grounds that the story was what his editors in New York had wanted. "The editors wanted the story to fit the image they had of Aspen," wrote Mary in conclusion. "The magazines have always been fascinated with the real Aspen . . . and the place they imagine Aspen to be."

I wondered how I could say to Mary that as far as I could see, the *Life* article was basically right: There *were* condos letting for

$2,000 a night; there *were* stores selling $250,000 saddles; there *was* a fax machine atop Aspen Mountain; the hospital *did* serve new parents a complimentary steak-and-wine dinner. Out on a walk one night, I saw a skinny guy in a Santa suit running down the sidewalk, probably on his way to a holiday party. My parents, at one time, would have assured me that wasn't the real Santa Claus but merely a man dressed up like him. The distinction between the "real" and the "imaginary" Aspen struck me in some ways the same as the one between the "real" and the "imaginary" Santa Claus: Both were inventions. Most visitors to Aspen would see something very similar to "the image" portrayed in *Life* and other magazines; that view of the place, in fact, would in all likelihood be one of the things that attracted them in the first place, the one the resort industry depended on. And there was nothing imaginary about it—that was a real Aspen. Another Aspen, though, represented by folks like those who worked at the *Times,* resisted identification with the celebrity scene, hated being lumped in with the high-profile "greedhead" entrepreneurs who needed the press coverage in order to thrive. They were the old Aspen. When he and others had moved to Aspen, publisher Dunaway told me, they had done it for love. "In those days you *couldn't* make money here," he explained. "There weren't ways."

Of course resort towns, at least the good ones, are always ambivalent about the media. On the one hand, they need press in order to survive: Aspen would wilt without the publicity that attracts skiers and other visitors. And yet when the press has anything critical to say, they feel victimized: "They won't give us credit for being a small town; they say we're just a resort" is a frequently heard complaint. It's an expression of the ambivalence at the very heart of a resort town, of any community of people who rely on tourism: You need the people from outside, and yet you fear the people from outside. You want them because they provide jobs and affirm that you live in a special place; and yet you spurn them because of their bad manners and the fact that you must serve them. (In Aspen the locals' insistence that theirs was foremost a community, not a resort town—a fact outsiders kept failing to recognize—raised the stakes even higher.)

This tension between a need for press and a dislike of outsiders' definitions never reaches a resolution in a resort town. But in Aspen it was showing its face more frequently as the outsiders' portrayals grew less flattering and more extreme. Aspen as it moved into the nineties was changing faster than at any time since its renaissance after World War II, and people talked about it all the time, worried.

Few people are in a position to assess these changes like Elizabeth Paepcke is. If there is one name in Aspen everyone knows (even if they can't all spell it), it is hers (pronounced PEP-key, or PAP-keh). Paepcke Park sits in the near center of town, on Main Street, and Elizabeth, eighty-eight, widow of Walter Paepcke, maintains a grand old house and summer garden in the West End, where she lives during those months of the year she isn't in Chicago.

The Paepckes were the founders of modern-day Aspen, of Aspen-as-we-know-it, of Aspen since 1945. For the nearly fifty years before Elizabeth dragged Walter to Aspen and they fell in love with it—or with their idea of what they wanted it to become—Aspen had drowsed along as a remnant of its former self, the booming silver town of 1879–1893. Originally a simple valley where Ute Indians summered, Aspen had been visited by miners from the boomtown of Leadville, Colorado, in 1879. The discovery of silver in the valley—of a mother lode, as it turned out, thirty miles wide—had led to its utter transformation in a space of ten years. In the 1880s, for example, the Hotel Jerome and Wheeler Opera House were built, as were the H. P. Cowenhoven Building, the courthouse, and most of the other best buildings in town. The boom—which may be measured in terms of the nearly $50 million in silver extracted from the area in just over six years—lasted almost precisely until the summer of 1893, when the price of silver collapsed on world markets, causing every silver mine in the state to close and the U.S. Congress, by fall, to quit its silver price supports through repeal of The Sherman Silver Purchase Act. The economy of Aspen promptly collapsed. By 1937, when André Roch was brought from Switzerland by a group of enthusiast businessmen seeking a place to expand the nascent American skiing industry, the town had six or seven hundred people, down from the fifteen thousand or so of its glory days.

If a developer's vision is grand enough, he may be known as a founder. Aspen was fortunate that one of the first developers to visit the sleepy town on the eve of the birth of skiing in the United States was a man with such a vision. The son of a German immigrant, Walter Paepcke had gone to Yale and returned to Chicago to manage the family carton business, which in his hands became the Container Corporation of America. In Chicago he was not only a prominent businessman but part of a world of high-thinking idealists that included philosopher Mortimer Adler (Paepcke was a student in some of Adler's original Great Books seminars), University of Chicago president Robert M. Hutchins, and Bauhaus designer László Moholy-Nagy. It was Elizabeth's world, too: Her father, William A. Nitze, was a distinguished professor at Chicago, and her brother, Paul Nitze, would become a prominent American statesman and arms negotiator. Elizabeth trained as a painter at the Art Institute of Chicago and introduced Walter to the Bauhaus modernism that became his aesthetic credo. As historian James Sloan Allen has described, the Paepckes' adoption of Bauhaus ideals was an important step in the design integration of different aspects of the Container Corporation—a uniform graphic on the product, the company letterhead, the sides of trucks, etc.—which pioneered the idea of an integrated corporate design image in America.

The genius of Walter Paepcke was his idea that just as he had "married" culture and commerce by bringing high design to his business, he could bring them together again by promoting in Aspen a ski resort with a high-culture component. Paepcke, in other words, imagined resort activities and cultural activities as complementary. Besides setting an appealing high tone for the small town that would become a source of its cachet, Paepcke had figured out an answer to the perennial dilemma of ski country promoters: what to do with all those empty beds in the off season?

For a few hundred dollars of overdue tax money, Paepcke bought properties that today sell for millions. He found like-minded friends to invest in other properties. He consulted his brother-in-law, Paul Nitze, then an investment banker, about starting up a skiing company and decided, in the words of Nitze, how they'd run the place: "Pussy [Elizabeth's nickname] was going to do everything that had to do with music, taste, beauty, that part of culture; Walter, the intellectual part; and I would do the parts having to do with the body. I would organize the ski corporation and make it work."

But how to let the world know? In an era before the dawn of mass marketing—which elite-minded Walter Paepcke would have disdained anyway, since it would attract the wrong people—he hit upon a brilliant solution. Friends at the University of Chicago had come to him for help in fund-raising for an event in commemoration of the two hundredth anniversary of the birth of German humanist Johann Wolfgang von Goethe. It was an event that appealed to Paepcke, following his ancestral home's recent humbling before the world: Rehabilitate German culture by celebrating one of its great figures. But the academic conference they had in mind seemed to him a bit too modest. Why not really do it up? Why not stage a major event—in Aspen?

Coming from the mouth of anyone else, the idea would have seemed preposterous: Aspen was still a ghost town, virtually unknown. But Paepcke pulled it off. To the amazement of the locals, the Goethe Bicentennial Festival of June 1949 convened in Aspen such luminaries of the time as playwright Thornton Wilder, Mortimer Adler, Spanish philosopher José Ortega y Gasset, and—on his only visit to the United States—Dr. Albert Schweitzer. Covered in *Life* magazine and elsewhere, it was justly described as "the leading cultural promotion of the mid-century." Main Street was still a dirt road and the Hotel Jerome had a single light bulb dangling over its decaying porch at night, but suddenly the world knew about Aspen. Along with gearing up the skiing company and other aspects of his investment, Paepcke sought to institutionalize some of what he had started with the conference, such as the high-minded dialogue taking place in a beautiful setting. The resulting think tank, the Aspen Institute, again sought to merge culture and commerce, this time by inviting American executives to sequester themselves for week-long immersions in the great questions of civilization. From the institute later sprang the music festival and design conference, two organizations that continue to lend summer in Aspen a vitality unprecedented for a ski town.

In 1960, Walter Paepcke died of cancer at age sixty-four. Other forces—such as the rise of the entertainment industry, and the Reagan legacy of a growing gap between rich and poor and an elite class that can buy into elite towns—now affect Aspen more acutely than did the will of one man. As Aspen seeks to create and sustain the shared memory that is a foundation of community, it often seeks out Elizabeth Paepcke.

I was fortunate to be able to meet Elizabeth Paepcke in the presence of her friends. Other old Aspenites at the luncheon table were Tukey Koffend, a longtime shop owner, travel writer, and community TV talk show host; Tom and Alice Rachel Sardy, longtime allies of the Paepckes (Tom Sardy was Walter's partner in the old Aspen Lumber & Supply Co., ran an adjacent mortuary, and also founded Aspen's airport, Sardy Field); and the hosts, Fritz and Fabi Benedict, he a former skier of the Tenth Mountain Division, Aspen's first registered architect and the designer of Snowmass Village, and current chairman of the music festival, and she the Paris-bred sister-in-law of former Aspen town manager and Bauhaus designer Herbert Bayer and daughter of avant-garde poet Mina Loy.

Though stooped and a bit frail, Elizabeth Paepcke seemed like a tall woman. A legendary beauty all her life (Andy Warhol, passing through in 1984, thought she resembled Katharine Hepburn), she remained striking. Her eyes, set off by snow-white hair, were a brighter blue than has yet been contrived by the makers of contact lenses. She was wearing a long skirt, a short cardigan, and Reeboks. She had a confident presence that was dignified without being offputting or pretentious. Before this meeting I had often—*too* often— heard her described with unreserved enthusiasm, but my skepticism ceded to a strange sense of feeling *lucky* to be seated on her right at the luncheon, and months later I would feel surprisingly honored to be asked to drive her home after a dinner party. It was as though the host of the party, a friend of hers, had entrusted me with something fragile and of great value.

What everyone but me at the table had in common was the old days, and talk turned to the way things used to be: Main Street rutted or impassable in the springtime mud, friendships strained by errant cattle in a neighbor's pasture, a boomtown legacy of matters being settled "with alcohol or dynamite." There was less dust now and she liked the pedestrian malls, but otherwise, said Elizabeth Paepcke, glancing through glass doors to the back patio, where cross-country ski tracks led into the woods, the story of Aspen was a "tragedy." The problem, she said without irony, was "too many rich people" and too many lawyers and realtors. "Walter never did a thing that wasn't for Aspen. He never made a penny on real estate." He left her with $700,000, she said, and "if it weren't for my grandparents [and her inheritance from them], I couldn't afford to live up here."

As she saw it, the year Walter died was the turning point for Aspen, the beginning of truly fractious politics and differing visions of the town. Elsewhere she had expounded at greater length, and with the inpunity granted a senior statesman, on what had happened to the hamlet she and her husband reinvented.

She told Mary Hayes: "Aspen is going off in a different direction from everything we cared about . . . I see bigger houses being built, more trees cut down. The environment where formerly we rode horseback and hiked is slowly, inch by inch, shut off from us by barbed wire fences and private property . . . My heart is broken."

She told the International Design Conference at Aspen in 1987: "We unfortunately . . . have now reached the limits . . . Are we going to kill the golden goose by feeding the animal until its liver becomes extended and we produce a pâté which is so rich that none of us can digest it anymore? What price glory?"

She asked *The Sunday Denver Post:* "Why do people want to buy a house here, spend $4.5 million or even $22 million, and then just spend a few weeks? . . . They haven't an inkling of what Colorado is, and they don't give anything to the town, they only take. It's become a town of glitz and glamour, no substance, a nut without a kernel."

Yet despite these pronouncements, Elizabeth Paepcke is beloved by Aspen. *Aspen Magazine* calls her "the conscience of Aspen." "The Paepckes . . . were rich with a difference," said one article (with an implicit comment about the "ordinary" rich). Practically no one will say an unkind word about Elizabeth Paepcke, and surely that may be because she does not deserve one. But there is more. As widow of the founder, she is a queen of sorts: She represents "real" Aspen, pre-image Aspen, ways that Aspen used to be, ways many residents wish it still were. Moreover, she stands for old values and old money, and we idolize those things in the manner of Ralph Lauren ads: through a professed love for the traditional, the elegant, the classy. Elizabeth Paepcke is old money incarnate, a remnant of the age of discipline and values.

Another reason Elizabeth Paepcke is queen could be that she is just, well, so patently admirable. As a former caretaker of her house—a Harvard-graduate-turned-land-surveyor—told me, Elizabeth Paepcke, blessed with looks, wealth, and intelligence, somehow resisted the temptations that can wreck similarly advantaged people and turned out well. Perhaps Aspen admires her so much because, though similarly blessed, it has not likewise succeeded.

Mary Hayes gave me permission to take a four-day weekend in early summer and was kind enough not to ask what it was for. In fact it was journalism, not exactly of the *Times* variety but of a kind quite appropriate to Aspen. The seed for it had been planted one night when I was still driving for Mellow Yellow.

It was not long after I had begun to tell the other drivers of my real agenda, trying to dispel rumors that I was a narc. Susan radioed around midnight to say that someone had called in and asked to have me phone them. I didn't recognize the phone number and I didn't recognize the voice when I stopped at a pay phone to call, but he told me he'd heard about me and thought there were a couple of people I ought to meet. "Why?" I asked. The drug-dealing backdrop of the cab world made me wary. He said only that they were good guys, told me where they there now, and suggested I drop by if I could.

It was one of the more venerable of Aspen's seventy-one bars. Two men seated at a dark table toward the back looked at me at the same time. "You Ted?" asked one. We shook hands, and they introduced themselves as Neil and Art; I immediately doubted these were their real names. They bought a round of drinks and then another, during which they asked about my work and told about their vacation. I felt I was being sized up. I still didn't know why they wanted to meet me, but the fact they had yet to say anything about it gave me a clue. Losing a lot of money with the cab not running, I broached the question.

"Uh, we were, uh, in a little business enterprise together," said Neil, the larger, more aggressive of the two. The sentence seemed hard for him, as if he were breaking a habit of some sort, a rule. He glanced quickly at Art, who was pudgier and more acquiescent. They were wondering whether to trust me. But to get what they wanted, it seemed, they had to. "Importers, you might say."

"Coke?" I asked quietly.

"No, uh, grass," said Neil, showing a flash of alarm.

They had brought "a lot" of marijuana to the country from the sixties to the early eighties, Art said, adding quickly, "But we're retired now."

We drank the third round. Where else would I be hearing this, I thought, amidst the antidrug harpoons of the eighties, but in Aspen? Here was the grist for the myths of a generation that I, then thirty, had grown up on the heels of, a source for the essential glamour of those days. Submerged for these many years, the tale was ever-so-cautiously breaking the surface. I listened and nodded as they struggled to tell me something without really telling me anything. It was taking forever.

"See, we want to save what we did," said Neil. "We've got some great stories, but we're no good at telling them. And the best storyteller of us all just died last year." They told me about their friend Carl, who, against the advice of all the others, got involved in the ever-widening cocaine trade with a group that had mob connections. He made a lot of money but was eventually betrayed and busted. The feds seized his cars and houses; his girlfriend left him; and after too much coke at a party, he suffered a heart attack and died. With him, I sensed, died a confidence that the stories could sustain them, that memories of the smuggling years would last them through middle age.

"The thing is," said Neil, "we miss it. It's the best thing we ever did."

That was enough for me, and when they sent a plane ticket to fly me to a reunion weekend they had planned in northern Florida, I headed for the airport.

Shells crunched under my feet as I approached the beach house. It was 2 A.M. and I was nervous: I had met only one of the five guys who were going to be there (Art could not attend because of "wife problems"). After the crispness of an Aspen spring, the muggy tropical air made me feel thick and slow. And I was ill prepared— less than a day before had I learned my destination.

I was carrying a garment bag and wearing some expensive clothes—my picture of these guys included a lot of thin-soled Italian loafers, double-breasted suits, and slicked-back hair. I wanted to look like I could appreciate the trappings of their world.

But as Neil from Aspen came to meet me at the screen door, I saw this was no Florida glitter spot—it was down home. Blond, frizzy-haired Neil, muscular and quiet, was dressed in rumpled khaki shorts, a torn T-shirt, and flip-flops; the big hand dangling at his side was wrapped around a Budweiser. I recognized his halting speech and air of military self-discipline from our single meeting in Aspen. Looking relaxed, he introduced me to Melvin, who appeared to be a bit younger (late thirties), more preppy, and fat. A third man, Kirby, appeared from around a corner, said, "G'night," and disappeared barefoot through the kitchen before we were even introduced. He was slight, I noticed, with shaggy red hair, sun-browned and -crinkled skin, and a missing tooth. He looked like some ne'er-do-well from your seventh grade class in Huntington Beach, with twenty-five years added on. The others, Russell and Bud, were already asleep. I relaxed some: This was a Southern seaside backwater, and they fit right in. Mel's Southern drawl was so pronounced I could understand only half of what he said. I took off my jacket, Neil grabbed me a beer, and he, Mel, and I retired to the dock on the canal that ran alongside the house.

It was still and very hot. We talked about my travel, about the two big boats they had tied up on the dock, about the end of the ski season. My reason for being there on this "Big Chill" weekend, and theirs, was avoided: It was the get-acquainted period, the getting-to-trust-you period. The only reference at all to the reason we'd convened—some of them for the first time in seven years—came as the clock headed for 4 A.M. and I was shown my room. Mel handed me a bound screenplay. It was titled *Florida Gold* and dated 1981, with an Aspen post-office box and the name of the writer—not Melvin—on the title page. "Here, you might want to take a look at this," he said.

"Whose is it?" I asked, thinking maybe I knew the answer.

"Oh, I wrote it, a little while back," Melvin confirmed.

I was up till dawn reading *Florida Gold*, the script for an action film that aimed, according to the anticlimactic prefatory note, "to describe the feelings of some of those who helped pioneer the marijuana business in the United States, and to dispute the common belief that all those involved are the violent gangster type." A filmmaker friend once told me that a screenplay to a dope dealer is like a memoir to a president: "They all write one sooner or later." But this was the first I had seen, and I was pleased to discover the opening setting to be something like the one we were in: "a medium-sized, old lake house somewhere in northern Florida, secluded among cypress and pine trees."

Six men, friends and drug smugglers all, had just completed a successful operation, had a party, and concluded they'd better lie low for a while. But a reunion was planned for five years later, on July 4, 1980, at a friend's bar. They gathered in 1980 as planned, cold-cocked a narc who'd been lingering around the bar, and contemplated changes in the pot-smuggling scene since the seventies.

TERRY

I wish I had about five or six tons of that old gold. Probably get $800 or $900, maybe $1000 a pound for it now.

LEO

Yeah, boy that's a lot of money for pot. We always thought we were damn lucky to double our money. We took nickels and dimes for years before that.

TERRY

I know. Nowadays no one'll do anything unless they can make $100 a pound. I guess we were just too early. We were tryin' to keep the country high and break in the market. Now it's gone berserk!

LEO

Yeah . . . hmmmm . . . (lost in thought)

TERRY

I can't believe the stuff is still illegal. I figured by the time 5 percent of the population started smoking, it'd have to be legalized.

LEO

Yeah . . . now over 30 million people are smoking.

TERRY

It was a lot easier to keep the country high when there was only seven or eight million smoking.

LEO

It's almost impossible to fill the country's needs now! There's a constant shortage . . . it's gonna have to change.

Nostalgia and a feeling of civic obligation ("fill the country's needs") propel the group back into one last run. It very nearly ends in disaster, but at the last minute friendship—faith in each other—pulls them all through.

I closed the manuscript and drew curtains against the brightening pink sky. According to the screenplay, the group had gotten out of the business when the world they were seeing began to look too different from the one they had started in, when cocaine moved in and business by handshake was over. I thought about the guys sleeping throughout the house. They were beginning to feel to me a bit less like potential enemies and more like big brothers whose day had come and gone, all a bit too soon.

I had come to Florida to learn something about the history of Aspen. But it took a little while to get there. Over the course of three days of waterskiing, fishing, driving at night in a big convertible, and just sitting and drinking on the screened-in porch, I learned bit by bit how, following high school, college, and stints in Vietnam, they had initiated trips to Jamaica, made contacts, and devised ways of bringing marijuana home—in old shrimp boats bought in St. Petersburg, in old airplanes bought from skydiving clubs (Neil had been a pilot in Vietnam), in Winnebagos so overloaded their axles had broken. The smuggling was fantastically lucrative, and was also something they believed in as a force for peace on earth.

They were hippies then, and the Southeast, though home, was not an especially congenial place. Flush with money and branching out, they went, on a friend's recommendation, to Aspen. It was 1972 and, said Neil, Aspen sent them even higher. Mel recalled their taxi drive from the airport: "The driver said, 'Where you guys from?' And I said, 'Gainesville.' He said, 'Wanta smoke a joint?' I looked at Neil and said, 'We're home!' "

Houses to rent were readily available, and some of the leading figures of the times, as far as they were concerned, lived there, too: Jimmy Buffett, Hunter Thompson, *Rolling Stone* publisher Jann

Wenner—they met them all. It was the kind of place where not having a regular job caused no suspicion and where dealers, in fact, were minor celebrities. They tried to avoid that kind of limelight, but they socialized sufficiently to establish a couple of new wholesale customers. Neil bought one house and then another, and then the others arrived for protracted stays—Art, Russell, Kirby, Carl, and Bud all were coming and going.

"Our dogs loved it there," said Mel, who had considered himself a resident. "I even went and bought me an old Dodge pickup truck like everybody had then, with a broom in the back—handle down, you know, bristles in the air. That was the style. You'd put your dog in the back, and use the broom to sweep out snow and the seeds from your bales of grass."

"That restaurant you met us at?" Neil added. "Used to be you could even smoke a joint in there, nobody'd say anything."

None of them had ever had so much luck with women, they said, as when they were in Aspen and in "the business." Almost without fail, according to Mel, "girls would hit on us when we were in the thick of things. It's something in your eyes, it's something about you." It was the drug runners' state of grace.

The others nodded. "People, they'd want to know, 'Who are you?'" said Kirby. "'Who are you guys? Are you rock 'n' roll guys?' We sort of had that air about us, that bigtime air. 'You get your money for nothin' and your chicks for free,'" he sang, after Dire Straits.

They told stories of hot-tub fellatio, of group sex, of "the black hole that is a party in Aspen," and the days required for recovery. Finding the right women, of course, was a little harder. Besides being gorgeous, the perfect candidate could not mind your extended absences, taking care of the dog, or never knowing the details of your work. Bud quoted the Eagles:

> Lookin' for a lover
> Who won't blow my cover,
> She's sooo hard to find.

"You should have been there, man, twenty-five years ago," Neil concluded, to nods of agreement. "There was no place like it."

They had settled down. Art, who had met me at the airport in a late-model Mercedes, was married, the father of two, and perhaps the most prosperous: He had buried, stashed, and otherwise saved enough money to buy a beer distributorship in a growing area, and it had flourished. Next best off was probably Neil, the only bachelor, who, through some front companies, had invested in Aspen real estate at a propitious time. Mel owned a video store and part of a small airplane but said he also had a lot of debts. Bud was close to getting a master's degree, but would never tell me in what or what his job was, though he did display an authority's knowledge of the cultivation of marijuana ("Now, *Cannabis sativa* is the American strain, and *Cannabis indica,* the Afghani, the kind that stinks—that's Asian"). His car was old and worn. He did say he'd never "held the same job more than six months in my life," until the present one, which he was at risk of holding for seven months. Russell ran a small commercial glass shop. After seven years of helping build golf courses at Caribbean resorts, Kirby was "sick of it. It's time to find a new career," he said.

"In the field of opportunity, it's plowin' time again," quoted Bud.

They had made and lost millions of dollars. ("Whenever we tried to launder money, we got taken to the cleaners," was how Mel put it.) Much of the money had been frittered away on life-style— luxury beach house rentals, fancy meals, fast cars, clothes, drink, drugs, and good-time girls—a long list of things that don't last. Easy come, easy go. Through it all, though, one thing remained constant: their trust in the group. None of them was ever caught, and trust was why. "Every one of us, is all we need," said Kirby, after "Yellow Submarine." They had never sold each other out.

Another favorite song was Jimmy Buffett's "A Pirate Looks at Forty." "It should be our theme song," Kirby said. As we sat on the porch the last evening, somebody put on the tape:

> I've done a bit of smuggling
> I've run my share of grass
> I've made enough money to buy Miami
> But I pissed it away so fast
> Never meant to last,
> Never meant to last.
>
> I have been drunk now for over two weeks
> I passed out and I rallied and I sprung a few leaks,

But I've got to stop wishin'
Got to go fishin'
I'm down to rock bottom again
Just a few friends,
Just a few friends.

Eventually, everyone started to turn in; some would be getting up early, to drive home or catch planes. Nervousness over our meeting had kept them from asking what I might do with their stories . . . exactly why, I wondered when I was left alone on the porch, had they invited me?

Part of the answer seemed obvious. They had a secret story, the details of which were fading with time. They wanted to tell it—the way anyone with a secret wants to tell it—and in me they had found a willing repository. If it came out as a piece of writing, perhaps it would provide that hedge against mortality almost everyone seeks. Also, they missed it, and getting together had provided a chance to re-create it, the time and the feeling.

Their nostalgia was about more than being rich. A comment Bud had made that afternoon stuck in my brain. "The great thing about this job," he told me, "was you didn't apply—you just did it." The path was different from the one others of his generation had pursued. They might be in the money now, but Bud bet they'd be "wondering if they missed out."

I wondered if he now was thinking the same about himself. The luster of being in the dope business had been fading for a long time. In the eighties there were other forms of rebellion, other routes to enlightenment. The need for secrecy, which was the legacy of the business, kept those years from being admitted fully into their present lives, kept them from making a transition. And, I thought, kept them thinking about it: The thought that your day has passed can also become a monkey on your back—the worry that opportunity knocks but once, once in a blue moon, and your one chance has come and gone very early in the game, leaving nothing as good to look forward to.

Wistfully, Bud had spoken earlier in the day of finding some other enterprise in which success would depend on the sort of friendship and trust that had made their business possible.

Nobody could think of one.

. . .

Walter Paepcke made boxes. In fact, local residents circa 1949 originally suspected that's what the industrialist had in mind for Aspen: a carton plant along the Roaring Fork, to be supplied by the bountiful timber of the valley. Paepcke, of course, had no such plans, but in a way his activities in Aspen constituted something similar: With his institutes and programs, he created a sort of container, a hollow structure whose contents awaited filling in. Planners and developers devise the framework of a place, but they can't give it character. It remained for those who followed Paepcke to realize the character of the new Aspen, to color in the outline, to fill in the box.

The children of the sixties were probably more influential in lending Aspen a character than any other group. The town's Paepcke-inspired air of utopian possibility fit well with the sixties desire for "paradise now." It was a young place, sufficiently in flux to have a sense of alternatives about it. It was in the mountains, far from cities and repressive childhoods, but close to nature. Commerce seemed something the town was *not* about—Babbitt lived far away. Small was beautiful, Aspen was both, and the young flocked to it.

An *ancien régime* was already in place, of course. Carroll Whitmire, the incumbent sheriff challenged by Hunter Thompson in the 1970 elections for sheriff, was a sworn defender of old values and tough enforcement and had to be gotten rid of before the streets were safe for marijuana. (Thompson lost by a 2–3 margin, but Whitmire was out a few years later.) Many old-time merchants had no use for the antimaterialist contingent: Bert Bidwell, owner of the Mountain Shop, on Cooper Avenue, was known to turn a garden hose on hippies dozing against his front wall. And across the street, Guido Meyer, of Guido's Swiss Inn, posted a sign that read, quaintly, NO BEATNIKS. Reactionaries complained bitterly of toenail clipping in public. But the resistance was outnumbered and fairly quickly lost out. A popular T-shirt slogan of the times, ASPEN: SOFT POWDER, HARD DRUGS, CASUAL SEX, summed up the ascendant ethos. Tourists were turkeys, and among locals there was solidarity. In 1967, my father pulled me out of third grade for a few days to go with him to Aspen. While he met clients on a sunny Friday in March, I joined the suntanned, long-haired, brightly dressed crowds out skiing Aspen Mountain. A guy waiting in line at the Bell Mountain chair was explaining to me about the nearby "underwear tree" (lift riders traditionally festoon its bare branches with dropped panties and bras) when I heard a cry go up from the crowd: Despite a lift line at least twenty minutes long, a young woman had dared to get on the double chair *single*. Fists were raised, snowballs were launched, and I saw her hide her face in shame. The underwear tree, the high-spirited unity of people in a lift line—these were things you didn't find at any other ski area.

A perennially popular film at Aspen's Isis Theater at the time was *King of Hearts*, with Alan Bates, in which a wartime raid on a French village leaves it abandoned except for the forgotten inhabitants of the insane asylum. They escape and run the town in their own whimsical, lunatic, oblivious-to-authority way, which many people will tell you is an apt metaphor for the kind of place Aspen was then, with city employees all taking est training, with Hunter Thompson running for sheriff, with a past mayor implicated in cutting down highway billboards, Halloween the most important holiday, cowboys entering the Jerome Bar on horseback, and developers and "straight" society, to some degree, held at bay.

It couldn't last, is the conventional wisdom. A favorite pastime among Aspen locals, these past forty years, has been pointing a finger at the moment when the battle for Aspen was lost. The dates, of course, vary, accordingly mainly to when the person arrived.

It is axiomatic of paradise practically anywhere that things were better some years ago. Cape Cod, the Florida Keys, Puerto Vallarta, Seattle: What hasn't changed for the worse? "You should have been there twenty-five years ago," Neil the dealer had said to me during our long weekend. Actually, you heard those words, or variations on them ("ten years ago" "twenty years ago" "thirty years ago") a lot in Aspen: They were visited upon the neophyte by practically anyone who had been there longer. With things in paradise nothing like they used to be, seniority had everything to do with status—only among senior citizens had I ever heard the past discussed with such reverence. Neil, however, said it differently; Neil really *did* seem to wish I had been there then. And not only that I'd been there—in fact he seemed to wish I had also been his age, been doing what he was doing, had friends like his. What he seemed to be saying, in so many words, was nothing more complicated than, "I miss my youth."

Nostalgia, for Neil and many others I met in Aspen, had a lot to do with peaking early. Well before middle age, he and his friends had had experiences and known a prosperity that none could reasonably hope to surpass for the rest of their lives. In this they had plenty of company in Aspen. If it was the kind of place that could offer what the ski industry likes to call "peak experiences," it was also the kind of place many people liked to stick around, past their very early primes. The upside was that it had become a cutting-edge retirement community for young adults, you might say, who had a base of shared experience; the downside was that among these youthful retirees, there was also a dispiriting feeling of "yesterday" and "what now?"

This was true across the social spectrum but especially easy to see with celebrities. The appearance of the country's hottest stars every Christmas in Aspen renewed the town's own celebrity status, but it also cast in sharp relief the stable of yesterday's stars who had been put out to pasture there. Jill St. John, Robert Wagner, John Denver, Claudine Longet (who married her local defense attorney), Suzy Chaffee, Chrissie Evert and Andy Mill, Glenn Frey and other aging rockers, Hunter Thompson and other semiretired journalists, former *Penthouse* pets, former race car drivers—the woods in Aspen were full of echoes.

Also subject to obsolescence were those who stayed in glamour jobs past their prime. To the aging ski instructor, for example, life presents a kind of poverty. Resort-town salaries increase little, if at all, with seniority, and if you hadn't moved into management by age thirty-five or so, odds were slim that you would. Seniority, indeed, is an impediment: There's social pressure against being a waitress past your thirties, and ski instructors, with job-related back, knee, skin (keratosis from UV rays), or sinus (from changing altitude in cold weather) trouble, received no worker's compensation. The moguls, the tourists, the very sun beat you down.

The premature demise of the ski bum was another painful milestone. Traditionally in Aspen, many low-wage jobs were held by Europeans and other, often educated, "ski bums," with the result that the maid making up your bed might have read the book on the night table and want to discuss it with you or that your fellow dishwasher might hold a doctorate in astrophysics. Workers in such an atmosphere were a sort of professional class in disguise and didn't really consider themselves servants. The rising cost of housing, however, made it hard for such people to subsist on minimum wage. When my ski-instructor friend Claire was forced to move into company housing in 1990, however, she found that practically all her neighbors were Mexican. They *did* consider themselves servants, which made it that much harder for her not to. The days of the ski bum, most agreed, were over; Aspen's unique class system was in its twilight.

In part this peaking early was a legacy of the sixties: What decade since has had such vitality? What do you do for a follow-up? Partly, though, it seemed an unwitting consequence of the culture they helped to create. The sixties' enshrinement of youth was adopted practically as a mission statement by Aspen, and living for the moment, "being here now," does not mesh well with the idea of long-term work toward the sort of goals that can only be realized later in life: a large family, an advanced degree, a career in a field outside resort management or real estate development. "Don't trust anyone over thirty," though it has been good to plastic surgeons, is not a credo to grow old by.

Stefan Albouy, a young man whose frame of reference was not the 1960s but the 1890s, had agreed by the campfire to show me his Compromise silver mine, and I held him to it: In January I was again following him into the dark, this time a hole in the side of Aspen Mountain.

The mine was Albouy's most controversial project, because it was literally in the middle of a ski slope. By driving a snowmobile up the face of Little Nell and tacking to a nearby evergreen a black plastic water bottle containing a special legal form, he had laid claim to the mine, which had not been worked in fifty years. The form hadn't changed since the 1870s, and neither had the law, a federal mining statute that allowed him to snap up the unpatented claim from the Aspen Skiing Company, which had let it lapse.

The law said Albouy not only could mine, he could put up buildings to operate the mine, gain access to the site, and haul the ore away. All of which Albouy and his friends began to do: They constructed a two-story log cabin and laid 18-gauge rail past it into the mine, through a new shed over the mine entrance.

The town, whose zoning prohibits most building on the mountain, was livid, as was the skiing company—but they had no re-course. It was a scenario similar to Albouy's marble quarry up Conundrum Creek: Legally, Albouy had the right. There was talk of the U.S. Congress making a special appropriation and buying out Albouy's marble claim—a senator had been by to visit, appraisals were being made. Some began to grumble that this was the oppor-tunistic Albouy's hope all along: big bucks from a sellout. But when he showed me the house and offered to take me into the Compro-mise mine, I began to doubt those insinuations.

Stefan wanted to save talk for the dinner we had planned after-ward in town; the exciting thing for him was the mine. He handed me a hardhat fitted with a miner's light, powered by a heavy battery pack that pulled down my belt, and strode out the door of the cabin, following rail tracks into the hole in the side of Aspen Mountain. I took a last glance at the skiers schussing through the turn known as Kleenex Corner, oblivious to us, and then turned and followed Stefan into the earth and back into time.

Our lamps provided the only light, which turned out to be quite a lot. The air was, surprisingly, warmer than outside: a fairly con-stant 50–55 degrees year-round, Stefan said. Heavy new beams and posts supporting the ceiling—10 × 10s and 12 × 12s—gave me confidence every few yards, but they were interspersed with old beams and old and new tree trunks. Walking into old mines was a major prohibition of my Colorado childhood; they were always collapsing and killing someone. But this route, Stefan's daily path, was cleared and renovated, so I followed.

Stefan's deep, stentorian voice was transformed by the mine; it took on the excitement of a child as his fingers ran over the tools, as his feet dodged the rail, as he narrated the story of the mine. Once it was worked by hundreds of men on round-the-clock shifts; those who labored during daylight hours, especially in winter, seldom saw real light; their paths were lit first by candles, later carbide lamps, and finally electric lights (Aspen's mines were the first in the nation to be electrified). They pushed out downsized railroad cars full of ore and dirt—the same cars he had restored outside, "one-ton end dump ore cars"—and tracks led all the way to smelters and full-sized trains below. Stefan loved the jargon and the machinery. As we passed them, he pointed out his electric ore car engine (the "Mansha Little Trammer"), which created no fumes, his Imco 12-B "mucker," which shoveled loose dirt ahead into cars behind, and the pressurized air tanks on wheels ("Universal Air Trammers") that powered the stope drills.

The tunnel began to wind, with all sorts of smaller branches breaking off, to the upper left, the lower right—you had to look hard to see some of them. Stefan paused to explain that what I thought was dust passing through my lamp was actually water vapor. You sort of had to move around the little cloud formed by your breath periodically, in order to see beyond. The clouds moved slowly by themselves, too: Stefan explained that a slight breeze came in from a tunnel opening on Spar Gulch, a major skier thoroughfare, a few hundred yards ahead. We were eight hundred feet in, but the tunnel went some six thousand feet further, under Bonnie's Restaurant, and then curved back out onto Shadow Mountain.

I began then to appreciate the extent of the mine. Stefan described a space Dante would have loved. In the blackness we entered an immense room without echoes; from where we stood, Stefan explained, there were forty levels down and five or six up. The lowest levels were below the water table and therefore, in the absence of pumps, underwater. He had traveled down five levels so far, he said, mainly using a rock-climbing harness or a bosun's chair and a bomber hoist. He had discovered cliffs five hundred feet high; and yet, even so, insisted he had probably seen only one tenth of 1 percent of the mine—a thought that delighted him. He tossed various rocks off the edge of the huge room, into the nothingness beyond the range of our lamps. Echoes of some rattled up from distant cantos after a few moments of falling; others you never heard.

We skirted the edge of the cavern on a narrow crumbling ledge. Once it had supported tracks, but now in many places the ground beneath the tracks had fallen away completely, so that, in a ghostly fashion, they ran out, roughly parallel, over empty air. To cross these, we jumped.

The space opened up by the removal of ore was called a stope, Stefan explained; it could be small or, like this one, gigantic, of an extent hard to contemplate. Stopes had names like Crib, Hooper, or Warnock—miners' names. In a smaller one, off a side passage, he showed me where a huge slab had separated from the ceiling, falling directly down—it was maybe fifteen feet square. That could happen at any time, he explained, and as we walked through one particularly narrow passageway, he advised that I not touch the walls, covered with condensation, or the wooden frames—anything that could destabilize the balance made delicate by the passing of decades.

Occasionally, he paused to point out traces of silver ore in the tunnel walls—millions and millions of dollars' worth had been taken out, but Stefan enthusiastically asserted there was much more left. Would he ever hit a big lode? Would the price of silver rise with inflation to make it really worthwhile again? "It just comes down to time," he said.

Over our meal at Little Annie's, a hamburger-and-beer joint in town named after another famous mine, Stefan told me he'd been a miner since childhood. Growing up within view of the tailing piles that streamed down Ajax and Shadow Mountain, he had become enamored of the miner's enterprise and had sought out old-timers like Johnnie Herron, "the last of the silver kings," who would tell him about it after school, over cookies. He burrowed beneath his family driveway and built a narrow-gauge railway into the greenhouse. The Colorado School of Mines in Golden had not worked out because it wasn't hands-on; what lured Albouy was "the romance, the geology, the danger, outsmarting Mother Nature, the whole atmosphere, the tunnels, the whole *chance* that goes with it, of hitting a strike." He pestered the owners of old claims to sign them over to him, eventually amassing the titles to ninety, including several more on Aspen Mountain.

His father, a French mountaineer, and his mother, a Red Cross nurse from Georgia, met during World War II. The family wasn't "antitourism"; indeed, his father, Stefan explained, was the first salesman in Colorado for Head's metal ski. But they had watched Aspen change. The house where he grew up was the Victorian on Main Street that now was painted bright yellow and housed a Chinese restaurant called Asia. "My room was that one to the left. You know, when you come in? Where the bar is?" Tourism had gradually made the family marginal, as old neighbors moved out, as miners died off, as town politics grew liberal and Aspenites began mining glitz instead of silver. All of a sudden I realized Stefan Albouy was the first person over age twenty I had met in Aspen who actually had *parents* in town. Stefan became visibly angry when he described seeing old ore cars and rail track taken from mines to be used as decoration at theme restaurants or around houses in town—"one of the biggest crimes," he called it, a strike against Aspen's soul.

I had been reminded of one such restaurant, the Aspen Mining Company, on the Hyman Avenue mall, back around the campfire near the Conundrum marble claim: The baseball caps of the men sitting around the fire that night all had similar words ("Aspen Mountain Mining Corp.") emblazoned above the bill. "No, we're not connected with them," Stefan had answered me with disdain. "That's what my *company*'s called."

Stefan and I said good night. Stepping out onto the mall reminded me of leaving the mine earlier that evening to discover skiers, tourists in all their brightly colored finery: It was time travel. I turned for more lightly trafficked streets and thought about Stefan while I strolled. Stefan's story was about land rights, certainly, but more than that it was about the meaning of the town, the state, the West. The history of the West is so brief that its meaning is perennially up for debate in a way that, say, New England's is not. The state seal of Colorado, miner Ed Smart had reminded me, depicted a pick and shovel. Mining had for a hundred years been what life in the Rockies was *about*. But the mayor of Aspen, arguing against Albouy, had stated that these days, "Aspen's mineral is the scenery." Tourism, now, was the region's lifeblood. The irony was that tourism, a fashion- and image-conscious business, did not usually reject anachronisms like ranching and mining; it simply subsumed them, converting them into objects of "color" and charm. Cowboy clothes were chic, ranches welcomed dudes, and restaurants—the old Shaft, the Mother Lode, Little Annie's, the Aspen Mining Company— mined a nostalgia theme. What the juggernaut of tourism could not tolerate, however, was disruption—and in deciding to be a *real* miner, Stefan Albouy was certainly that.

Chapter V

Willing Seduction

Working at *The Aspen Times* was much more fun than the alienated, nocturnal life of a cab driver. I was in the stream of things, meeting people, using my writing skills, more a part of the life of the town. I saw my reporter friend Paul every day, and I liked the others I worked with. I liked my editor and I liked the *Times*. I started going out to lunch a lot, making other friends, meeting for drinks after work. For the first time since I'd arrived in town, I'd begun to feel *included*.

Summer days in Aspen were sunny and dry, usually in the seventies and eighties. I shed my Sorels and parka and, to dress more like those around me, visited sporting-goods stores for a new work wardrobe: shorts, tennis shoes, and polo shirts. Everybody I knew, it seemed, was into mountain biking, so I raided the bank and bought myself a bike, too. Then I realized you couldn't really wear regular shorts to go mountain-biking—you'd feel out of place—so I went back and bought cycle shorts, sunglasses, a helmet, and a pump. Now I could ride with the best of them.

It was shortly afterward that Claire, my ski-instructor friend, walked into the *Times* office to place a classified ad. I had just come in from a meeting and saw her eyes pass over my new work togs: a pair of teal-colored cotton cycling shorts with NIKE in big letters up the side, cross-trainers with a strip of something fluorescent sewn in, and sunglasses pushed up on my head. I knew she thought of me as a sort of serious intellectual, and I saw her face break into a wide grin. "You've been infected," she said gleefully. "I *knew* it would happen."

"What are you talking about? I'm just trying to stay cool!"

"Aspen's gotcha, Aspen's gotcha! You thought you'd just study it, but Aspen has you in its *grip.*"

Attracted by the commotion, Paul came up as Claire was leaving. We both watched her go, admiringly. "You'll find there is a massive infusion of women into your life here," he said soberly. "It's unstoppable."

Helping the process along, Paul introduced me to good restaurants, good trails, and a lot of his friends. I found myself, to my surprise, getting asked out on dates.

One invitation came from Claire. A native Californian, she had come to Aspen from Jackson Hole, after briefly attending the University of Colorado. She was brown-eyed and sandy-haired, drove a Jeep, and was incredibly fit: After days of teaching on Aspen Mountain, I heard someone say, she would often go to the Aspen Club, "just for some upper-body work." I suggested we go for a bike ride, and she agreed. "Road bikes or mountain bikes?" she asked me. Flustered, I answered mountain bikes, because it was all I had.

We rode the bike paths out of town to Maroon Creek and then turned to take the winding road up Castle Creek to Ashcroft. Her hair blew in the wind behind her; I followed, just to watch her body work. She was all muscle, all tanned, all determination. I had planned on a leisurely sort of recreational ride, but for Claire, riding was a workout. She began to outpace me and I started to sweat. Now and then, as she reached a curve ahead of me, she would look back, notice where I was, and indulgently slow down for a while, but she seemed unable to keep up the slower pace. Finally, I had to surrender: Could the top wait for another day?

She didn't seem disappointed and in fact looked pleased; she mentioned a day the next week when we could try again, or maybe play tennis. She was going to visit a friend, she said when we had cruised back down to the bike path, and wouldn't be riding with me back into town—I accused her of planning an assault of the Maroon Creek Road to complete her workout. She laughed, didn't deny it, and then—the best part of the afternoon, the day, the week—she moved her bike next to mine and gave me a long hug and a kiss.

She was a long, lithe muscle, and for a moment my chin rested on her tanned bare shoulder and her windblown hair brushed my cheek. We were both damp from exertion. It was going on seven or eight months, and Aspen was looking better all the time, much better.

Denver, to my dismay, was looking worse. Every time I drove down there, it seemed, I would notice another flaw that hadn't struck me before. A recurring one was smog: There is a point, when you descend from the mountains of the front range to the Great Plains and Denver, when your car passes through the elevation where the worst smog hovers, a great dirty blanket that you realize you will thenceforth be breathing as long as you're in the city. The highway then passes through areas of the sort that in Aspen would be confined to an out-of-the-way area like the Airport Business Center or pushed downvalley. Except, from certain angles, all of Denver had started to look like a much-worse version of Aspen's Airport Business Center. There were industry, loud trucks, poor people walking on dirty sidewalks.

My neighborhood wasn't the nicest, and that never really bothered me except for moments when I felt guilty. All eyes would be on me, I felt, when I pulled up in front of my duplex and began to unload all the expensive ski gear: the Gore-Tex shell, the boots, the skis and poles, or the mountain bike from on the roof rack. I had the only sports rack on the block. One day a homeless guy walked by while I was unloading. Without ever stopping to think about it, I began to feel a bit annoyed about the guilt: In Aspen you *never* had to be ashamed of your gear. And when I took my bicycle out to run to the post office or grocery store, I had to carry a big Kryptonite lock, because I was back in the city. In Aspen you didn't need more than a little cable lock, if that. You didn't need to worry about your car stereo if the car was parked on the street overnight. You weren't punished for *having something*.

Though I'd more or less ignored the fact while I was still living in Denver, upon return it became increasingly apparent that, Aspen or otherwise, my friends and I were heading in different directions. Specifically, many of them were getting married. Of these, more and more were having children. They had less time for beer with a buddy, less time to throw a ball around. At dinner parties I felt like the sympathy guest—the odd man out. In Aspen, by contrast, being single in your thirties or even later wasn't a handicap at all. On the contrary, it meant you were at the center of the action.

There was another change that totally surprised me. When, in Denver, I had occasion to go to an expensive restaurant or a fashionable night spot, I no longer felt intimidated by them. Imperious waiters, doormen, other patrons—they had no power over me. On the contrary, I found it easy, if I was in the mood, to look down on them. Aspen's clubs booked better acts, Aspen's restaurants were more up to date, Aspen's fashions reflected coastal trends long before Denver. The hipness of Aspen was unassailable, and if you lived there, you somehow took it with you when you left.

And the people! For two months I'd been looking forward to an arts reception to which I'd been invited at the governor's mansion. This ought to be a great chance to meet some new colleagues, I thought, some like-minded people with literary sensibilities. Perhaps there'd be an intriguing woman to ask out. But it was not to be. After half an hour I ran into a novelist friend who had come with similar hopes and had them similarly dashed. "A wasteland," he concluded (and, after several months, moved to Santa Fe). After the exotica of Aspen, I had to admit Denver seemed very plain vanilla, very middle-class; home, instead of comforting, seemed dull.

Actually, I didn't admit it, because a very faint voice in the back of my brain whispered there was something unsupportable about the idea. But I felt it. And when I heard, through the grapevine, that an ex-girlfriend was telling people I had "changed," it annoyed me and made me want to leave even more.

Of course, it still was slightly nervewracking to arrive back in Aspen, like passing through the gates of a fancy club or college, a place with its own set of rules. But the more I did it, the easier the passage became, the feeling disappearing sooner and sooner.

At summer's end, after the design conference, the film festival, Aspen Institute symposiums, and most of the music festival, came the Aspen Writers' Conference, a two-week-long workshop at which published authors lectured and taught aspiring writers. I was leading the nonfiction workshop, which I vastly enjoyed. As faculty, however, I had an implied obligation to attend the lectures of fellow faculty, and after long days of work followed by nights out drinking, this could be difficult.

I was at the Aspen Community Center one afternoon at such a lecture when a notebook hit the floor, jolting me awake. I sat straight up. It was my notebook. It had been in my lap. I looked straight ahead and remembered: Rilke. The poet at the front of the room was reading aloud a lengthy scholarly essay on Rainer Maria Rilke. Not having a particular stake in the German poet, I had been drifting in and out. I glanced at the distinguished writer in the molded plastic chair to my left. He appeared not to have noticed my gaffe but was certainly just being polite. I took some deep breaths and resolutely held open my eyelids. I glanced around the room in desperate search of something of interest.

Outside it was sunny, breezy, green—a gorgeous day. A wall of sliding glass doors, mostly open, offered a constant reminder that we were inside and that outside was . . . Aspen. At least the lecture halls of England and New England, where I had spent years listening to lectures, had seldom had windows. You had been inside there, no doubt about it. You could forget. And anyway, it was always cloudy.

A woman's eyes met mine as my glance headed back up front. I had noticed her before, in the first hour. She was stretching, yawning, moving her sunglasses back up into her brown hair: antsy, like me. She shifted in her chair and glanced back at me again—it was me she was looking at, wasn't it? Not somebody she knew in the next chair? Or behind me? I looked at her again and she looked at me again, right through the studious gaze of my distinguished colleague, intent on Rilke. Embarrassed, I tried to seem as though I hadn't noticed. Rilke's mother, declared the lecturer, snaring me momentarily, had often dressed him in girls' clothes . . .

As the lecture moved into what sounded like concluding thoughts, I watched the woman in front rise and walk over to the glass doors. She wore a long skirt, a white oxford shirt, and a sweater vest—a stylish, grown-up, prep school kind of girl. She looked well heeled, unapologetic, somehow even proprietary over the proceedings. Her skin was olive-colored. The last words were hardly out of the lecturer's mouth when she came up to stand practically in front of me and ask, "Are you doing anything for the next hour?"

Have we met? I wanted to say. Did you have something in mind? All I could think of was all the people nearby who could hear. She had an elegant smile, perfect white teeth. The second lecture would begin in fifteen minutes. Like a nerd, I turned to the distinguished writer. "What should I do?" I asked, sort of joking.

"Go," he said, hardly looking up.

I went.

She drove a vintage white Porsche 356 convertible, and after we bought a six-pack, she asked if I wanted to meet Hunter.

"Who?"

"Hunter S. Thompson. He's my daughter's godfather." Dr. Hunter S. Thompson. A daughter. Jesus. I drained my beer and opened another.

The hills were green but the air rushing over us was dry; it was about seventy-five degrees. Across the valley rose craggy peaks, the largest ones snowcapped and windblown. Nearby was a small herd of exotic cattle, Scottish Highlanders, which we passed at double the 35 mph speed limit.

We pulled up off a dirt road and into a short dirt driveway. Peacocks scattered, some jumping onto the large silver photographic-equipment cases that spilled out the back deck of a rental car onto the driveway. "Hmm, wonder who's here," said Alison, my guide.

The front door was open, and I followed her in. "Annie!" cried Alison, entering the kitchen.

"Oh, I'm glad you came!" said the tall, large-handed woman who hugged her. She was Annie Leibovitz, the celebrity portrait photographer from New York whose shots filled *Vanity Fair*. She had been preparing to photograph the door of the refrigerator, upon which someone had taped the photo of Gary Hart, with Donna Rice on his lap, from the *National Enquirer*.

"Hunter freaked out. He left. You've got to go find him," Annie said.

"What do you mean? What happened?"

In preparation for her shoot, Leibovitz had taken some Polaroids of Hunter, sort of "rough drafts." One of them, at the side of a road, had reminded Thompson of one of the last portraits of comedian John Belushi, taken by Leibovitz not long before his death by drug overdose. Apparently, the journalist, known for his fondness of illicit drugs, had found the photo prophetic. He had jumped into his Jeep and disappeared.

"Oh, Hunter!" said Alison with a sigh. "He's probably down at the tavern." We climbed back into the Porsche.

The Woody Creek Tavern is one of the last authentic-seeming places in Aspen. It's a roadhouse with a pool table, a well-trodden carpet patterned to look like a parquet floor, and a stuffed wild boar, usually clad in a T-shirt or Santa hat or other seasonal garb, over the entryway. On either side is a trailer park. The drink is mostly beer and the food mostly burgers. There is a bar with five stools, and seated at one of these, drinking a Molson, was Hunter Thompson.

Tourists, thanks to "Doonesbury" cartoonist Garry Trudeau, will have no trouble recognizing this man. The dark glasses (Photo-grays, actually), the cigarette holder jabbed into the side of his mouth, the bald, sweaty pate: Between puffs on his cig, the tavern's most famous patron was eating a ham sandwich. This did not make it any easier to understand what he was saying. Thompson is a mumbler.

"Nff ng going back coz eed flgg nyshe k," he said.

"But, Hunter," said Alison sweetly. "*Rolling Stone* paid a lot of money to send Annie out here. She needs to get a good picture."

"Mmmgngiylllfu. I'm glg n thass not t ka shay."

"Oh, I see. But, Hunter, this is for their big issue, right? The anniversary issue? You *have* to be in it. Why don't you come back with us?"

Another beer, much cajoling, and half an hour later, Hunter came home. He and Annie seemed to reconcile. But it was only midafter-noon, with the sun still high and the light harsh. We shooed the peacocks, which Thompson raises, off the deck, and Thompson produced a large color TV and a half-gallon of gin. Then Hunter, Annie, Alison, and I watched the news, and were joined by Maria, his girlfriend. She was from Phoenix, much younger and more attractive than he. Hunter, thin, tall, and gawky, seemed all knees and elbows. He was again wearing shorts, white knee socks, Ree-boks, and a baseball cap; his rarefied appearance, virtual unintelligi-bility, and jerking manner made you wonder whether he was an imbecile or a genius. Though the weather was warm and he did not seem to have a cold, his nose ran constantly, in the thin, watery way children of the eighties will recognize; Maria would reach over to wipe it dry for him. I tried to chat with him during commercials, but he was not especially a *communicator* as the term is generally understood.

After we had drunk half the gin and watched our fourth identical half-hour of CNN, the group broke up, with Hunter, Annie, and the entourage of her assistants heading off to take advantage of the superior light of late-in-the-day Aspen, and Alison and I bound for town and an early dinner. A few months later, posted on the wall of the Woody Creek Tavern, I would see the photo that came out of that session, printed across two pages of *Rolling Stone.* Dr. Hunter S. Thompson, gonzo journalist and weirdo of his generation, was dressed as we had seen him that afternoon, and leaning way back on the seat of a parked Harley-Davidson motorcycle, the iconoclast on the icon.

As Alison's Porsche accelerated to fifty-five on the McClain Flats Road back to Aspen, I thought about the first line of Thompson's *Fear and Loathing in Las Vegas:* "We were just outside of Barstow when the drugs took hold." The year was 1971; getting high was a form of social protest. What was it in the late eighties? Increasingly, an anachronism—though for Hunter it was more likely an affirmation of identity, a reflex. I'd heard he'd seen a doctor recently, when one of his arms started contracting involuntarily. My brain was aslosh in gin, which seemed wholly appropriate.

Alison insisted on sushi. She owned a large share of the first restaurant we tried, she said, but there was no cutting the waiting line, so we went across the street to another, where she also seemed to know everyone. I was, at the time, a confirmed sushi skeptic, but Alison promised to eat anything I decided I didn't like. We drank sake. The California roll was delicious, the *tekamaki* and *hamachi* definitely edible, but I had profoundest doubts about the raw quail egg, which was presented on a tiny pedestal. Alison ate one to prove they were good, rubbed my back, and I was a goner: I popped it in my mouth.

That's as far as it got. I couldn't swallow it. Absolutely, positively, no way: I would blow that fish all over the bar. I shook my head emphatically at Alison and reached for a big cloth napkin. But she stopped my hand with hers, leaned in front of me, and volunteered, "I'll take it." Then she opened her mouth and kissed me, the gooey egg flowing into her mouth, and I was saved.

Or was I lost? Somewhere around that moment, Aspen took a hold of me. When the conference was over, I noticed one day that at some point during the summer I had stopped taking notes for my book. I had been keeping myself at arm's length for too long, I felt, and it was nice just to relax for a while and go with the flow. I just knew I had sampled something I wanted more of, before I got too old. Was seduction ever really "unwilling"? A part of me I had always kept in check seemed to have found an opening. I felt that dreamy languor of the lost sailors of Odysseus, thought about the addictive fruit of mythology. What was a lotus, anyway?—I thought I still had a slight taste of the Aspen version on my tongue. A taste of gin and quail egg.

Chapter VI

A Positive Difference on the Planet

I'm on a flight to Australia with my Aspen photographer friend Nicholas DeVore III. The plane is a Flying Tigers 747 cargo jet, with no windows; our fellow passengers are eighty-seven thoroughbred racehorses, eight bison, and six miniature Spanish ponies. For our passage, DeVore has agreed to document the proceedings photographically and I in writing; then we will try to sell the article. We put together this arrangement at a party in Aspen attended by the twenty-eight-year-old in charge of North American operations for the International Racehorse Transport company, which organizes these flights.

Nicholas will be traveling for several months following the flight, and his wife has sent him off with a good-luck crystal. Quartz crystals are enjoying a vogue as New Age amulets that ward off sickness and promote healing; they are worn by many in Aspen in necklace pendants or other jewelry. The one Nicholas is carrying is too big for that, though. It's about the size of a lipstick, with points on either end, and he keeps it in his pocket, where he turns it over in his hand during idle moments.

During takeoff, one of the horses spooks. The spirited animal pulls loose the rope tying her harness to the front of a stall and rears up as the plane accelerates. Nicholas and I and several handlers watch in alarm as she kicks and bangs her way out of the stall, then bolts down the aisle toward the front of the plane. We scatter to let her by, but one brave handler grabs her harness rope, hangs on, and slowly brings her under control.

When the commotion settles, I notice that Nicholas is holding his leg. There seems to be some blood.

"You okay?" I ask, lending a hand. "What happened?"

"It's the crystal," he says with a grimace. He reaches into his pocket. The crystal, in his sudden movement, has cut through his pocket and into his thigh. As the plane climbs into the sky, we both start to laugh, sharing the nervousness of the horses.

"Fucking thing malfunctioned," says Nicholas.

Johanna and I end a morning of errands with a visit to Quadrant Books, Aspen's oldest bookstore. The store is on the ground floor of a gaily painted two-story Victorian house, and just inside the door we see an old man who looks as though he might be the original occupant, a left-over miner, rumpled and stooped, with suspenders holding up his dungarees and wire-rimmed specs. His kitchen appears to adjoin the bookstore; he sits in a wooden chair, heating water on a potbellied stove. His feet are warmed by two furry dogs that curl around the bottom of the chair. "Hello," we say, but the old man does not answer.

There's a wall of popular books: Stephen King, Danielle Steele, some Penguins, and a few standards of American literature. But there are several freestanding shelves and a longer wall of books on more arcane topics. There are *Seth Speaks*, by Jane Roberts; *Reflections*, by Shakti Gawain; and *Codependent No More*, by Melody Beattie. "It's sort of a New Age bookstore," Johanna murmurs as I examine the Castañeda.

A shuffling noise alerts us to the presence of the old man, directly behind us. He is unsnapping an old sunglasses case. From it he raises up a string; at the end of the string is a dark wooden pendulum. The old man drops the pendulum and it starts swinging. We turn around, because it seems rude to have our backs to him.

"Your order is God's Angels," he announces presently, peering up at Johanna. The pendulum is tracing figure eights over the floor. "They will come for you soon."

This catches us off guard. "They will come for me? When will they come for me?" asks Johanna.

The old man watches the pendulum. "January third."

Johanna glances at me, sort of wide-eyed. I know she doesn't take this *too* seriously. "What does that mean, the angels will come for me January third? Am I going to die?"

"No, no," says the old man, the proprietor. "They'll just take you up."

"Take me up? And when will I come down?" This strikes me as a key question. The old man doesn't look up from the floor, his solitaire version of a Ouija board.

"April fifteenth."

"Oh good, in time for taxes!" says Johanna, sort of laughing— laughing, it seems to me, with the hope that the old man will laugh with her, that even if he doesn't see it as a joke, he'll realize it sounds strange enough that one ought to have a sense of humor. But he doesn't laugh. He just stands there watching the pendulum.

Wayne has been in Aspen three months. Alison met him at the bar at Mezzaluna. He was throwing the I Ching, and that intrigued her. He's quite a bit older than she is, so it probably made him feel good when she approached him.

He tells his story freely. For years he lived in the suburbs of New York City, with his wife and three children. His commute wasn't bad; he managed the development of new software for IBM. But then suddenly he knew it wasn't the life for him. He left behind his family and moved to Aspen. When he wasn't seeing Alison or planning a trip to Nepal with her or breaking in his new hiking boots (identical to hers), he was sitting at his laptop computer, programming it to tell the reader what the runes—characters of an ancient alphabet, said to be magical—said about his life.

One day I ask him to use it on me. He enters my name, date of birth, and something else like favorite color and pushes a key. Representations of the runes appear on the screen, an array of little tablets, each highlighted momentarily as the program does its work.

Then the printer comes alive and churns out a lengthy horoscope. The first section reads:

WHAT SHOULD TED KNOW ABOUT HIS LIFE NOW?

Current Situation: Retreat

You have reached a fork in the road. Old skins must be shed, outmoded relationships discarded. This situation indicates a radical severance and that a peeling away is called for. Real property is associated with this Rune of acquisition and benefits. However, the benefits you receive, the "inheritance," may be derived from something you must give up. The separation called for now will free you to become more truly who you are.

Do: Shed, release, and retreat if necessary.

Avoid: Avoid attachment to things that will impede your progress.

"This sounds like *your* horoscope, Wayne," I suggest with a smile.

"No," he says. "They're all different."

"Do you program for a hobby?"

"Well, sort of," says Wayne. "But this also qualifies as work. I already sold the rights to the program, to a company in California, for nine thousand dollars."

The New Age, I have noticed, has no problem with making this sort of magic.

Saturday night it's a tough choice. I'm torn between an invitation to a special session with the son of Black Elk ("he's going to be doing sweat lodges"); a tepee gathering with Jessica, a secretary at the *Times* who has put together a group of people to have crystal readings; and going with Marciela, an Argentinian friend, to a party thrown by an artist friend of hers ("There'll be interesting people. You won't be disappointed."). I've had a sauna at the Aspen Club already, so the sweat lodge doesn't sound too good, and the previous crystal session mainly involved placing a number of industrial-size clear white crystals in special patterns on the carpet and then sitting amidst them and hearing what it all portended for us spiritually.

With my tolerance for things spiritual and esoteric thus at an ebb, I cast my lot with Marciela. She picks me up in her sleek blue Acura, and soon we are at a sprawling single-story house. Marciela doesn't ring the bell: Kathleen, who's throwing the party, is her friend. Kathleen's throwing the party for Eli. ("Is he her husband?" I ask Marciela. "Mm, sort of," replies Marciela after a moment's consideration. "I would have called you sooner," she adds to me, "but Kathleen only remembered yesterday that today was his birthday." "Mhmm," I say.)

At first it looks like a regular party: guys at the pool table, people gabbing around the bar, white people ages twenty-five to fifty. But groups of guests keep appearing from the big house's back hall, ooohing and aaaahing. I take a stroll to see what's going on.

Eli, thirty-four, is leading a tour through the house's major New Age paraphernalia. He's a thin man, wearing jeans and a white cotton Mexican shirt, with shoulder-length dark hair. There's something demonic about his bright smile: He looks sort of early Dan Fogelberg, with a touch of Charles Manson. On an easel in front of Eli is an oil painting, still in progress, of a monster from his dreams. It's devillike, with the eyes of a cat and the throat muscles of a human anatomical chart, such as he has on the wall in front of his drafting table. "Are you a painter?" I ask.

He doesn't leap to answer, and I wonder if this is a question Eli doesn't much like. "Oh, a little here and there, now and then," he says finally. When I asked her what they do, Marciela said she didn't really know, and now I wonder who is rich: him or her or both.

I am allowed to tag along as Eli shows three other guests "some of the things we have back here."

There is a machine that lets you breathe positively charged ions, filtering out all the bad, negatively charged ones.

There is a light machine. It has interchangeable lenses, which allow the creation of a number of colors. It sits at the foot of a bed and shines on the person lying down. You shine it on you for a couple of hours a day. It's set for magenta. Eli prefers a purple. It looks expensive, makes a fan noise, and you can feel the heat.

In another room, a small, heavy canister hangs over the pillows from the ceiling—the polarizer, Eli explains. With you and the box in one configuration, it makes you healthy (you have to be lying on a north-south axis, I think Eli says); in another, it recharges you sexually. "But it's not working quite right," Eli laments, raising a number of intriguing questions.

Finally, sitting amidst pillows, prisms, and low-wattage lamps is a small pyramid, constructed of metal tubing. I've seen these in pictures: You sit in them and meditate. They're supposed to help you tap into the Power. I want to sit in there, but Eli says not now—maybe he feels I would bring in the wrong energy, defile it somehow. And who knows, he may be right.

When we leave the party, Eli touches Marciela's arm. He holds up his other hand, palm toward Marciela, fingers together like the Buddha, and says to her, "White light."

"White light," replies Marciela, smiling, as we leave.

"What light? White light what?" I ask her, outside.

"White lights means magic, like, you know, white magic, good vibes," Marciela explains to me.

"Ah," I say. "Hmm."

Back when I was fourteen, a new kid came to the neighborhood.

He was a year older than I, and his name was Maharaj Ji, or "boy guru Maharaj Ji," as the papers called him. A portly kid, he didn't go to school and he didn't have friends, he had followers. They were members of his Denver-based church, the Divine Light Mission. These followers, all grown-up Americans, bought him a house on a corner five blocks from our house.

The boy guru tended to stay indoors, and after the initial excitement of his presence in our midst wore off, we thought about him mainly when we walked to school. There were bodyguards constantly stationed in a sedan outside his house, and we tried to stare them down as we walked by. Even this became boring until, on the young master's fifteenth birthday, we beheld a thirty-foot yacht, bought by the followers for their "divine master," and parked squarely across the front lawn. Why they bought him a yacht, in Colorado, we never understood. Frankly, in those days of first driver's licenses and borrowing the family station wagon, we were much more interested in the guru's next present, an English Jensen convertible. An apparent precursor to the guru Bhagwan Shree Rajneesh, founder of Rajneespuram in Oregon in 1984, whose followers bought him eighty-four Rolls-Royces, the boy guru Maharaj Ji was a great fan of expensive conveyance. Soon he had a Mercedes 280 SEL and then a black-and-silver Maserati Bora. When one summer day he was ticketed next to our local shopping center for doing over 60 MPH in the Maserati in a 30 MPH pedestrian zone, I felt much better about him. The fat kid was human after all.

It was only about fifteen years later that the *The New York Times Magazine* got wind of the large number of, um, *spiritual* people in my state. "Colorado's Thriving Cults" was the cover story on May 1, 1988. Cults, by that time, was actually not the best word to describe a more generalized movement of New Age thought in Colorado, a movement that really started when counterculture types, who had been attracted to Colorado in the 1960s by its cheap land, relative isolation, and mountain mystique, blended in with the many young professionals drawn by the economic boom of the 1970s. Mothers of my friends would have had nothing to do with Maharaj Ji and the Divine Light Mission (cult), but they were sort of interested in Shirley MacLaine and Windstar (New Age), and one or two were known to sport the occasional crystal.

These were movements mostly of the white middle class, of people who had been brought up going to church but for whom church had ceased to provide meaningful answers for life's new problems. The search for new wisdom fueled a booming industry of soothsayers and self-helpers. A profusion of groups and activities, some more cultlike than others, sprang up, aiming to help participants "heal" psychic damage, "align" themselves if they felt unbalanced or ill at ease in the world, and find harmony in personal relationships. It seemed some friend or friend of a friend was always trying to get me to a meeting of the church of Scientology, or the groups known as Choices, Lifespring, or Insight—they would "change your life," was the vague but consistent promise. Easier to consider—if only because they did not make demands for all your time, all your commitment, or all your money—were therapies like acupressure, transcendental meditation, macrobiotic diets, or flotation tanks, all helping you deal with the increasing stresses of modern-day life.

Boulder, next to the mountains, and Aspen, nestled in them, were always larger capitals of this sort of thing than ordinary Denver, down on the plains. And so I guess I was not too surprised, two months after my arrival at *The Aspen Times,* to be invited to a UFO landing.

Larry Koss invited me. He came to the *Times* office looking for John Colson, the reporter who, if not an adherent, at least seemed receptive to some New Age ideas. But Colson was on his way out the door to Telluride, to "cover" the annual bluegrass festival. To the nervous Larry Koss, he recommended me.

Koss had done a lot of thinking about UFOs. Not only had he

taught a class about them the year before at the Colorado Mountain College, he was presently trying to organize a symposium in Aspen entitled "The Choice to Acknowledge Extraterrestrial Contact." He handed me a proposal by that name, in a plastic report folder, with the subtitle, "An Historic Symposium and Major Motion Picture Examining Cultural Implications Inherent in Acknowledging the Existence and Presence of Extraterrestrial Intelligent Life." The symposium, which he was working hard on, was important, even vital, he said. But something even bigger was brewing. It was three nights away. "It's larger than anything you've ever been in before," he said. "What's about to happen may lead to an awakening exponentially greater than the Copernican revolution."

Larry Koss looked over his shoulder, but Reporters' Row was empty. There was going to be a landing, he whispered. I carefully took notes, to avoid having to look him in the eye. Two weeks earlier, at an appointed time, a light had appeared on the horizon. As a result, a woman was being flown into town, a woman who had been abducted previously by UFOs and could get into contact with them. Five other people there would speak about their experiences, Larry said, and their fear. "It's not about a UFO, it's about divinity," he explained. "We'll bond. We'll go outside. And Cynthia will establish contact."

I was being invited, along with *Times* photographer Frank Martin, because Koss did not want this event to go unwitnessed by the press. The press was important to launching the new Copernican revolution. Koss instructed me to "stay off pot and liquor till then," wear warm clothes, and bring a folding chair, ten dollars, and a contribution to the vegetarian potluck. "Be willing to have your life altered beyond anything you can imagine," he said finally, staring at me like a man possessed. I scribbled away frantically.

Frank, the photographer, had his doubts. There could be a story for me whether or not the thing landed, he said; but for him, there would only be a story if it did. Which it wouldn't. "And besides," he added, covering his bets, "the lighting at night is always a problem."

Koss had requested that I not tell any others, so I was left to ponder alone the impending evening, three nights away, that would alter my life. I read and reread Koss's précis. "Benefits to You," it read at the end: "Gain the satisfaction of enabling the most signifi-

NO POSITIVE DIFFERENCE ON THE PLANET

cant shift of consciousness in the history of the planet" and "Be at the forefront of information that will influence the entire course of human events." It was as though Koss expected the Second Coming. I couldn't get my mind off this idea of millenarianism—that some impending event would spell the end of the current world and the beginning of the next one. A professor of mine had been a big fan of *When Prophecy Fails,* a book that traced the growth of a flying-saucer cult whose leader specifically predicted the time the members would be hauled into space aboard a UFO. Cargo cults in numerous south-sea islands predicted the arrival of white gift-bearing saviors. Many speakers at Windstar, closer to home, had predicted an imminent revolution of consciousness, which would usher in a New Age time of planetary peace and unity. Like many religious movements, the New Age was shot through with apocalyptical predictions. What would happen, I thought, when the saucer didn't come? Not knowing me, how could Koss risk ridicule from an outsider?

The answer came when Larry delivered notes to me and Frank at the *Times* the day of the landing. "Please don't feel offended, but I need to forego having the press there. Some of the people are too sensitive to it right now. Maybe next time. I'll inform you of the results. Larry Koss." That's when I learned that someone *had* been eavesdropping on my conversation with Koss that day: The ski columnist, Josephine Pettit, a reporter with a mean streak, had seen Koss at the counter and greeted him with the words, "The flying saucers landed yet, Larry?"

I felt bad about that—but I still wanted to go.

It was just getting dark when I drove up the driveway to the big-windowed house outside of Aspen. Larry Koss was standing right around the corner from the front hall, where I added my shoes to the pile already there. I held my breath.

"You didn't get my message?" he asked, looking surprised.

"What message?" I said. "Isn't she coming?"

"No, no, she's here. It's just that . . . well, come on in." I let out my breath, relieved.

Most of the thirty or so people there seemed already acquainted. I felt lucky to know only a couple of them—a woman who worked in the *Times* typesetting room and was married to a county commissioner, and a habitué of the Nature's Storehouse natural foods store. Neither seemed to find my presence unusual. I added some bottles of juice to the vegetarian smorgasbord taking shape in the kitchen. A middle-aged woman told me she had been fasting, which made me recall Larry's dietary strictures—I had drunk a beer the night before. Would people know?

Present were members of white-collar Aspen—a ski shop owner, a real estate broker—and blue-collar Aspen—a carpenter and his wife—with the oldest a woman, probably sixty-five, and the youngest a brother and sister in their late teens. Eyes seemed wide-open, the crowd earnest and expectant, open to the possibility of a life-changing event. I began to pet the cat, which I will do whenever possible in a room where I don't know many people—a big, fluffy black thing, with an extra-long, curly tail. A man sat down next to me. "Have you met Nostradamus?" he asked. "Not formally," I replied. He picked the cat up. "He and Caroline [the owner of the house] have been together a *long* time. Many past lives. They've been reincarnated together. Previously, Nostra was a monkey—notice the tail?" I nodded knowingly. "Where'd she get him?" I asked bravely.

"Oh, he just showed up at the door one day, as karmic cats will do," the man replied.

"Yes, I guess they do," I said amiably.

As we finished dinner, Larry Koss introduced our alien connection. Her name was Cynthia Smith. Narrow-shouldered and broad-hipped, she wore a long peach-colored sweater. She had blond hair and would describe herself, later that night, as having "big brown eyes." Larry glanced out the picture windows, excited but nervous. "It's pretty dark," he said. "Let's get started."

I feared the group of us, scattered around the living room on cushions, carpeted steps, and low couches, would have to go around and say something about ourselves, but all Cynthia Smith wanted to know, by way of introduction, was how many people in the room had been "abducted." By space aliens. Five people raised their hands. We would want to hear from them later, she said, but in the meantime, she would tell us about herself.

Though she was from a town of five hundred people in Texas, her reputation, from the power of her spiritual and intuitive powers, was worldwide. She had worked as a consultant to Steven Spielberg on *Close Encounters of the Third Kind.* In addition, she had worked with numerous police departments that needed help in locating missing persons. That rang a bell in my head—*That's Incredible!*, that's where I'd seen her! Having been told the particulars of a case, she had, according to the show, intuited the location of the grave of a missing person for a Texas police department.

Having established her credentials, Cynthia Smith downplayed them. We all have psychic potential, she said, but most of us are not open to it. Negative energy is your enemy; you have to acknowledge the possibility. It was like Larry Koss's "Choice to Acknowledge" symposium—crouching down for the leap of faith. Having a spiritual teacher, of course, was useful. Cynthia Smith's had been a traveling vaudevillian.

Her first vision was of Jesus. In response to a question she replied that, yes, it was okay to go to church. There were no contradictions between psychic phenomena and the church. She herself, in the course of past life regressions, had made it back all the way to 180 A.D., and had found nothing disappointing about the early Christian era.

Smith spoke calmly from an easy chair. As she did, she produced a tassled, "Native American" leather pouch, and brought from it a long crystal. This she rolled around in her palm, explaining that many crystals came from outer space and had their power rejuvenated by lying in the earth a while. Staring up at her raptly were the two teenagers; Cynthia took a liking to the boy, a well-coiffed, *GQ*-type of guy.

"We've hugged in a previous life, am I right?" she asked him, nodding slightly. He grinned broadly and nodded back. She handed him the crystal in her hands.

"Hey, thanks!" he said.

"It's not from me," she replied mysteriously. Instead of returning to her story, then, she stared at the boy a bit longer.

"You've been, too, right?" Shrugging and grinning, he looked back at her. "Abducted?" she said. He just stared at her, and I imagined his bind: If he said no, he would ruin her spell or risk contradiction; but if he said yes, he would have to tell the story of it. Or maybe she was making him wonder if he *had* had an abduction experience. "Well, why don't I just tell everyone about mine?" she said, saving him.

The details were sketchy, like a person recalling a dream. Cynthia Smith was sitting in a coffee shop with a friend when it happened. She was lifted right out of there and into the spaceship. A TV in the ship had allowed her to look down on the table where she had been sitting moments before. The craft had lots of buttons in it. She felt she was in good hands, and consented to let the aliens do everything they wanted to with her—but she would not tell us exactly what this was. The little mark on the left side of her nose was not, after all, a chicken pox or acne scar, but the "needle mark" left when the aliens inserted their hypodermic, the other pockmark, on her forehead, where it came out. Just like in the movies, they had huge eyes, pointy in the corners, but their other features were small. The communication was all telepathic. It was not her only abduction experience, but it was the only one she was going to tell us about. As she finished, all the lights in the room dimmed slightly for an instant, the way they do when a furnace or central air conditioner goes on. "Good, good!" said Cynthia Smith, looking around and smiling.

There was a lot of conspiracy, in regard to UFOs, on the part of the government. The government is keeping valuable UFO info from us—she knew, she had asked a general whose name could not be revealed. Furthermore, she added solemnly, "NASA is controlled by the government."

"You know the space shuttle, the one with the teacher? Well, did you see the little flash right before it went? That was the laser." Many in the audience nodded, rapt. Cuba, also, had warned us beforehand that the attempted launch of the *Challenger* would be used to humiliate us. The Cuba-alien conspiracy? Why would the aliens, whom she had described previously as benevolent, want to do something like that? They were angry at us for polluting the heavens with satellites and all that other junk we send up there, Smith explained. I wanted fervently to ask more questions and flesh these theories out, but this was an audience with an oracle, not a press conference.

The charge about a government conspiracy I had heard somewhere before—it was a repeated concern of UFO fans, that they were being kept in the dark. Larry Koss's proposal had even opened with a blunt reference to it: two quotations from speeches by President Ronald Reagan, both to the effect that the world's leaders fixate on the differences between nations instead of what they have in common. But Reagan had said, "If suddenly there was a threat to this world from some other species from another planet, we'd forget all the little local differences" and become united members of humanity. Koss commented, "While true we presently seem to lack 'hard evidence' of extraterrestrial contact (or public access to such evidence), recent events throughout the world, including statements of our President and Commander in Chief, suggest the possibility . . ."

"It's important to have three or four bowel movements a day," continued Cynthia Smith. She had digressed into a discussion of the seven chakras and the centrality of the colon in trying to answer a dietary question by a young woman who appeared anorexic. This was a hard discussion to follow, but it was determined by Smith that the woman's problems were probably caused by candida, a yeast infection. Holistic thinkers who put stock in candida, I later learned, blame it for everything from poor memory, allergies, depression, and fatigue to the sudden death of the discoverer of King Tut's tomb. In this case, though, the symptoms were clearer. "It causes a lot of gas, right?" Cynthia asked the woman, who nodded feebly. One hesitates to disagree with a psychic authority, I thought again— to a crowd of believers, it would be saying more about you than about her.

With the presentation in danger of stalling, Larry invited a woman in the back of the room to give an account of her abduction experience. Like many of those attending, she had been a student in Larry's UFO class. But, though Cynthia Smith had said the universe is full of only positive energy, this woman described her abduction as frightening. When she was lifted up through the ceiling, it scared her to death. Tears came to her eyes as she spoke. She couldn't figure out why it was so horrible and asked Cynthia Smith what she thought.

"Have you ever had hypnosis?"

"Only a past life regression."

Smith suggested that hypnosis, which she normally opposed, might help. Once you got past the bad stuff, she said, the rest was all good.

Koss, still glancing every few moments out a window and into the night, asked Smith if she could maybe move onto the subject the two of them had been discussing earlier—a clear reference to tonight's landing. It seemed to me the moment of truth.

Smith answered by closing her eyes. Four years earlier, she said presently, she had seen a sign in a dream, in color, that spelled out A-S-P-E-N. She didn't know then where Aspen was, but she did know she'd be going someday. And sure enough. But today, as she climbed a mountain enshrouded in storm clouds, something told her the landing would not be tonight. Disappointment clouded the face of Larry Koss.

He should be glad, I thought—a greater psychic than himself had gotten him off the hook for the Big Landing. But, forget his reputation, he was ready for that thing to land. Others stared out the big, dark windows. "It *will* happen here," Smith said firmly.

"When?" asked Koss.

"I'm not allowed to say. But it will be landing. There will be indisputable evidence. The mother ship is circling now. It will be in Aspen."

The evening broke up soon afterward, everyone having a goodbye embrace with Cynthia Smith. One drunkish guy, who had brought Budweisers to the gathering, asked Larry about paying for a private session with her before she left. Larry said she was to leave in the evening, so how was the daytime? "I just happen to have tomorrow open," Cynthia said.

A plea was made for ten-dollar donations to help defray the airfare. Slowly, at the tail end of the crowd, I made my way out the door and down the driveway. At my car, I looked back. Cynthia was back inside. Alone on the porch, unaware anyone was watching, Larry had his head tilted back. He was staring up at the stars.

Even in Aspen, UFO enthusiasts were on the fringe. Other parts of the New Age were an accepted feature of everyday life. Among my beats at *The Aspen Times* was John Denver's Windstar Foundation.

My first exposure to Windstar came in the form of encounters with one Rio de la Vista, Windstar's PR person. Rio would submit to me, usually at the very last minute, Windstar press releases she wanted in the *Times*. "Windstar Offers Grand Canyon Adventure Raft Trip and Retreat," they would say, or "Windstar Hosts Valley Kids for Earth Day." When there wasn't room for them all, she would request that I call and let her decide which was more important. Often, later, she would call back and change her mind. I was annoyed by these calls—while most people were grateful for free publicity, Rio felt *entitled*. And I will admit, I was annoyed by her made-up name, which in Spanish meant "river of the view."

But I had faith there was more to Windstar than its PR. It was one of the big things happening in Aspen, an innovation with a national reputation and, within the New Age community, a mainstream appeal. By coming to understand Windstar, I hoped, I could learn more about Aspen, about the New Age, and about why they fit together so well.

Founded in 1976 with $3 million from John Denver's recording success—and sustained by $15,000 a month from him in subsidies— Windstar was the realization of the childhood dream Denver had described to me: a place in the mountains where people like him, who had felt like spiritual outsiders in the culture at large, could find kindred souls and together "seek new solutions" for a troubled world. Located in the Snowmass Creek Valley, a few miles from Aspen, its 985 acres comprised a tract "roughly in the shape of a bowhead whale," according to the literature. On them were offices and classrooms, summertime tepees, and the fifty-foot diameter Biodome—a greenhouse that produced fish and vegetables year-round.

But Windstar was not about bricks and mortar. Rather, it was about consciousness and changing the way people think. In our interview, John Denver had outlined for me an idea of social progress that I came to understand was a fundamental precept not only of Windstar but of the New Age movement as a whole. The idea is contained in a book called *The Hundredth Monkey*; the model it presents has been suggested by other scientific studies. John Denver had leaned back in a chair and told it to me as a kind of parable. To quote from the book:

> In the 1950s, scientists were studying Japanese monkeys on the island of Koshima. They provided the monkeys with sweet potatoes dropped in the sand; the monkeys liked the sweet potatoes, but hated the sand. Then, an 18-month-old female named Imo found she could solve the problem by washing the potatoes in a nearby stream. She taught this trick to her mother. Her playmates also learned this new way and they taught their mothers, too.

In the following years, all the young monkeys learned how to wash the potatoes, as well as all those adults able to learn from their children. Those adults unable to learn from their children continued eating the dirty potatoes.

Then something startling took place. In the autumn of 1958, a certain number of Koshima monkeys were washing sweet potatoes—the exact number is not known. Suppose that when the sun rose one morning there were 99 monkeys on Koshima Island who had learned to wash their sweet potatoes. Then let's further suppose that later that morning, the hundredth monkey learned to wash potatoes.

That's when it happened.

By evening almost everyone in the tribe [all the monkeys] was washing sweet potatoes before eating them.

The added energy of this hundredth monkey somehow created an ideological breakthrough. Soon, colonies of monkeys on nearby islands, and then on the mainland, began washing their sweet potatoes, too.

Thus, when a certain critical number achieves an awareness, this new awareness may be communicated from mind to mind.

Although the exact number may vary, the Hundredth Monkey Phenomenon means that when only a limited number of people know of a new way, it may remain the consciousness property of these people.

But there is a point at which if only one more person tunes in to a new awareness, a field is strengthened so that this awareness is picked up by almost everyone!

The Hundredth Monkey, written in 1981, is about creating a movement to prevent nuclear war. But its lesson, embraced by much of the New Age movement, is this: You may be the "hundredth monkey." The energy of your enlightenment, in other words, may be the increment necessary to suddenly change the world. The harmonious, productive, god-worshiping epoch to be ushered in by this change is the New Age. Windstar, one could fairly infer, wanted to help create that first group of monkeys.

"Order about fifty of those, will you?" John Denver had yelled to his secretary, holding up the book, when he had summarized the story for me. "We'll pass 'em out."

What was a bit harder to understand was exactly the sort of change Windstar favored. Its official mission statement declared that the foundation "expresses a profound belief in humanity's ability to live in harmony with one another and the earth." That could mean almost anything. But elsewhere, I read that "Windstar is an organization of people who are taking a stand for a peaceful, sustainable future." "Sustainable future" is New Age code for energy solutions that are nonnuclear, farming solutions that focus on small-scale organic produce, environmental policy that preserves wilderness, and political policy that reduces armaments: a roster of policies to engender "planetary health."

Amidst all this, though it was hard to be sure, was the suggestion of a lot of new ideas for how to run the world. That was something I was in favor of, and I welcomed the chance to attend Windstar's big summer conference, the third annual four-day "Choices for the Future" symposium.

Sprinting out in jeans, blazer, and an open-necked shirt, John Denver helped set the tone of Choices III by hugging his introducer long and hard. Hugging was one of the things this would be about. There was thunderous applause.

It was the first morning of Choices. I and fourteen hundred others were gathered under the big white music tent in the Aspen Meadows on the west side of town. Rows of seats sloped gently down from level ground in a grand semicircle to the stage. Light entered in a gentle diffusion from the white canvas overhead but beamed in from the small entryways. When Denver told us he wanted the conference to be "a model for each of you of how you'd like that world to be out there," I looked around me. About two hundred people were from the valley, and most of the others looked as though they could be—white, aged thirty to sixty, upper middle class, casually dressed, and appearing, like our host, earnest and positive. They had paid airfare and condo rental and the $350–$625 fee required to come to Choices. A model for how we'd like the world to be? I realized Denver was talking about the example of personal behavior: of promptness, participation, and not littering ("I don't want to see a piece of paper left on the ground anywhere!"). People nodded.

I looked around again. This was not your typical conference, and these, apart from the demographics, were not your typical conferees. They shared no profession or company, they were not aficionados of cars or antiques, they were not there to buy or sell. The American mania for association, described by Tocqueville, here took on an unusual new flavor: People came to Choices because of a feeling, because they believed it might be important for their souls. These were people who had experienced some crisis of purpose, people who, though they looked a part of it, had taken exception to establishment ways of looking at the world and were seeking new ways to rebuild. They were people with plenty of money, plenty of choices, who wanted to do something good in the world but were not exactly sure what or how. They came not just to hear panels but to *relate*, to emote, to get straight, to meet kindred souls.

Aspen was a good place for seekers because it was a young town, unburdened by traditions, that carried the promise of a future waiting to be made. Santa Fe, though not a young town, seemed to hold a similar promise of alternatives, and John Denver next introduced someone he had met there. Dennis Becker—a man who was so close to him as to be "like a brother," said Denver—had recently led the Windstar board of directors on a "vision quest." The fortyish Californian walked onstage, hugged Denver, and assured us that it was "a privilege to co-create this event," that he was sure we were all "committed to making a positive difference on the planet."

Next he tried to explain what the conference was about. The previous years' symposia had focused on futurism and hopeful trends in the world, but this one's theme was, specifically, "Ethics in Action." It seemed designed to counter the criticism, heard in some quarters, that Windstar was long on talk but short on results. Becker said he wanted to help "evoke a commitment to action in the place in our lives that's most appropriate for us.

"That may mean only creating a space for positive well-being in yourself," he conceded, appearing to reassure the crowd that this conference wasn't really for *them*, the beneficiaries of these good works, if we didn't want it to be; it was for *us*. This seemed to me a rather quick retreat from the "Ethics in Action" theme, saying that working on yourself was enough, but Becker, in the manner of Windstar, aimed to be inclusive.

His next words made me think he'd given a lot of motivational seminars; he asked us to "imagine the difference [it] could make on the planet, with fourteen hundred people walking out of here . . . people who are predisposed to take positive action . . . It's exciting, isn't it? Exciting!" There were shouts of agreement. "This is a congreg— . . . a *gathering* of bright lights," he corrected himself. "There's a possibility that exists here of a transformational event that has the possibility of shifting a lot of people, both in this room and out of this room—really, really making a difference." The level of enthusiasm in the tent grew. It was a rousing speech to the first hundred monkeys. But as I clapped along I found myself wondering: Were these people going to have more effect on the world than fourteen hundred ordinary volunteers? Especially if they hadn't yet decided what to do?

Witnessing was next, with John Denver, Phil Donahue-style, inviting audience members to "share" the reasons why they had come. After initial shyness, the participants—*believers* seemed a better word—started waving their arms eagerly, and "runners" rushed into the audience with wireless microphones.

"I've been going to a lot of workshops and trying to figure out all my life what I want to do when I grow up, and I have great anticipation that this weekend will help me decide." The audience applauded. "Great!" said John Denver.

"I'm committed to living the discovery of what [life] can be."

"I've been going through some major, major personal healings in my life. A month ago I was at John's concert in Boston, which was a major healing for me."

"There's got to be a better way to run the world, and I think this is it."

"So much to say, so little time! It's great, you know, it's so funny 'cause it's getting together with other people. And all of us sitting together, and everybody's rubbing elbows and it's called space and getting together!" (Applause)

"I've been on my own vision quest for the past couple of years."

"I also was present at John Denver's concert in Moscow, with 'Children as Teachers of Peace.'"

The meeting broke midmorning, with participants slated to reconvene under smaller canopies outside, for seminars on topics such as "Personal Relationships" and "The Joy of Service." All were so full, though, that the only place I could find a seat was at a session on "Leadership Development."

A couple in their thirties led the workshop. David Gershon had introduced himself during the opening session as "an evolutionary scout . . . walking on unknown trails and finding the strategies that work for me personally." "I honor you, John," he had said, "for creating this opportunity for me." He and his wife ran the Empowerment Workshop, "a personal growth training in which thousands of people throughout the world have participated." Both had big smiles.

But most of the two-hour session was concerned not with empowerment or leadership training but with letting the audience know about the First Earth Run, which the couple had organized, and seeing how people responded to it. The First Earth Run, designed "to celebrate our possibility to live in harmony with each other and with the planet," involved mainly, as far as I could tell, the export of jogging from California to countries of the third world. A videotape was shown, opening with shots of a crying black mother and her starving child, of maimed kids suffering, of third world misery. Then torch-bearing joggers appeared, resulting in scenes of people cheering and smiling. ("The Masai had a total knowing of the power of the flame," intoned Gershon.) The runners went through sixty-two countries, Olympics-style, "to celebrate our possibility for peace." In the background was a kids' chorus, singing a "We Are the World"-type song. The lesson of the film, according to Gershon, was that "we can create the world we want, we will create the world we want. It will be." The couple had worked free on the project for three years before its realization in 1986; they evidently were people of means.

Gail Straub then took over: "We know that feelings happen during that film, and so we'd like to stay in the heartplace and hear how people are feeling about . . . this vision." The "languaging," I could see, was an essential part of the New Age project. One woman's response contained a reference to "sharing a traffic problem" with a Denver truck driver (i.e., colliding with him). Another man was crying, following the film, "because of joy and excitement."

"Any other questions and/or feelings?" Presiding over this, Straub and Gershon had the beatific, unflappable look of saints. The sight of them evoked for me John Denver's opening imprecation that the Choices symposium provide for us a chance to be "our better selves." I liked that idea. It seemed an update of the Christian concept of grace, of divine influence acting in a person to make that person pure and morally strong. If you made a conscious choice, you could be a better person.

And yet you had to wonder about the depth of Windstellar goodness. Aspen, with its low-density living, pristine surroundings, and high standard of living, was an easy place to feel one's better self emerge. You didn't get cut off in traffic too often in Aspen. Street people didn't approach you for change at outdoor cafés. You did not have to live in fear of the needs of your neighbors. The way acquaintances of mine in Aspen talked down about life in the city, life in Denver, life among the poor or handicapped or even the unattractive, one could even suppose they thought they were better people for living in a better place.

But to really wear that mantle of goodness, it seemed to me, you had to be tested. If the test wasn't convincing, you just looked smug.

On my way to lunch, I stopped at the official notice-board. An unofficial-looking poem had been tacked to it:

I was hungry . . . and you formed a humanities club and discussed my hunger.
I was sick . . . and you knelt and thanked God for your health.
I was naked . . . and in your mind you debated the morality of my appearance.
I was lonely . . . and you left me alone . . . to pray for me.
You seem so holy,
So close to God.
But still I am lonely & hungry & cold.

The next day, the poem was no longer there.

By mistake, I took Leo Buscaglia's chair.

It was the next day. Though I hadn't read any of his numerous books on relationships (*Love; Loving Each Other; Making Love a Choice*), I arrived early at the circle of chairs outside the Music Tent, where "Dr. Hug" was supposed to eat lunch. I was well into my potato salad when a throng of people arrived, Buscaglia in the lead. One of them whispered in my ear, pointed to the RESERVED sign on the back of my seat.

"I'm sorry." I leapt up. "I'm in your seat."

"You are not!" Buscaglia chided me. "And if you were, why, I'd just have to sit in your lap."

The psychologist, UCLA professor, and authority on love took the seat next to mine. But, asking if I'd hold his paper plate and iced tea, he was soon standing up again, making time for the people who had formed in a long line to meet him, shake his hand and, usually, give him a hug. He had green eyes, a salt-and-pepper beard, and by the looks of it, he relished every minute.

I wanted to ask him a few questions for my *Times* story, but worried that he hadn't had a moment to eat. So I asked him if it was okay to ask him a question. One question.

"One question? You can ask me six questions!"

"You've been hugging people for half an hour. Everyone wants to meet you, to hold your hand. People want to tell you what makes them happy and sad, and you listen. Do you ever get worn out with other people's stories?"

"I want to give everything back that people give to me," he answered. "Everyone in this group has so much to share—you couldn't get at it even if you had days. You go to bed exhausted, but you sleep well." He handed me his tea again so that he could shake hands with another admirer.

"Leo," said the next in line, a tall, rugged-looking man.

"Yes?"

"Leo, I've got AIDS, and it's so hard," he said quietly, breaking into tears. Buscaglia hugged him for a full minute.

He spoke to the forty-odd people gathered around about his approach to life. You need to project a sort of unconditional love at the world, he said, the kind espoused at Alcoholics Anonymous meetings. People will react accordingly.

"How you walk into a room makes all the difference. I always walk in wagging my tail and hoping someone's going to pet me, and they almost always do. I'm the most petted man in the world."

"Leo, you probably won't remember me," stammered yet another admirer, approaching Buscaglia. Buscaglia hugged him anyway.

I asked if he wasn't afraid of strangers.

"I love people," he replied. "If I have to be afraid of the very thing in the world I love most, I'd rather be dead."

He turned toward me and stared, nose-to-nose, from perhaps an inch away. Everyone around laughed. "It's so hard to be angry at people if you can go like this to them," he said.

He had nearly died of a heart attack recently, he admitted. But in the wake of the open-heart surgery that followed, "I have become so much more aware. The sound of an aspen leaf can overwhelm me and send me into tears." At the waves of warmth he exuded, several people around him were already weeping.

"Life isn't a goal," he said then. "If you're so bent on accomplishing something or getting somewhere, you're going to miss the flowering peach." Several cameras were aimed at him.

He spoke of how important a gesture of love it can be simply to want to share a room with someone—even if you have nothing to say to that person. "Don't just do something, sit there!" he directed the woman on his other side, placing a hand on her knee.

He reiterated the theme of his recent children's book, *A Memory for Tino*, that "life is only the accumulation of memories. Start early creating beautiful memories." A Holocaust survivor had told him that while in a concentration camp, one memory that sustained him was the vision of his wife's hair falling over her shoulders when she let it down at night.

Someone told him of her pain. "That's the purpose of pain—to learn," Buscaglia said. "We listen to physical pain, but we never listen to emotional pain. You know, everyone says, Keep a stiff upper lip. I'd like to pour that on their heads!"

A call from inside the music tent beckoned us to the afternoon session; it was time to go. But in my mind there was already a memory, of the sort of thing I had hoped to hear at this conference.

There were other things I liked about Choices: the kids' program, Earthkeepers, which tried not only to keep children "occupied" but to teach them something; the singing, with John Denver performing one night with a Soviet singer; and the slow, circular movements of tai chi dance, which an expert named Al Huang led participants in twice a day.

But as far as other guests, Leo Buscaglia was a hard act to follow. Rio's press releases promised workshops with "some of the nation's brightest thinkers." More appropriate might have been "the hottest self-improvement managers of the eighties." Among the presenters were Paul Hawken, of Smith & Hawken, the garden-supply outfit, on "growing a business"; Ken Blanchard, author of the *One Minute Manager*, on ethics in business; actor Dennis Weaver *(McCloud)* on "commitment"; and futurist Barbara Marx Hubbard on "global citizenship." Jay Hair, head of the National Wildlife Federation, spoke on environmentalism, and Atlanta mayor Andrew Young spoke on urban politics.

Weaver, a part-time minister, insisted that "instead of trying to rearrange what is outside of us, we should try to find out what is inside of us," and drew a standing ovation by saying he would return to Windstar the $5,000 honorarium check he had been given for coming. ("I didn't realize our honorariums were so large!" John Denver commented later.) Barbara Marx Hubbard described her efforts to produce a worldwide broadcast full of good news, not just bad. A world 900– number would be available for viewers anywhere, at least in places with phones. She invited us to envision, for a moment, the reality of world cooperation, and then got everyone to crouch down and then leap up in a cheer: "GO-O-O, PLANET!"

Back in general session, Dennis Becker was dealing with a sort of sticky question. Someone had said she agreed with the need for commitment but wondered what the best causes were to become committed to. Were there bad causes? Could you commit to the wrong thing?

Becker responded with a warning against being judgmental, against prescriptions of what were good causes and bad. "When we say something is right or wrong, we diminish our own effectiveness out there," he said. He denigrated "that right/wrong game, that righteousness game." Instead, he said, we need to "speak the language that promotes inclusion." "The language of peace," John Denver then called it.

Later, as I bicycled home, I thought about this advice. The conference was titled "Ethics in Action"—and what were ethics, if not prescriptions about right and wrong, judgments of value. Could changing the world ever *not* involve judgments? It occurred to me that a Klansman could pass through Choices with racist ideals unchallenged, emerging secure in his sense of his own commitment. In a sense, I thought, a Klansman would be one of the more advanced participants, since at least a Klansman would know what he believed in.

The idea that *attitude* is the important thing reminded me of Mel, down in Florida. He retained the latter-day hippie belief in enlightenment through pot smoking. "If only we could have gotten LBJ to smoke some reefer, we would have been out of Vietnam like *that*," he said, snapping his fingers.

But pot and positive thinking had limitations as panaceas. Positive thinkers had the smiles of full stomachs, not the anger and desperation of empty ones. They didn't want to hear the dialogue of desperate people, the words of anger and "self-interest." Becker and Denver's "language of peace"—a well-intentioned reaction to demagoguery and calcified thinking—really amounted to never saying anything disagreeable.

Sunday morning under the tent. Denver and Becker wanted to know what the conference had done for people, and people were eager to tell. Hands and arms waved frantically in the air. A woman recounted how part of her spirit flickered out years ago upon the death of a child. But the gathering, she said, had revived her. She was deluged with applause and hugs. A Houston man in cowboy hat and tennis shoes pledged to connect needy food banks with wealthy corporations, and there were loud cheers.

The speakers continued to proclaim their renewed or freshly found hope—hope for themselves, hope for mankind, hope for Earth. The cheers validated the stories, sparked more stories. Afterward, on the lawn, participants mingled with the presenters, as well as Hugh O'Brien and newsman Rolland Smith, and did what they did at the movies: They laughed; they cried. But at Windstar, the experience counted for more, because it went both ways. The movie stars—along with the pop singer, the New Age celebrities—would talk back to you.

While Windstar proclaimed itself to the world at press conferences, John Denver concerts, and television documentaries, I was fascinated by another Aspen New Age group that you could learn about mostly through hints and gossip.

Names were what initially got me interested in the Alive Tribe. Numbed by the stacks of press releases for New Age events like the "Seeds of Change" conference (aiming to create stores of native farm seeds in order to save them from genetic engineers), the "Coming Home" conference (working to get the United Nations to recognize Aspen as the country's first "healthy city"), and a zillion codependency support groups, I was always invigorated to come across a name as strange as, say, Joyous Heart.

"Joyous and her partner offer a light- to very-deep Swedish style massage," according to the circular she sent the *Times*. "They also provide upon request Cranial Sacral Therapy, Deep Tissue, Shiatsu, Acupressure and Polarity." In the program for an upcoming dance concert, I noticed that one of the dancers was named Sunshine Canyonland. Edith, back in advertising, tried to stifle her giggles as she showed around a Pitkin County legal notice for the name change of one Jonathan R. Bernoff—he had just become Sky Canyon.

A cameraman in the credits at the end of a local film production was listed as Sequoia Sun. A former editor of *Aspen, The Magazine*, in her goodbye letter to readers, supposed that in Maine she was going to miss phone calls like the one from Sapphire Blue, trying to interest her in signing up for a Domain Shift weekend.

Engaged in the never-ending search for better housing, I would come upon ads for roommates in the *Times* classifieds. "Nonsmoking veg. seeks same for roommate. Cat OK. Domain Shift graduate preferred. $700," read one that I saw on a Thursday afternoon, when the paper was hot off the press. I leaned into reporter John Colson's cubicle. "I keep seeing this phrase—what does it mean?" I asked.

"Oh, they're talking about the Alive Tribe," he explained. "Domain Shift is what they call their weekend encounters. I went to one of the sample lectures they give, up in Snowmass. You go to see if the whole weekend's right for you. Just the evening costs, like, ten dollars."

"Is it like a cult?"

"A cult? Well, yeah, I guess so. People who get into it change their names and stuff, to show their new identity. You know, like Summer Eternity? It's New Age, though—they don't come and take you away, or anything. Lots of people have done it."

He mentioned a couple of folks I knew. Much more than most cults, the Alive Tribe seemed well integrated into the life of the larger community. It had another big following in Marin County. "You know, I think Jane even has one of their tapes." We walked back to the shelves of the reporter I was filling in for, and Colson pulled out a cassette tape I had noticed for sale in Quadrant Books. "See?"

Domain Shift: A Way Out. A Dynamic Lecture and Guided Meditation, was the title of the tape. On the cover was a couple embracing in front of a mountain and a setting sun, and smiling at the camera. They wore loose-fitting, saffron-colored clothes, like Krishnas, but more stylish, with fancy accessories. The man had a sparkly scarf tied around his neck, and seemed to be wearing blue eye shadow. The woman, shorter, shapely, with a big head of hair backlit by the sunset, wore large dangling earrings and a wide silver belt. "Guided by Diamond and Angel Fire Ecstasy," said a line at the bottom. I repeated the names out loud, impressed.

"That's them," said Colson. "Everyone revolves around the amazing energy of Angel Fire." We took a closer look. "She must be great in bed," he mused. Besides the lecture, participants were made to dance in a circle, make different sounds for different emotions, "other touchy-feely stuff."

"But isn't Angel Fire the name of a ski area in New Mexico?" I asked. Colson just grinned; it was. I asked about their philosophy.

"Well, it's New Age stuff. Domain Shift is built upon est and a whole raft of shit since then. They don't ask you to worship *them,* but somehow you feel that's how you're going to make progress." Colson hadn't forked over the $800 for the four-day weekend session.

I was fascinated by the idea of the cult: the energy it took to make yourself different from everyone else, the alternative beliefs, the group dynamics of a communal family, the possibility of finding new truths. Spiritual certainty was, for me, a very seductive idea. But I also had some doubts. I told Colson that as a newcomer to the movement, I would probably feel out of my depth at a long weekend.

"I doubt it," said Colson. Aspen, as he saw it, was full of seekers. The New Age seekers said little you didn't already know, but they put it in a context—chose new words for old ideas, etc.—that made it seem original and insightful. The weekends were designed to make you feel you just had an overpowering, once-in-a-lifetime spiritual experience. His experience with similar things was that this feeling usually wore off.

I decided to let the Alive Tribe introduce themselves to me, so

I went home and played the tape over my stereo system. The first few minutes were Windham Hill-like acoustic guitar music. Then a man's voice, with the self-conscious calm of a progressive FM disc jockey, began to speak. His first word sounded like, *mmbreathing*. He said it again. "mmBreathing. This lecture is for the purpose of opening new possibilities." He spoke slowly, hypnotically, inviting the listener to relax and to consider the opportunity of "releasing a domain based on denial and survival and receiving a way out—a Domain Shift."

A woman's voice—Angel Fire Ecstasy—took over. She sounded accessible, Californian, and very serious. "Breathing," was her first word, too. She elaborated further on the ways that she and, presumably, everyone else listening, had been damaged as we grew up, of how we were willing "to give up ourselves and who we were in order to survive." Her search for an alternative way to live had led her through various therapies, spiritual disciplines, and psychoactive drugs, but had ended, she suggested, with the revelations of Domain Shift.

Diamond didn't say much about himself, but later I heard from a friend who had known him in Minneapolis. In that life Diamond Ecstasy, né Daryl Jameson, had been a musician and lothario, a "professional attendee" of workshops and a trainee at the Gestalt Institute. Apparently, he had been a longtime seeker, too.

Over more guitar music at the end of the tape, Diamond invited the listener to "make a commitment now to yourself and to God to heal yourself and to be restored in full alignment with all aspects of your being, including being restored to your appropriate place, time, form and relationship to all of creation. If you want to heal, you can. mmBreathing."

I doubted whether a weekend retreat could actually restore me to full alignment with all aspects of my being. But I was impressed with their boldness and curious about their philosophy, and it seemed cowardly not to try.

I applied for a spot in the next Domain Shift weekend.

Since the turn of the century, the sign on the high wooden ranch gate had welcomed guests to the Horseshoe Bend Guest Ranch, a place of hunting and fishing, horses and steaks, cookouts and canoe-ing. It was not far from Aspen, a drive down to Basalt and then up a long, high side valley. But in 1987 the place had been transformed by one Rob Krakovitz, M.D., into the Rocky Mountain Health Ranch, a New Age spa, complete with vegetarian food, conference facilities, and a new attitude. It offered "a daily program of ritual, study and meditation." At the *Times,* Dr. Krakovitz had pestered me to attend an open house, but I had had conflicting appointments. I tried returning his numerous messages, but always would get his machine, which had an announcement that closed with the words, "Wishing you optimal peace and well-being." Dr. Krakovitz and his wife, it turned out, were themselves Domain Shift graduates; the use of the Rocky Mountain Health Ranch by the Alive Tribe seemed a marriage made in heaven.

The high valley was heavily timbered and very scenic. Road cuts revealed the almost bloodred soil and sandstone that underlay everything. For a long way, the winding road followed the Frying Pan River, a gold medal trout stream teeming with rainbows, cutthroat, and fly fishermen. It passed a preserve where one could see Rocky Mountain bighorn sheep, with their curly, croissantlike antlers. It was littered with rocks that had tumbled down the eroding mountainsides and, right before the ranch and the end of the paved road, with the carcasses of so many chipmunks you wondered if some mass migration was under way. Slowing down my car considerably, I still squashed two or three, a bad omen.

Though we had been asked to arrive "on time or up to twenty minutes early," the Alive Tribe themselves were late. Twenty-five or so of us initiates lounged about on the sunny porch, but it was not very easy to meet the others—these were people skeptical of the ways of polite society, including the idea of going around and introducing yourself, shaking hands. Some had arrived in pairs or seemed to know each other from previous Tribe gatherings; these people chatted. About half, I later learned, were from Denver or Aspen and the rest were from across the country. I scrounged an old plum from a mostly empty bowl and took a seat on the lawn. Items of dude-ranch decor—wagon wheels, white-painted rocks bordering gravel walkways, a flagpole, antlered animal heads on the walls, a guest book—clashed with the Birkenstock sandals, the men's earrings, the beaded medicine pouches, and the sweaters from the third world. A hot tub was being installed behind the lodge; you could hear the plumbers clanging.

An hour or so later, a purple van whooshed into the parking lot in a cloud of dust. Old hippies, I thought, but then noticed the others looking up expectantly. This was the official vehicle of the Alive Tribe. Out climbed Diamond and Angel Fire Ecstasy—I recognized them from the photo on the cassette box—and two others, Rain and Laser NightSky, M.D. Diamond and Angel Fire sort of disappeared, while Rain and Laser began registration. Both were tall, lanky, and dark-haired; Laser's white muslin outfit and dark, bearded face made him look more than a little like Renaissance portrayals of Jesus Christ. Rain explained to us that she was a doctor, too, a chiropractor. They, in their late thirties or early forties, looked like old hippies who hadn't given up, hadn't forsaken the counterculture but had changed with the times, from social rebellion to the personal-enlightenment business. And business it was—as we all wrote our checks for $800 to "Multi-Dimensional Research and Expansion" (MDRE), the corporate name ("Sorry, no scholarships," Laser told me unsmilingly when I pleaded writerly poverty). I realized the total, for twenty-five people, would come to $20,000. Even with the expense of meals and lodging, it made for a tidy profit for a weekend's work. How fitting, I thought, looking over the orientation materials, that the Alive Tribe had an 800 number (1-800-331-MDRE).

"Congratulations," Rain and Laser said to all the participants as they paid their bill.

We trod up a short hill to the new conference building. It consisted of one large room, newly carpeted, with sliding glass doors opening onto a wooden deck that overlooked the lake. It was surrounded by tall pines. Leave your shoes at the door, we were instructed. There were chairs, but they were solely for the Alive Tribe. We were expected to sit on the floor. This gave some annoying individuals an opportunity to show off the lotus position.

Two things had been set up in the otherwise empty room. Toward the back was a long table that contained raw, unsalted nuts and fruits and the makings of herbal tea, as well as a selection of MDRE publications and tapes for sale, for our breaks. At these tables, behind us, Rain and Laser NightSky, M.D., would often sit with their Apple Macintosh computer, doing paperwork. But as Diamond and Angel Fire Ecstasy came in, we all gathered around the really important end of the room, where the chief couple took a seat and began to hold forth.

They had constructed for themselves a sort of stage, more of an altar, really. Big potted palms and other plants on either side of two low rattan chairs evoked something between an ancient Egyptian throne room and a fern bar. Laid out on the carpet in front of them were a variety of bizarre-looking implements, which might have been culled from a witches' coven or an exhibit at the Museum of the American Indian: some huge feathers (from the tail of an eagle, no doubt), a small brass pot, filled with twigs, a deer antler covered in bead work, and a smooth black rock. Near the antler was a handheld microphone. This was because, as with any American gathering of over ten people these days, the organizers had seen fit to provide a public-address system. Large stereo speakers were mounted on the wall above them on either side; and powering the whole array was a bank of amplifiers and a huge mixing board, all within arm's reach of Diamond Ecstasy, who, he confirmed, was once the soundman for a rock 'n' roll band.

The first thing you had to notice about Diamond were the plum-colored eyelids behind his aviator-style eyeglass frames. The eye shadow was set off by a dark eyeliner. His irises were bright blue, and what was left of his head of blond hair was cut a short, spiky length all around the shiny top. His beard was a bit darker. He wore tennis shoes, baggy black shorts, and a black sweater loose enough to reveal a necklace underneath—a gold chain with a pendant of four crystals in a cross formation, held together by gold wire.

Angel Fire had a stronger presence, seemed less mellow. She was petite, with long, teased, hennaed hair and a loose-fitting cotton outfit, which contained certain of the colors in abundance among those seated around me: tie-dyed pink, purple, and aqua. Her big dangling earrings were enamel camel heads, with pyramids and an aqua sky in the background.

What followed was an immersion in a new language and a radically new way of looking at the world. My familiarity with Wind-star and the New Age, and the human-potential movement that preceded them, helped me understand the antecedents of some of what I was told, but with other ideas I was completely at sea. Gathered in that room were a number of people who had paid to be told—or had already decided—that the worldview they grew up with was invalid, and were awaiting a radically new version. Maybe other people didn't take it on so literal a level; maybe for some, it took the form of suggestions for tinkering with one's outlook, rather than creating it anew. But the Tribe was serious about imparting a profoundly new way of living and thinking, as attested to by the way they talked, the way they taught, and the thick, photocopied Domain Shift guide we were handed as we settled on the floor.

Diamond started off. "We ask that you fully presence yourself in the space," he said, which sounded like his take on the est-ian bid to "be here now." Part of the challenge here, I could already see, was going to be translation. What Diamond seemed to be saying was simply: *pay attention.*

He asked that we be "impeccable" in our habits—be prompt, make your bed, don't litter, in other words. But *impeccable,* I knew, came freighted with extra meaning from the mystical books of Carlos Castañeda, one of which was for sale on the table: Impeccability was a divine attribute, implying holy. In other words: *Cleanliness is next to godliness.*

Diamond then undertook to teach us all how to breathe correctly—under the theory, I suppose, that if you're going to get people to switch domains, you've got to start somewhere. His method, which seemed to me opposite of what is instinctual, involved first filling your stomach as you breathe in through your nostrils, then filling your chest, and then emptying both by pulling your stomach in. We all tried, but weren't nearly vehement enough. Diamond repeated, the sides of his nose virtually flattening out as all that "cool air" came rushing in. The microphone, held near his face, made it seem that Diamond's nose was next to my ear. He exhaled. "Breathing is a choice," he said. We tried again. The noise of all that air rushing in and out of sixty nostrils made it sound like a huge Lamaze class.

"mmBreathing," said Diamond. The lecture began.

The world we were brought up in, they said—the Denial, or Survival Domain—a world thousands of years in the making, was based on a system of denial and repression (of feelings), of not telling the truth. It meant living according to society's expectations, not your own feelings. It was an irresponsible life, in which other people decided things for you. It was a life resigned to empty goals and

scrambling, to looking out for number one. Its results were addic-
tions and feelings of guilt and powerlessness. Today's world leaders,
raised in this domain, emphasized not an innate "silent knowledge"
and freedom but rationality and linear thinking. Today's major
political problems all derived from problems of self-image—whether
others liked you or not—and self-obsession.

But there was good news: The old domain was disintegrating.
"There is nothing we can do to prevent its downfall," said Angel
Fire. And by following their teachings, we could hasten the arrival
of the Freedom Domain.

"I too acknowledge that there's a whole world dying," said Diamond, adding that it didn't bother him. He had chosen to "invalidate the old continuity," to "stabilize and establish myself in a whole
separate context" in order to heal himself.

The woman next to me, who had been listening raptly, raised her
hand. She confessed that she was worried about the prospect of
positive change in the world, given the way things were going—the
horrible life in the ghettoes, the trouble in South Africa, the limited
number of people of higher consciousness.

"You shouldn't be," Diamond said. The woman started to cry.
Angel Fire added that the crisis on the planet was a wonderful
opportunity. There was trouble, because individuals used to the old,
addictive system were in rebellion and competition against God.
But all we needed to know, she reassured the woman, was what our
appropriate roles were, not how it would all turn out.

"Thank you!" said the woman in gratitude.

Diamond looked beyond her, out the window. "mmBreathing,"
he said.

The participants, but not the Ecstasys or NightSkys, ate lunch in
the healthy dining room of the Health Ranch. I was one of the few
people who seemed motivated to socialize: Others ate their vegetarian stuffed peppers quietly, asking others only to pass the yogurt or
the bulgur. The point of this, it dawned on me, wasn't for us to
progress as a group; it was for each of us to confront ourselves
individually. There were no nametags and no introductions.

Still, over the course of the long weekend, I spoke at least a few
words with most of the others in attendance. There was Crane,
fifty-something, who wore a tie-died T-shirt, drawstring pants, and

had a tanned, bearded, wrinkled face. Diamond had pointed him out during the morning as an example of one who, once addicted to the old continuity, was now going through withdrawal. It wasn't easy, and that's why he was back at Domain Shift for a second time. Hanging from Crane's gold necklace was perhaps the ultimate New Age pendant: a gold dolphin, clasping a long quartz crystal between its tiny flippers. He had a small property-management firm in Denver, he told me. I felt sympathy for Crane: Time seemed to be running out for him to get it all together.

Saving money by sharing a tent with Clyde—"under the stars," as he put it—was a guy in his twenties named Lapis. He had an asymmetrical haircut and two feathery earrings dangling from one lobe. He looked at you intensely when you spoke to him. There was a short New Yorker, who wore a yarmulke, named Neal. There was a handsome man from Snowmass, whose thin legs were wrapped in floral-patterned Lycra, who often lay on his back with a large marble in his navel during the Ecstasys' lectures. I was frequently distracted by a nubile young blond woman, whose tiny nylon shorts kept creeping up her buttocks and who demonstrated, through frequent stretches on the newly carpeted floor, the incredible limberness of her body.

There were two professional women from Denver in their thirties—a paralegal and her friend, a nurse—who had arrived in a Honda. Along with a tall emergency-room doctor from Oklahoma named Robert, we shared one of the rustic, two-room health ranch cabins. One young couple looked as though they might live in a trailer park in Glenwood Springs. Another, a more upscale Seattle couple, were self-confessed veterans of a number of "intimacy seminars." They frequently touched, not only each other but those near them. A third, older couple could have stepped straight from an L. L. Bean catalog. There was a kind-looking woman named Corinne, whom I had originally approached on the porch as we were waiting for the Tribe to appear. She had met a woman from Aspen at a Choices retreat in Winter Park the weekend before, a ski instructor named Claire—did I know her? Yes, I did, I said, and was relieved to speak with someone who seemed to be coming from a place I could "relate to." But then she told me she was a member of a group called the Global Family, badly estranged from her punk daughter, and about to move to a communal household in San Francisco.

I had listened to a Global Family tape that was distributed free at Windstar—a few minutes of Barbara Marx Hubbard reading something called the "Declaration of a Positive Future"—and now I looked at this woman in puzzlement. What had gone wrong in so many people's lives that they were seeking a new life as radical as what the Alive Tribe espoused? Why the interest in a total break with the past? And what was it about Aspen that made them think the answer was here? At least, I thought, most of these people still used their given names, but one of the kitchen staff had been telling me that the Health Ranch held frequent renaming ceremonies. This was a place where you could get rid of the baggage of your name, try to completely reinvent yourself.

The group was summoned back to the conference room by Laser NightSky, M.D. Diamond was already there; he instructed us to take our pillows, grab a blanket, and find a space to lie on our backs. When everyone was so positioned, hypnotic New Age music filled the room, and with it the airy, amplified voice of Diamond Ecstasy: "mmBreathing. We are now going to the Optimum Level of Being to breathe, to feel. We can utilize this experience to align our emanations and align with the emanations of God."

This was like the after-lunch nap at camp, I thought, only fancier. And Diamond apparently didn't want us to sleep, exactly—"Don't go unpresent," he directed. He kept talking, repeating mantras we might want to adopt as our own.

"I am totally integrating all aspects of my multidimensional being, including my Spirit and Will. I am aligned with impeccable timing. I am experiencing eternal full-being ecstasy now. I release all excess density and I am manifesting the optimum form for myself at all times."

Following this came more lecture ("sharing information") and more breathing. We learned to scream into our hands, a useful way to relieve stress since, after all, you could do it anywhere. And then it was time to all stand up and jump around and practice these things. Diamond led the group in this metaphysical aerobics and got us all to blink our eyes, turn our heads left and right, move our fingertips, all the while *mmbreathing! mmbreathing!!* We breathed in unison, then, imitating Diamond, we danced while making these sounds: "Hey hey hey hey, hee, hee, hee, hee, hi, hi, hi, hi, ho, ho, ho, ho, hoo, hoo, hoo, hoo." They were, I suddenly realized, basically the vowel sounds of our alphabet. We shook our arms up and down around our heads, and lifted our knees, like a Jazzercise class gone berserk. "Pull up on your genitals and anus!" commanded Diamond. From inside the body, he meant.

The Ecstasys, like John Denver, had promised us a "safe space" in which to perform these rites, but unfortunately one middle-aged participant did not have the requisite conditioning and stepped the wrong way on her ankle. As she dragged herself in anguish off to the side, I waited for Diamond to stop the exercise and go to her aid, or at least for one of the participants on either side to lend a hand. But some subtext of being here just for yourself, of *individual* healing—of the basic narcissism underlying the whole enterprise— had somehow already made its way into peoples' heads, and no one made any move to help. A minute went by. I danced my way over to her side of the room, stopped, and tried to help her get comfortable. Soon after, the dancing ended. Laser NightSky, M.D., came up and told me he'd take care of it. When the day's session was finally over, at 11 P.M., and the woman still hadn't returned, I asked Laser how she was. "She left," he said, expressionless.

His curtness confused me until the next morning, when we all reconvened in the conference room. After breathing a little to warm up (herbal coffee not having opened all the eyelids), Diamond and Angel Fire discussed responsibility. The main point, not too controversial on its face, was that we are all responsible for what happens to us. But then Diamond elucidated: We were responsible for our own realities or situations, he explained, because we and we alone created them. We were responsible, for example, for our health. This did not just mean we were responsible for keeping clean and getting exercise. "Illness," said Diamond, "is not accidental." In fact, he added, "There are no accidents." "There are no victims, either," Angel Fire piped up. If you got sick, was the drift, it was because you put yourself in the situation for that to happen—because you "created the space." "We create our own reality" was shaping up to be the recurrent theme of the weekend, and this was one of its more radical implications.

Some people stretched, some yawned: Most of the participants either seemed familiar with or immediately accepting of these ideas. But others, like me, had questions. One woman, sensing it was relevant, told how her infant had been born with Down's syndrome; the book *When Bad Things Happen to Good People* had been of great comfort to her, she said—had they read it? Angel Fire, refusing to engage this idea, simply repeated that we were all responsible for everything that happened to us.

I thought of a friend of mine who lived in Boulder. For four years she had been battling breast cancer. She wrote some articles on the subject of cancer to educate herself, in the course of which she interviewed two therapists. They told her about one distraught patient's failure to benefit from creative visualization. "They're going to tell me creative visualization is bunk," she thought. Instead, one of the physicians commented that the patient "really didn't try hard enough" for it to work. They faulted the woman for her own sickness, in other words; they blamed the victim. This attitude angered Juliet, reminded her of the old view that women who get raped must be "asking for it." According to Angel Fire, "Life is how I want it to be."

I raised my hand. "What if you're on your way to lunch today and a drunken cowboy comes around the corner and runs you down in his pickup truck. Would that be your fault?" I asked Diamond. "It won't happen," was his reply, and the shortness of his tone reminded me of Laser's, discussing the fate of the woman with the twisted ankle. Suddenly, I understood: They felt it was *her* fault! And they had no patience for self-inflicted injury.

Diamond moved on to his next point: Death itself was a choice, he maintained. "More people die because they believe they will than for any other reason." The belief itself, he explained, triggered the body's death processes. "Immortality," added Angel Fire, astoundingly, "is a possibility." In fact, she said, Rain and Laser NightSky's new book, *Bring Your Body Along*, was a look at "the support systems for immortality."

But some in the group were a step or two behind in their thinking. "So should you tell someone who's dying that it's their fault?" asked one of the women from Denver. A murmur in the room said no. But Angel Fire said yes, adding that you had to take them past questions of fault, to blamelessness and learning to live with it, being content with your responsibility. "That would be the best way to die," she concluded.

The discussion continued, but I stayed back with my own thoughts. This aspect of New Age thought—that we were all masters of our destiny—struck me as quite reactionary. Were crack babies responsible for their mothers being addicts? The attitude of the Alive Tribe seemed to me the arrogance of people so insulated from misfortune, who so took for granted the luxury of making their own choices—"creating their own worlds"—that they faulted anyone who had not shared in their good fortune. Rather than luck, they credited their own worldview. "There go I but for the grace of God" was not the credo here. That Aspen, with its surplus of money and leisure, was a crucible for this kind of thinking made a certain sense.

Still, there was something very American about the idea that the self could be perfected, that happiness is within our grasp: It was an update of the idea of the self-made man. The notion that one could change one's situation by changing one's consciousness, that one was to a large extent responsible for the conditions under which one lived, had an Emersonian underpinning. Certainly, it was one of the assumptions behind the utopian re-creation of Aspen shortly after World War II: a faith that the living could be better, that a place might be perfectible. Maybe this was the reason for the growth of New Age thought in Aspen's soil.

Lunch that day was silent, speech prohibited, for the purposes of promoting our inner knowing and meditation. It was just as well, I felt; I had a lot to think about.

The afternoon of that second day, thankfully, arrived on a lighter and less directed note. The lost continent of Atlantis, we learned, declined due to too great a reliance on high technology—"they overamped their crystals," according to Diamond. Angel Fire confirmed someone's question about the Harmonic Convergence—Aspen *was,* along with Stonehenge, Peru's Nazca plains, the Great Pyramids of Egypt, and other sites, one of the world's great spiritual energy centers. Similarly, the world's great cathedrals were built upon the "acupuncture meridian points of the earth," where galactic energy was sent up to benefit pagans.

Even more intriguing were the snippets about Alive Tribe family life. What would it be like to grow up in such a strange communal family? I had wondered. We learned that the kids—with names like Light Dreamer Eternity, Serene Dancer, and Juniper Paradise—were home-educated. We learned that they had a Yorkshire terrier named Ally, which they had selected after meeting about sixty other puppies in Denver. "He eats a lot of tofu," Angel Fire confided. We learned the Alive Tribe had traveled to Disneyland but that the kids had been disappointed by the Pirates of the Caribbean ride, among others, because it depicted so much violence. They had been similarly disappointed by other kinds of "shallow entertainment" that society had told them were "fun," she said.

"It's been so fun watching our kids invalidate the old continuity," said Angel Fire. That sounded like a lot to ask of a kid; I wondered if they were social outcasts. At least, they sounded normal in some ways. Jade Moon Ecstasy had confessed one day to buying some doughnuts in town. And Ruby Joy Ecstasy, six, had expressed to her mom a normal-sounding aversion to a typical American chore, though perhaps in odd language: "It is just overriding my will to do the dishes."

My spirits were also lifted in a rare moment when Diamond, following a dance session, asked if we had any feelings to share. The woman from the couple who were schooled in intimacy wanted to let the group know a concrete sign of the progress they had made at the Domain Shift weekend. "I just wanted everyone to know that I haven't ovulated or menstruated in four months, and it's been a problem," she said. "But this morning, I noticed for the first time that I have ovulatory mucus!"

"Hey, that's great," said Diamond, not too enthusiastically.

After dinner, Diamond lit the cedar twigs in the little pot and used the feathers to waft the fragrant smoke through the air of the conference room. We held hands and danced in a circle, and when we were finished, someone heard the call of a coyote. But then the bathroom door opened, and we realized it was just the sound of the toilet running.

Next, the person who had been on your right in the dance circle became your partner for a session of painful massage, apparently inspired by Rolfing, the spinal alignment regime which holds that portions of your body store emotional pain, which can be released with the proper manipulation. Diamond, taking a volunteer, demonstrated the technique: The receiver was to lie on his back, while the masseur, on his knees at the receiver's side, extended his fingertips and pushed below the receiver's rib cage, into his body cavity. Diamond encouraged the volunteer to yell as this happened, since that was how the pain left the body. Then he dug in. It looked painful, and sure enough, the receiver yelled. Diamond pushed hard, and he yelled some more. "You may be able to feel the backbone if you do it right," he told us.

Diamond turned down the lights, turned up the music, and it was our turn. Compelled to choose, I thought I'd rather administer the pain than receive it, to begin, so my partner—a thin, middle-aged man to whom I hadn't spoken—lay down in front of me. I pushed gingerly on his stomach and immediately felt uncomfortable. I didn't even know this guy, and here I was going to probe for his backbone? "Did that hurt?" I asked. He shook his head. I was seized with the horrible thought that, rather than pain, this rubbing might give him an erection. He wore loose maroon sweatpants, but there was no sign. I delved in again, panicked that I might feel the outline of his liver or a kidney . . . maybe I would give him a hernia. I continued to probe around.

Suddenly, Diamond appeared at my side, on his knees. "Having some trouble?" he asked. "No, um, I think I've got it," I said defensively. "Do it like this," he responded, jabbing his long pointed fingers into my partner's gut.

"AAAAAAaghhh!" cried my partner. Diamond delved again. "AAAAAAAAAgghhh!!" came the louder cry. "See?" said Diamond. "Like that. Now, let's see you."

I pushed hard and got a yelp. Then, as Diamond turned away, I pushed halfheartedly. This wasn't my thing. I continued on, best I could, for another ten minutes or so, until Diamond announced it was time to change positions. The thought filled me with dread. I told my partner to sit tight and went to talk to Diamond.

"I can't do this," I told him.

"Why not? Are you afraid it will hurt? It doesn't hurt."

"I'm not comfortable, I guess, exploring the body of someone I don't know."

"Did he mind? He didn't seem to mind."

"I mean, I guess I'm not comfortable with him exploring *my* body."

"Why not?"

I was tired. We had been in session for fourteen hours so far that day. "I'm just not."

Diamond looked at me. "You mean you want to leave the group?"

"Just this exercise. I think I want to go to bed."

"I think you want to leave the group."

"No, no, just this. This is all that bothers me," I lied.

"I think you should talk to Laser," Diamond insisted.

"I think I'm going to bed," I answered. Then I left.

It was a vast relief to be outside. I tied my shoes, then walked down to the pay phone at the lodge. I called home, where my friend Seth was staying for a couple of weeks. It was about 11 P.M. Seth answered.

"I need to talk to somebody."

"Ted, I think you need a drink," he said.

"Meet me in Basalt?"

"Sure, okay. Where?"

I told him the name of a bar. "If we both leave now, we'll get there at the same time, in about twenty minutes." I found my car keys and headed down the mountain.

I felt like I'd escaped from prison. It was pure joy to listen to KSPN on my car radio—music of our own had been "discouraged"—and I took a subversive glee in the prospect of having a drink. And Seth: a physicist, he had been my roommate during graduate school, and he knew me about as well as anybody did. He knew me well enough to listen while I talked—on and on and on. He knew me well enough to remark on the language I'd been repeating to him: Words like *energy, vibration, domain, perturbation, radical transformation, density, critical mass,* and *alignment,* he suggested, all had been borrowed from *his* discipline, physics. The words had gained currency and power from the success of hard sciences like physics, which in many ways represented the most rational branch of human knowledge; the irony was that the Alive Tribe members were no fans of rationality. In fact, had they known about it, they might have considered the Enlightenment to be one of the worst developments in recent Western civilization.

Finally, Seth knew me well enough to suggest that emotional

repression—that bugbear of the outmoded Survival Domain—was something most people had to have in order to get up and go to work every morning. When making a living came first, some desires had to be ignored. "Hallelujah," I said to Seth, downing my drink. I would repress my aversion to the Domain Shift. I would drive back to the ranch that night.

They snagged me at breakfast. My roommate, Robert, the M.D., seeing me looking tired and a bit strained, was giving me a neck rub when Laser NightSky approached and asked if I would accompany him up to the conference building. I knew it was about the previous night; I felt as though I was being called into the principal's office.

"I hear you walked out last night," he said as we walked up the short dirt road.

"Not 'walked out.' I didn't want to participate in the last exercise. I discussed it with Diamond, and then I left."

"Why did you leave?"

I repeated my reasons: that the abdomen-probing caused pain, that it was popped on us as a surprise, that I wasn't comfortable sharing in invasive procedures with someone I don't know. That all the screaming was too much. That I was tired after about fourteen hours of seminar. This little conversation took us inside to the altar, where Diamond was seated, preparing for the day, chatting with three or four other participants. One was the older guy whose stomach I had been rubbing. Diamond peered at me from under his plum eye shadow and gestured toward the man.

"It didn't hurt, did it?" he asked him.

The guy was a perfect teacher's pet. "It hurt while it was happening, but I was so glad when it was done," he said. "I felt like something dark and terrible was moved out of there, like—"

"See?" said Diamond.

I didn't deny the man's response. I simply said that it wasn't for me.

"And how do you feel about it now?"

In truth, I had the gravest doubts. Domain Shift asked me to throw away some of my most cherished beliefs. Why had I worked so hard in college, for instance, when "inner knowing" was the only important kind? Why had I volunteered on political campaigns if my personal attitude was the only one worth focusing on? What would happen to my relations with family, friends, and almost everyone else I knew if I exited their Survival Domain and cast my lot with these dubious visionaries? This challenge they presented, actually, had made me feel more certain than ever of who I was, of my true identity. It was hard having your worldview challenged for upward of twelve hours a day, and frankly, I was feeling a bit touchy. A big part of me wished I were back home, watching something brainless on TV. A larger part of me, however, didn't want to waste the stake I'd made in the Alive Tribe. I wanted to stay and learn more about them.

"I think I can handle it now," I told Diamond Ecstasy. "I feel I can be present today. I'd like to stick with it."

Diamond said okay and Laser nodded, but I knew they'd be watching me.

The day started with breathing, with questions about the previous day's remarks on health, and with Laser solemnly reminding everyone to lock the bathroom door, so that no one's privacy was interrupted inadvertently. "You weren't too concerned about our privacy last night," I felt like saying, but didn't. People asked about how different sorts of New Age training fit in with Domain Shift, and Diamond and Angel Fire responded that mostly they fit in well. "We've just taken them all a step further." In fact, said Angel Fire, we would do rebirthing that afternoon. She warned people about another New Age fad, however: past life regressions. "Everyone claims to have been an Indian or an Egyptian," she noted. "Why wasn't anyone a housewife, reliving why her Kirby broke?"

Despite everything, I liked Angel Fire for that, and I liked Diamond for the guided meditation he led us on next. "There's a pink cotton ball in a turquoise bowl," he said. "mmBreathing. It's rolling around and around, faster and faster. It's edging up the side of the bowl toward the brim. But still it's going faster—it's leaving the bowl! It's flying up into the sky carried on the wind. Finally, it's starting to head down. The cotton ball is heading down, down, slowly, until it lands . . . right here—" he touched his heart "—in you. You are the cotton ball." There were noises of delight in the room, and mine among them. It was one of the more striking images to pass through my mind lately.

We danced, all at the same time but alone, and then piled up our pillows in front of us.

"Close your eyes and extend your hands like mine," Diamond instructed, palms upward. "You are preparing to receive." The level of the hypnotic New Age music increased. "Something is missing in your lives," he intoned. "What is it? What's missing?"

This was a surprisingly powerful question—something is probably missing from everyone's life, whether a loved one, a former hopefulness, or certainty . . . it tapped into the hollowness inside almost everyone. Some started wailing and swaying—but prematurely. For Diamond had an answer.

"What's missing? It's not a car. What's missing? It's not a house. It's not a partner. What is it?" A note of unusual vehemence was creeping into Diamond's normally placid voice.

"*It's you! It's you!*" he said suddenly. The surprise announcement had a big effect, and those around me all seemed to drop their heads onto their pillows. "*You never got to develop something! You never got to be something! There is something you were forced to look away from.*

"*Come find yourself!*" he cried. "*Come home! Come home to yourself!*"

Everyone was sobbing except him, Angel Fire (who was chatting away with Rain as we went through these emotional paroxysms) . . . and me. But I put my head on my pillow.

Coming home was the New Age update on the sixties *finding yourself*. Both meant getting in touch with something essential about who you were. It was especially resonant, I thought, because home was something most people there, and most people in Aspen—perhaps most people in the country—had lost. Most in Aspen had grown up somewhere else and had left, or had grown up in many places and had never had a home, at least in the traditional sense. A song popular in town at the time, by James McMurtry, had the refrain, "I'm not from here, I just live here." But home remained a potent idea, and everybody wanted it. And if home was now simply a clear sense of self-identity, it seemed attainable.

The Alive Tribe was engineering a very emotional morning. The "home" exercise greased the wheels for what came next. It was described in the Domain Shift manuals as an "Express & Release" session, and I'd heard of similar things from seminar-going friends. At first it looked simple: As Diamond demonstrated, it involved stacking the pillows in front of us again and then pounding them with our fists and forearms. Diamond emphasized that for the release to work, we had to *really* hit the pillows hard, and he proceeded to do this—again, with a vehemence that was startling.

"Now, you try," he instructed us, and the room was filled with loud thumpings and breathing. "Harder—come on, really hit them." It was tiring if you kept it up as he directed. "Exaggerate the feeling." He kept encouraging us, and then came the surprise. "The pillows are your mother," he said quite baldly. "You need to tell your mother the things you never told her, the things she kept you from saying. You need to get free of your mother."

I expected the room to grow a bit quiet with this emotional manipulation, with the surprise of its intimacy, but instead, the noise grew. They trusted Diamond. This was what people wanted. Some became upset almost immediately.

"Mom, how could you?" demanded a forty-year-old man named Phil, tears streaming down his face. "How could you do that with my bike? Damn, damn, damn!" He pounded harder with every curse.

"Go for it!" said Diamond.

"No, no, no, no!" cried a young woman. "It was my idea! You're so stupid, Mother, Mother!"

For a while, also, we were our mothers and the pillows our kids; the role-playing was to "reintegrate fragment personalities and for resolving conflicts," Diamond said. Some people ended by hugging the pillows; others pounded them till the exercise stopped. Having always gotten along pretty well with my mother, I ran out of steam after a few minutes. But I saw Laser watching me from the back of the room, and kept pounding and moaning as best I could.

I was relieved when Diamond said we could stop—the idea of expressing your innermost feelings about your mother was not, to me, the sort of thing you'd want to do with a room full of strangers, under the direction of people you'd essentially *hired.* But then he said it was time for our fathers, and back we all went.

With my emotional and physical resistance to the exercise, I found it utterly exhausting. The mother exercise had lasted about half an hour; I was pooped and placed my face on my pillow after about ten minutes. That's when I felt a tap on my shoulder.

The big face of Laser NightSky, M.D., was staring into mine. He wore upon it an expression of sympathy that I found totally unconvincing. He was on his hands and knees, again in his all-white cotton outfit.

"How are you doing?" he intoned. "Are you participating fully?"

"Oh, it's hard," I said sadly. "I don't feel so good."

"It *is* hard," he said with the professional concern of a therapist. "But you've got to feel. Can you feel?"

I felt he was picking on me. I wanted him to leave me alone. "Yes, I can feel." Idiot, I thought.

He stared at me for several seconds, not saying anything. I was getting angry. I couldn't believe I was paying to participate in this fool's charade. I prayed he would leave.

"Is this working for you? What do you feel? Tell me what you feel."

I couldn't hold back anymore. "Laser," I said in total candor. "I feel like hitting you in the face." And I did: I felt like knocking his fucking teeth out.

He recoiled, scooted back a foot or two, and alarm clouded his face. "But you agreed," he said. "This would be a safe space. There can be no physical violence—"

"I'm not *going* to hit you, idiot! You just asked what I felt like, and I told you."

Laser scooted away. I hit my pillow with renewed vehemence. The exercise took on a new life for me.

But it couldn't last. In a few minutes Laser returned, with Diamond standing behind him. They summoned me to the back of the room.

"We don't think this is working for you, and we're prepared to offer you a pro-rated refund," Laser said. I accepted. He wrote out the check on the spot, and Diamond, sensing a diminished chance of violence, returned to his altar. Laser handed me the check. I wished I had quit before they fired me. But it was over.

"We honor your process," said Laser, offering his hand. I didn't believe him, but at least he was a good sport.

Chapter VII

The Chances You Take

Dismissed by the Alive Tribe, I walked to my room, dazed. I packed and climbed into my car. There was nobody to say goodbye to; I felt lonely, like the kid expelled from school, my defiance fast dwindling. It was hard to concentrate as I drove down the windy valley. Three long days had left me exhausted, abused, confused about the ending. I just wanted to get back to the real world, as represented by my house, my old routines, and my old friend. I wanted to chat with Seth, drink some beer, take a long, hot bath, and go to bed, in precisely that order.

The hour-long drive seemed to take forever. When I arrived, the house was empty, but five minutes later Seth pulled in.

"God, am I glad to see you," I said. "You won't believe what happened today." I began describing what had happened in the hours since we met, but then noticed he seemed strangely removed.

"What's going on with you? Are you okay?"

Seth seemed to gather himself. "Um, well, Ted, not exactly. You see, Heinz fell."

"What? Oh, that's right, you were going climbing." Heinz Pagels, a celebrated physicist, was Seth's dissertation adviser and an avid hiker. "He fell? Is he okay?"

"Well, I don't think so. I don't know. He disappeared."

Seth explained: After lunch atop 14,018-foot Pyramid Peak, which is a demanding but not a technical climb, he and Heinz had been descending along a narrow ridge. There was a path in the middle of the ridge, with steep drops on either side. Heinz was in the lead, Seth a few paces behind. Heinz, forty-seven, a fellow at the Aspen Center for Physics, had previously climbed Pyramid seven times. He was a tall, slender man who had some weakness in his ankles from a childhood bout with polio. As he made a small hop over a gap, he landed on a rock that proved unsteady and lost his balance. Almost before Seth could notice, he was gone, sliding down a steep, gravelly chute and then dropping out of sight.

Seth called to him repeatedly but got no reply. There was no question of following his path down the couloir, because there were no hand- or footholds. Seth, hearing only silence, ran down the trail to see if he might intercept Pagels's route. But the trail angled away from where Heinz would be, and sheer cliffs blocked the way. Despairing, Seth ran the rest of the three miles down to the trailhead, near the Maroon Bells parking lot, and waved down a shuttle bus. The driver used his radio to call the police, who called Aspen Mountain Rescue; the first ones on the scene ascertained that a team on foot would take hours to arrive where Heinz had probably fallen, and that, with sunset impending, they might not even find him, so vast was the terrain. They ordered in a helicopter and advised Seth to go home, shower and change, and return within two hours.

"So now I've got to drive back," Seth concluded. I had never seen anybody with his expression; he was trying for composure, but the effect was pure dread.

"I'll drive you," I said.

They had emptied the Maroon Bells parking lot when we arrived and were admitting only rescue personnel. The famous Bells—huge redrock domes—and the handful of high peaks around them were the area's most popular climbing sites and, consequently, the scene of most of Aspen's outdoor disasters. Two years before, while leading a rescue training workshop, the leader of Aspen Mountain Rescue himself, Greg Mace, had slipped on a snowfield, lost his ice ax, and slid to his death on boulders on the Bells. (A nearby mountain had since been renamed in his memory, Greg Mace Peak.) The rescue workers took the risks of outdoor recreation very seriously.

I had played squash with the current president, a dentist named

David Swersky, at the Aspen Club, and also knew the rescue leader, Dick Arnold; he'd flown me once, in his private plane, to Telluride and back. Dick was directing this operation, and he waved Seth and me over to where he was studying a looseleaf notebook of aerial photographs of all the peaks in the area. Pyramid Peak, with its distinctive pinnacle top, had several pages devoted to its many faces. Seth tried to pinpoint his and Heinz's route and the exact spot of the fall, to help the helicopter pilot.

The rescue personnel scattered from the parking lot when the copter arrived, and it set down in the middle. Seth climbed into its Plexiglas bubble, along with the pilot and one of the rescue team's top climbers. The climber was famed for having recently hung off a helicopter skid to rescue someone from a ledge; he carried rope and other equipment, which seemed to me a hopeful sign. The helicopter lifted off toward the high valleys.

Their return was desperately awaited for the answer it might bring to the question no one had dared to discuss openly: Was he alive, or was he dead? In the best of all worlds, I could imagine the copter carrying Pagels himself. He had managed to save himself by grabbing on to a branch or getting his shirt snagged on a rock, just as they do in cartoons.

Twenty minutes later, as the rotor slowed, the wind died down, and dust settled, Seth climbed slowly out of the helicopter's bubble. He walked toward me, and everyone else walked away. He appeared scared and stony-faced and looked at me for a long time before saying, "He's dead."

This was real sadness, true sadness. Days later, crying again, I remembered the overwrought sobbing of Domain Shift and felt it had happened months or even years before.

There was a lot more to be done, and unfortunately, only Seth could do it. With a sheriff's deputy and a psychologist, we drove to the house of Heinz's wife, Elaine Pagels, a well-known professor of religion at Princeton, and their children, ages three months and two years, where Seth broke the news. The next day the local papers called, and the day after that, *The New York Times*—Heinz had been a professor at Rockefeller University in Manhattan and executive director of the New York Academy of Sciences. Seth had to retell the story of the fall to each of the reporters, again to the police, and then, numerous times, to Heinz's associates at the physics institute and at Rockefeller University. There was a funeral service. There were more visits to Elaine. There was a trip with Elaine to the coroner's office, where she had asked to view the body. But the coroner persuaded her not to: "It would give you the wrong idea of how he died," he said, which was instantaneously. Heinz Pagels had fallen between fourteen hundred and two thousand feet, the height of one to one and a half Empire State Buildings. A rescue worker had called recovery of the body the next day "an unpleasant task"; rocks had torn it into several pieces.

Every year, six to eight people are killed, on average, in the pursuit of outdoor recreation in Aspen. In Colorado as a whole, the annual figure is much higher. Skiers hit trees, lightning strikes hikers, whitewater rafters go under, hunters mistake each other for game, Jeeps flip, cyclists miss a turn. Of course, the risk is sometimes part of the attraction. Other times it is not.

Seldom, however, does one get to contemplate the question in the manner we did following the death of Heinz Pagels. *The New York Times* obituary alerted me to Pagels's 1982 work *The Cosmic Code: Quantum Physics as the Law of Nature,* an account of particle physics and quantum mechanics for the general reader, which is also a personal meditation on the universe. At the end, Pagels discusses mountain climbing. "The rewards I wanted were of sight, of pleasure, of the thrill of pitting my body and my skills against nature," he wrote. Like many climbers, he dreamed of falling. One wonders, though, how many of them have dreamed of it with such prescience: "Lately I dreamed I was clutching at the face of a rock but it would not hold. Gravel gave way. I grasped for a shrub, but it pulled loose and in cold terror I fell into the abyss."

The similarity of this imagined death to the actual one is breathtaking. The passage raises the age-old question, crass in its oversimplification, Did he fall or did he jump? Of course he fell; Seth saw him fall. *The New York Times* wrote he died "in a mountaineering accident." The question is, Was he the one to blame? Was he responsible for it? I was annoyed that the reading of Pagels's words recalled for me the philosophy of Diamond Ecstasy: *There are no accidents.* Diamond, I knew, would have said he jumped; to him, every accidental death was a suicide. But a competing precept, visible on bumper stickers all over Aspen, was that pearl of California surfer wisdom, SHIT HAPPENS. It was more forgiving, but was it more true? Both, it seemed to me, were probably true, in varying proportions, at different times. If Pagels had stayed home and watched tennis on TV instead of going climbing, you could argue, he'd probably be alive today.

But one point about life in Aspen is that the vicarious life is not enough. For people like Heinz Pagels, watching sports is a poor substitute for the real thing. This attitude lends the town vitality, a spiritedness. But there are consequences. The Pitkin County coroner, Dr. Steve Ayers, told me Aspen's is "a weird population—the percentage of death from fatal injury to illness is skewed." In other words, more Aspen people die from some kind of accident than from illness than in a normal population—than in Denver, for instance. One explanation Dr. Ayers offered me for this was that Aspen's was a younger, more active population, with individuals inclined to take more risk than in the population at large.

Also, though, you had to consider whether people in Aspen, people who'd chosen something other than a routine way of life, might be people with more angst than others, people with more complexities, uncertainties, people not part of a community, people living harder, people with more reasons to die.

For Pagels, in his book, the fall wasn't the end. In the dream, while falling, he realized that "what I embody, the principle of life, cannot be destroyed . . . It is written into the cosmic code, the order of the universe. As I continued to fall in the dark void, embraced by the vault of the heavens, I sang to the beauty of the stars and made my peace with the darkness."

One must hope that's how it happened.

I remember as a child standing on a narrow balcony circling the very top of the Duomo in Florence. The immense red-tiled dome of the church beneath me curved away out of sight, and I pressed against the wall at my back. Imagine sliding down those tiles, I thought, imagine the speed, the ride. What an experience it would be, if you had arrived at the point of choosing a last experience.

I held tight to the railing. I was terrified by the drop. I was terrified by my interest in the drop.

. . .

The natural state of a skier on a mountainside is to accelerate. From the moment you get off the chair lift, this is what your skis want to do. To learn to ski is, essentially, to learn how to control this tendency, to learn how to slow down. The main mechanism of control is a turn: snowplow, christie, parallel. Beautiful skiers have learned beautiful ways of slowing down.

As a restless high school senior, I landed a weekend job ski-instructing at the Breckenridge ski area. Breckenridge was owned by the Aspen Skiing Corporation, and the instructors studied the manual of the Aspen Ski School, one of the best.

As an instructor, you are admired for the quality of your control. It is a different paradigm of performance than ski racers have: Racers are admired for their ability to go fast. I spent three days with members of the U.S. Ski Team during a World Cup race in Aspen in 1989 and was not surprised when Jeff Olson, the leading American men's downhiller, told me that what he liked best about his job was, in a word, the *speed*. I tagged along with the lanky Montanan during some of his training runs, rode the lifts with him, asked questions. As I watched Olson sidestep down the course, plan his moves, commit the terrain to memory, and finally ski the thing at breakneck speed, it dawned on me that I had misunderstood racing. I began to appreciate that though it doesn't look like it, downhill racing is about control, too. It's about successfully *minimizing* your control: making as few turns as possible so as to arrive at the bottom in the shortest time possible.

Thoughts come into your mind when you ski, in the way they do when you're driving alone down the highway. Thoughts that have been lingering, waiting to take shape. One day I was skiing Ruthie's Run, a long, popular intermediate "cruising" run, which was also the start of the World Cup downhill course, when Jeff Olson came to mind. I remembered him at the starting gate, wearing helmet and skin-tight suit, psyching himself up in the seconds before the race to be as daring and brilliant as possible. Like everyone around them that day, I was admiring of the skiers, in particular of their guts, of how fast they dared to go. Compared to Olson's, I thought that day, my own technique seemed ornate, overly fussy, studied. It was midway through my second winter in Aspen, and

I was thinking I had been perhaps too careful in my life, too much in control.

This feeling stirred me on Ruthie's Run, and I began to go faster. I had never been the racing "sort," the fast car "sort," but my time in Aspen made me feel it wasn't too late to start being visceral. My skis chattered and my legs began to ache as I began making longer, faster turns, going further without a rest. I angled off Ruthie's onto Aztec, a short and very steep stretch of the World Cup course. Aztec appeared to be empty of skiers, and as I reached its face I crouched into a tuck. It was the feeling you have when, on a stretch of empty road, you decide to see how fast your car can really go—is the speedometer marked up to 100 just for show, or can the car go that fast? Only, the stakes seemed higher: When skiing, not only are you the driver, you are the car.

On Spring Pitch, at the bottom of Aztec, I was lifted by a rise in the terrain and shot into the air. Jeff Olson would have prejumped this, gotten aloft before the slope dictated it, thus landing sooner and maintaining a kind of control. But I was not a racer. And in the air, truly out of control, I lost my nerve. The instant my skis rejoined the hard pack, I cranked them around sideways into a skid, trying to stop. But the slope crossed a roadcut, and the lip sent me sprawling. I lost a ski and slid to a stop not far above a class of skiers. The instructor turned to look at me. Had I been further down, I would have been lectured about endangering his class—but I was out of reach.

I stood up, shook the snow out from under my jacket and from the wrists of my gloves, reassembled my hat and gloves, recovered my ski, and tried to collect myself. It was the fastest I'd gone in my life. I had scared myself, panicked. Caution was the proper lesson to be learned from this, but in a way caution was what I was trying to exorcise. Perhaps I'd been too much the careful skier, too much my life's shepherd. I got back in the lift line, to see if I could do it better the second time.

A photograph appeared on the front page of *The Denver Post* the winter before my arrival in Aspen. It was a close-up of the snowy face of a mountain next to the Breckenridge ski area. Following a night of heavy snowfall, seven skiers had ducked under the Breckenridge boundary ropes in order to ski that steep face. The desire to put your tracks on fresh-fallen snow seems to be, in some cases, irresistible. The photo showed where the seven had started their run: Any skier could feel the ecstasy of their first few turns. And then the horror of what happened next. Halfway down the picture, the snow suddenly ends, and a jagged line shows where the huge slab of snow the men were skiing on suddenly broke off and began sliding down, leaving bare rock beneath. The caption explained that in the avalanche which began at that jagged line, three men were killed. It wasn't until a few days later that rescuers discovered a fourth.

I cut out the picture and tacked it to my bulletin board. It was a cautionary tale, more vivid than words, of how dangerous back-country skiing could be. I skied a lot—carefully, I liked to think, and wary of steep, unstable slopes with new snow. But everybody makes mistakes. I couldn't help thinking of those guys, skiing in unison, finishing a third graceful telemark turn and starting a fourth, tracking the untracked snow, suddenly noticing, against all expectations, that the snow they were skiing on was moving downhill too, adding to their speed like a moving sidewalk . . . wondering, what to do when the firmament does not hold.

That was a bad year for backcountry skiing: Eleven people died in Colorado avalanches, up from an annual average of four. But the accidents did not dissuade avid skiers. Aspen is the starting point for two excellent systems of cross-country ski huts—wilderness bunkhouses, connected by trails marked on U.S. Geological Survey topographic maps, which allow skiers carrying food and sleeping bags to spend up to several days on a ski tour through national forest. The huts were heavily booked all season, and I was among the guests. I skied on the Tenth Mountain Division trail system, which stretched from Aspen toward Vail and was named after the alpine corps of soldiers trained near Leadville during World War II. The other system was named after Alfred Braun, its founder. The Austrian-born Braun, an avid nordic skier, built and maintained a chain of high alpine bungalows between Aspen and Crested Butte. For a nominal fee you could reserve them, in a back room of his miner's cabin on Main Street.

It was over the taxi radio, that first January of my first winter in

Aspen, that I first heard the news: A morning avalanche on Pearl Pass, not far from Braun's Tagert and Wilson huts, had left three skiers missing. By dinner two of them, men from Boulder and Glenwood Springs, had been found dead. But still missing was Krystyne "Teeny" Jeung, thirty-eight, the emergency room head nurse at the Valley View Hospital in Glenwood Springs and a Glenwood Springs city councilwoman, and her dog, Bear.

The three were part of a group of thirteen cross-country skiers who had begun their trip the day before. Led by Roy Poteet, of Carbondale, an experienced mountaineer, they had skied late in the day from a parking area at the ghost town of Ashcroft up into the vast Pearl Basin. They had rented the Tagert and Wilson huts near timberline for a weekend of skiing and a possible ascent of 14,265-foot Castle Peak. Some of the party made a foray up into the basin late that day to check conditions.

That night it snowed lightly, and Sunday morning the group assessed the idea of a climb. New snow added to the instability of steep slopes they'd have to negotiate on a trip up Castle Peak, and bad weather was expected. So plans were revised, and groups of two and three skiers headed out into the fresh cover of snow to try some turns in the basin.

Poteet, thirty-one, the group leader, John Logsdon, thirty-two, of Boulder, Teeny Jeung, and Bear were one such group. Poteet was an ad salesman at *The Glenwood Post* and a disc jockey at KDNK, Carbondale's public radio station. Logsdon was a cabinetmaker. Jeung and the dog were later said by her brother to be very close.

All were experienced skiers. All were aware they were entering dangerous terrain: Poteet and Logsdon wore avalanche transceivers, useful to rescuers in locating victims; Jeung had loaned hers to a friend. All had probably seen the two signs posted en route to the huts, warning skiers of the avalanche hazard. All three, approaching the top of the basin and presumably ascending to its jagged rim, were traversing a steep face when the snow beneath their skis detached from the mountainside in a giant slab, eventually crumbling and burying them all.

Two nearby skiers in the group, George Russell, of Boulder, and Joy Kor, a nurse who worked with Jeung in Glenwood Springs, witnessed the aftermath of the slide: One moment they had seen their friends, and the next they were gone, the snow on which they were standing scraped completely off the rocky ground. The avalanche had traveled six hundred feet and in places was up to three hundred feet wide. Russell and Kor called across the basin to another couple, Ron and Diana Osborn, of Glenwood Springs. Diana Osborn skied down for help, and the other three headed for the slide.

The only sign of the groups was a ski tip, which Ron Osborn began to dig around. A short time later, he found the ski attached to the body of John Logsdon. Logsdon, encased in the heavy, compacted snow, had suffocated.

George Russell removed Logsdon's avalanche beacon, switched it from transmit mode to receive mode, and followed the signal across the slide deposition to where it was strongest. With Osborn's help, he began to dig. Three or four feet down, they found the body of Roy Poteet, the trip leader. The coroner later concluded that he, too, had died of suffocation.

There was no sign of Teeny Jeung or her dog, and ten rescue volunteers, arriving shortly before dark, failed to locate her. They placed the bodies of Logsdon and Poteet in olive-green body bags and took them down to the Tagert hut, to await evacuation by sled the next day. The Osborns, Russell, and other members of the group all left for town, traumatized. The next day, Monday, would be the first day of Colorado Avalanche Backcountry Safety Awareness Week.

When my friend Paul arrived on the scene the next day to cover search efforts for *The Aspen Times*, the bags startled him. "It seemed odd they were unattended, just left there on the snow that way," he wrote in an unusual first-person story in the paper. But by then, the urgency and hope of the day before had yielded to a somber grimness. Sunday, it had been a rescue operation; Monday, after twenty-four hours buried in the snow, no one expected to find Teeny Jeung alive. "This would be, at best, a recovery," wrote Paul.

Searchers were being towed to the site behind snowmobiles, water-ski-style, their faces protected by masks, goggles, and hoods. Winds roaring up to sixty or seventy miles per hour made the twenty-degree-Fahrenheit day seem bitterly cold. Since he was not a member of the team, Paul skied up under his own power, across barren Zhivago Flats near Ashcroft, and then up a steep road through the woods to the Tagert hut. There, by a raging fire, search details were being formed: Three avalanche dogs and twenty-one volunteers were dispatched to the high country. Paul followed them up on skis, above tree line, into the open bowl and gale-force winds, which sent snow shooting horizontally "like a sandblaster." Fluorescent-orange marker flags had been set in the snow to guide workers to the site. A bare patch of unskiable terrain required the workers to take off their skis; "the wind pulled and yanked," wrote Paul, "jerking our skis around, trying to pull them out of our hands."

Finally arriving at the avalanche site, Paul, who came to take photos and observe, found himself instead recruited into a probe-pole line. It was like a giant fine-toothed comb: A row of workers, maybe fifteen across, line up a foot and a half apart from each other and methodically sink thin twelve-foot aluminum probe poles straight down into the avalanche deposition. They move forward as one, hoping, and yet not hoping, they'll hit something that feels human. The snow was deep; too often the poles went down their full length, leaving unexplored the depths beneath. In the thin air of 12,700 feet, the work was exhausting. Among the workers were ski patrollers from several ski areas, the crosses on their jackets implying a sense of security.

But the weather in Pearl Basin seemed bent on thwarting human intention. Blowing snow meant you could see ahead of yourself only occasionally, and a sense of chaos reigned. "The yelping of avalanche dogs, the shouts of probers, the stereophonic squawking radios fought the wind for dominance . . . When it whipped up you heard nothing but a roar," wrote Paul. The radios were warning of a worsening storm, the base camp wanting to know when the rescuers would be coming down. Finally, a gust whose speed the workers estimated at seventy miles per hour blew one prober over, and the rest of the people on the probe line fell like dominoes. A man's heavy pack blew away through the chunks of avalanche debris, into oblivion. Someone smart decided there was no further point in risking the lives of rescuers for a corpse.

"The descent was a circus," wrote Paul. "Traverse. Kick turn. Traverse. It was purely survival getting out of there. Rescuers . . . were checked in one by one at the Tagert hut." Below, skiing on the flats near Ashcroft, "the wind pushed me down the road. I could lean back on it and rest. The barbed-wire fences were singing in the gale."

Teeny Jeung was not found that day, and the storm hit with a vengeance. More snow fell, deepening her tomb, and the wind built up huge cornices on the ridge above the accident site, new avalanches waiting to happen. Those who understood how snow accumulates in the high country, deeper and deeper until spring, knew what this meant: Teeny Jeung would have to wait.

All winter long, playing my part in the expensive, efficient transportation network that moved thousands of tourists quickly into and out of Aspen, I had thought about Teeny Jeung. Her fate was some sort of foil to all the Aspen hype and promo that fueled this massive visitation. The constant revelry of the people I drove would sometimes put me in a dark mood, because *I* had to *work*. At times as we drove by Castle Creek Road I would be tempted to spoil the party, to tell new arrivals that there was a body up there, waiting to be found; that the technology did not exist that could extricate a gentle cross-country skier and her dog from a huge pile of snow, 4,700 feet above Aspen.

The Japanese have a word, *aware* (ah-WAH-rey), that signifies beauty that is passing—that of a butterfly, for example. If civilization persists in Aspen another two thousand years, perhaps the sensibility will arise that can invent a word in English for another kind of beauty, the beauty you can sense looking up at a wind-torn, jagged peak, beauty that is dangerous.

Coming to work at *The Aspen Times* in April, I inherited the avalanche beat from Paul. David Swersky, the rescue leader/dentist, said I could accompany the next expedition to the site. He called me late in the evening of June 26. A ski had been found in an unexplored area of the avalanche deposition, he said. A Jeep would be leaving the headquarters cabin at 5:30 A.M.

I was there on time, but spent the next hour and a half eating breakfast with Phil Weir because the avalanche dog was late. Weir is fortyish, short, blond, and muscular—I often saw him working with weights at the Aspen Club. His boyish looks had been just what Benson & Hedges was looking for in a model for a cigarette ad the year before. He had unsuccessfully pursued a pretty friend of mine who taught skiing in the Powder Pandas program at Buttermilk Mountain. He was one of Mountain Rescue's most gung ho members. "I think we're gonna find her today," I remember him saying excitedly. "I really think this is it."

We were waiting for Max. Max, a young Doberman pinscher, was specially trained to reconnoiter avalanche sites and sniff out bodies beneath the snow. Christine, his owner, finally pulled in around 7 A.M., having overslept. She fussed and fretted over Max while Phil and I readied the rescue team's old Jeep pickup truck. In good Aspen fashion, Christine thought the world of Max. So much so that as we drove through the chilly morning air up Castle Creek toward Ashcroft, she thought that Max had better not sit in the bed of the truck lest he catch a cold. From his spot in the middle of the Jeep's front seat, Max gazed through the back window at me, crouched down behind the cab, trying to stay out of the wind. He looked nice and warm.

We drove up the paved road along Castle Creek, past the ghost town of Ashcroft, and then onto the steep, winding dirt road leading up into Pearl Basin. Just above the huts, the truck could proceed no further. We parked it and hiked out of the narrow timbered part of the valley into an awesome open, rolling terrain—Pearl Basin, ringed by jagged peaks and ridges. High above to the left, Pearl Pass, 12,700 feet, led to Crested Butte, about twenty miles away across the Elks. To the right a huge, undulating series of wind-scoured knolls comprised the bowl. The hike took about forty-five minutes. It was a beautiful day, and the way was lined with wildflowers; snow remained now only at the highest elevations. Still, there was something foreboding about it all: Our route on foot nearly traced the path the skiers had taken that morning. I had never seen the avalanche site, but as we approached I was gripped by the same sort of inexplicable certainty as Phil Weir, an overwhelming intuition that yes, this was going to be the day, and yes, I was going to be the one who found her.

I could see the site before they told me: one long tongue of snow at the foot of a steep slope at the very top of the basin. You couldn't see the whole deposition at once; it curved around a knoll. It had shrunk a lot since last they saw it, Phil and Christine agreed, and the melting surface had smoothed out from its original chaos. The thought that there was a dead body under there, present but invisible, made the snowy area seem similar to the sea or a dark lake, holding a hidden malevolence that, if fate decreed, you might bump into.

Before others of us could leave our scent on it, Christine and Max worked the slope. Max thought he smelled things in three other places, but deep holes we dug at those sites yielded nothing. We took a seat on the huge flat stone now known to rescuers as Lunch Rock and awaited the others.

The sheriff and rescue-team leadership had decided this day to make a big push; by now, they felt, she was probably findable. We were soon joined by four more workers, including two sheriff's deputies, and then by noon a helicopter had begun to ferry up ten more volunteers from Ashcroft, including Dr. Ayers, the county coroner. Lunch Rock was covered with packs and box lunches. Everyone held either a shovel or a twelve-foot probe pole. By the official description, these were selfless volunteers, missing work to perform a needed task for the community. To a smaller number of people I knew in town, they were crisis junkies, for whom the idea of injury or rescue carried an adolescent fascination.

Whichever was true, they worked hard. Probing was the main task of the day, and we did it for ten exhausting hours. One person directed the line, with the same commands repeated countless times during the day: "Okay, lift probe. Probe left. Probe right. Step forward." Another two held a cord tight in front of the poles, to make sure we all moved forward a uniform distance, in a straight line. A fourth person responded to calls from probers who thought they might have found something. A flag would be placed near the pole in question so that a shovel crew could follow up by digging a hole.

Sometimes the poles would pierce the mass of snow easily, but more often, some obstruction would be encountered on the way down. The trick was knowing whether that object you hit was just another chunk of ice or rock, suspended in the melting mass, or whether it might be . . . a corpse. The problem was, no one knew what a corpse would feel like. If it was frozen, would it feel just like ice? Would it have some give? If a probe pole hit a parka, would that feel bouncy? The leaders didn't know, either. We were all going by intuition, hoping we would know when we hit it.

Most chunks of ice could be pierced with repeated blows, and probe poles sunk the rest of the way in. But you couldn't help wondering, as you sunk a probe pole through some obstacle, whether you hadn't just sunk a probe pole all the way through her. Graveyard humor was rife. The prober next to me, an expert climber I will call Nils, asked me to push on his pole, to see if I agreed he had found something. It was definitely resilient. "What do you think, a pancreas?" he asked, grinning. We flagged it and moved on. The shovel team later found nothing. The feeling, behind all the macho joking, was one of profound ambivalence. You wanted to find her, but you didn't want to find her. To be lucky would mean to be unlucky. It was a strange combination of treasure hunt and walk through a minefield.

In midafternoon, gloves were drenched and backs were stiff when we got the most encouraging sign of the day—a prober struck metal. Work on the line was immediately suspended as the shovel team dug down six feet to get to the source: a ski pole, bent nearly in half. We probed carefully in concentric circles around the area, but nothing more was found.

The weather turned cold and windy as the sun set behind the ridge above us. Leaving the deposition area, now perforated with hundreds or thousands of tiny holes and severely pockmarked with thirty-five or forty big ones, we tied a streamer to a probe pole on the edge of snowfield that had become our helipad, to help the copter pilot negotiate the gusty wind. I was ferried out on the fourth trip. As I climbed into the bubble, Nils ran under the whirling blade and stuck a heavy black bundle of rubberized fabric on my lap, with an order to take it down. It was a body bag. It wouldn't be needed that day.

The copter's engine gained rpm's, and in a roar of wind and rotor noise we lifted off the ground. We had risen perhaps fifty feet when, despite the accelerating motor, the copter began to lose altitude. I looked over, alarmed, at the sheriff's deputy seated next to me. "Wind," he said tersely. Like a huge hand, the gust pushed us down to perhaps twenty-five feet off the ground, then twenty, then below. I found myself tightly grasping the body bag. Moments later the wind released us, and the copter rose. "Shit," I whispered. We swung around and headed downvalley. Nobody said another word about it.

·   ·   ·

Rescue leaders weren't ordering anyone, but they strongly encouraged two team members to visit the site every week, just to take a look. Fairly new to the team, Chris Myers and Jim Angevine were eager to make a good impression. Besides, said Chris, twenty-six, "I'd been maxed out. I wanted to get out, and this was a reason to get out. Also, I had not been up there, and there's a natural curiosity."

"We didn't expect to find anything," said Jim, twenty-nine. "We were gonna go up, take a quick look at the site, and climb a peak . . . maybe Greg Mace Peak or Castle Peak or something. It turned out to be quite a different day than we had anticipated."

Though not close friends, the two got along well enough. Chris, who lived in Aspen for two years, had researched problems of energy-efficient lighting at Amory Lovins's Rocky Mountain Institute in Snowmass for several years before moving on to a spin-off company that provided such lighting. Blond, single, and of medium build, he moonlighted as a disk jockey on KSPN. Jim, shorter, also blond, but not as talkative, had been in the area for several years, too, working as a part-time ski tuner and for property-management firms in Snowmass.

They met at the Mountain Rescue bungalow at 8 A.M. on Saturday morning, July 18. Separately, they both commented to me about how beautiful the day was, remarked on all the wildflowers in the high country. The sky was blue and the winds were light. They hiked in shorts, T-shirts, gloves, and hats, " 'cause it was still pretty cold up there," said Chris.

Jim had been there before and led Chris to Lunch Rock. Since spring, it had stood high enough above the surrounding snow to provide a dry place to sit, eat, and rest. That day, it stood even higher. "Jim was amazed, I remember, at how much snow had melted." Besides Jim's surprise, Chris remembered "a real heavy air"—despite the fact they were at 12,700 feet. "We'd been real talkative going up, and then we were kind of quiet—there was just this feeling, that sensation of the macabre. You're going, This is weird, why should I even *want* to do this?

"We radioed in that we had gotten to the site, and we started to check things out." They dropped their packs on the rock, had a drink of water, and looked around. "And from there," said Chris, "we could see something sticking out of the snow in the upper snow patch. And we went over. And sure enough, it was Bear's paw."

The dog was higher up in the avalanche chute than anyone had expected, given the magnitude of the slide. It made the searchers reexamine some of their assumptions.

"At that point we decided to continue a visual search of that entire chute up above the snow actually, in the rocks, too, just to make sure there wasn't anything up higher," said Jim. "And we continued walking the entire snowfield, too—we wanted to try and do it in sort of an orderly manner and make sure we weren't, you know, looking at something and focusing on or touching one area when maybe there was something lower or higher." They found nothing, and went back to the dog. "It was a very furry dog," said Jim, not a pure Lab, as they had been told, but a mixed breed. They uncovered parts of it, gingerly, because the body was so close to the surface it was no longer frozen. "The fur, if you touched it, would come away from the body. And exhuming that, it was pretty bad." The smell of decomposition filled the air, and turned their stomachs.

"I guess it's like any—if you're walking through the woods and there's a dead deer or something like that, it's the same—I guess it's been described, and it's pretty accurate, as a sickly-sweet aroma." Thinking the better of it, they re-covered the dog in loose snow, radioed a report of its discovery to headquarters, and got on with the real work. Using two of the thin twelve-foot-long aluminum poles that rescuers had left at the site, they started probing all around the dog. It was frustrating, time-consuming, and exhausting. After a rest, Jim said, "I decided to exhume the dog a bit more, just to make sure there wasn't a hand holding the collar, or something like that. And we both had this very strong feeling, that's all I can describe it, that she was very near the dog. Just a gut-level feeling. While I was doing that, Chris continued to probe around the area of the dog, and he was probing in one area just to the side of the dog and he was still hitting ice very shallow. And I called in to say that we were getting ready to suspend the search."

Jim slowed down as he began to tell what happened next. Words no longer flowed. "At this point, Chris just said, 'You know, I feel like there might be something down here.' And I had this digging iron that I'd been using [about twenty pounds] to dig out the dog, and I took it over to around where he was and I said, 'Well, I'll knock some holes through the ice so you can probe down below it.' And the first hole I punched through the ice I contacted the body. There was no mistake about it at all. Absolutely no doubt—if you're striking a soft body. It gives and, you know—there was no doubt in my mind. I asked Chris to put his probe pole down through the same hole that I did, and immediately, 'Yeah, this is it.' And we took some shovels . . . it was less than a foot below the surface of the snow. And we shoveled out a little bit, and we uncovered a small patch of . . . definitely clothing. And at that point, although we didn't have the entire body . . . I called, and told them that we definitely had found her."

Chris and Jim dug out the snow all around the body. It was lying even with the surface, which made the job easier, but it was also encased in ice, which made it harder. She was surrounded by ice, Jim explained, because she was warm when she died, and this melted the surrounding snow: the sole effect *she* had on the tremendous force of the avalanche. The only exposed skin was her face, which had a thick mask of ice on it. "We did leave that ice on her face till the very last, because it did cover the face," said Jim. "You could see it was a face behind it all, but it wasn't like, looking right into the face. It provided a certain amount of relief to us to do that. I know there was a lot of trauma to the body, so it's very possible she died very quickly . . . It was obvious there was damage to the skeleton—the hip, leg, were in awkward positions, and when we dug around below the head, there was blood, frozen blood in the snow behind the head. So it's, um, at least I hope that maybe she never even knew."

That seemed likely, according to Dr. Ayers, the coroner. Most avalanche deaths occur from suffocation, and normally, "from the time of encasement [in the avalanche], it's a few seconds to thirty seconds of consciousness." Rare survivors of avalanches, he said, "recall they passed out almost immediately," and revived only upon being dug out. "It's like being set in cement."

The worst of it is then, for Jim and Chris, was the waiting. For three hours, alone with the bodies of dog and woman, they awaited the deputy sheriff and two others who would help get her down from the valley. They kept busy for the first hour or two, cleaning up and carrying to the road the probe poles, shovels, marker flags, and other rescue paraphernalia strewn around the site: The long recovery effort was almost over. Then there was nothing to do but wait. Antsy and frustrated it was taking so long, Chris went on a hike up the ridge above the slide site, "so I could sort of look out over the whole area. And it was gorgeous, but I kept imagining what it had been like."

He wondered if the skiers were to blame. "Everybody says, 'God, they were stupid,' but you know, we're all human and we all do make stupid mistakes." He was thinking it could have been him that made the stupid mistake.

Jim sat on Lunch Rock and stared down valley, his back to the excavations.

Finally, the others arrived. They cracked the ice mask to remove her from the slope, and lifted her up. "And I'll tell you, you've never seen people move so fast as when they're putting someone into a body bag," said Jim. "You put it in, zip it up—and it's a terrible thing to say, but you're dealing with a thing then, rather than a person." They slid the bag down the remaining snow to where they had left a litter and a one-wheeled device the litter could be attached to, and thence rolled down over the uneven surface. After discussion, they left behind the dog—eighty more pounds would have made the evacuation extremely difficult.

Arriving at Ashcroft, they were surprised by a reporter and photographer from *The Glenwood Post*. "I guess they heard about it on the police channel," said Chris with a grimace. His was not the attitude of a hunter with a trophy. "They pretty callously put a picture of the body bag in the back of the pickup truck on the front page of their paper, which I still think is extremely tasteless. And at that time they asked a lot of questions, and we were pretty vague, very brief, and we didn't give 'em anything, and said you want to talk to somebody, you talk to a spokesperson, and we never let our names get out."

The body was delivered to the morgue, and the group split up. As Chris and Jim parted, Chris suggested they get together later on, maybe to go over it. But Jim, who had spent a long time on Lunch Rock with his back turned to the body, didn't want to. He wanted to go home, deal with it on his own. "It didn't start settling in until a few hours later," he told me. "I thought I had it under control and tried to go to bed, and then I had images. And you just can't shake those images."

My conversation with him came five months after the fact. "If you had called me up, like, the week after, I would never have agreed" to talk, Jim said. It's one reason he wanted to avoid talking to reporters. "I was having enough trouble dealing with it without continually having to relive it. Someone asks, 'What was the condition of the body?' or whatever, and instantly . . . [I see it]." But slowly, he said, it was getting better. Slowly, the images faded.

Everybody is curious about death, especially in the twentieth century, when there is less of it than ever before in the United States and the lion's share of what there is is the experiential domain of police officers and morticians. Chris Meyers was no exception. But the experience of looking death quite literally in the face was more than he had bargained for.

Leaving the morgue, Chris said, he realized "I, oddly enough, had to go to a CPR final in half an hour—I was already late, it was in a half hour, and I had a forty-five-minute drive to Carbondale. So I was driving down there, and I was very, very careless. I wasn't thinking, I was just gone. I was thinking, I've gotta get to this CPR final, I've gotta get there, I'm late, I'm late." On narrow Killer 82, he passed two cars at a high rate of speed. "And I got blinded by the late-afternoon sun, so I had no idea what was coming towards me or if I'd make it by. Then I got back in [to his lane] safely, and then I just started . . . I slowed my breathing down, started thinking, wait a second, you know, this makes no sense. Got down to Carbondale, you know, ran upstairs to the CPR final, and everybody's around the room, performing CPR on dummies, and I walked into the instructor, she's an EMT in Carbondale, and I said, 'Look, Barb, I'm really sorry I'm late,' and she goes, 'I know'—she'd heard—and she goes, 'Now are you okay?' I said, 'I'm fine.' She said, 'Are you ready to take this?' And I said, 'Yeah, yeah, no problem.' She goes, 'Look, go take a walk.' I hadn't even made it out on the walk, and I just lost it." Chris started sobbing. "Yeah, big-time. It's even comin' back now. It's gettin' it out that'll settle it."

"So I went out of the building, and I was bawlin' like I never had before. And I still don't know why. And I just went over and just walked down the street, found a deserted building on a side street, and sat against it and, like—I still did not know why I was crying,

I just, like, I, somethin', you know. All this pent-up energy, un-
released emotion. I was probably there for ten minutes, trying to
sort of control it. And finally I thought I had controlled it, and I got
up and walked across the street and got a glass of lemonade and sat
down. Now I guess it was about six-thirty, almost seven, and I was
just drinking that and . . . somebody from the CPR final came out
and said, 'Yeah, I know how you feel, I knew her too,' and I didn't
know her, and I just started crying again. The guy must've felt
really bad, because I just lost it. And all he said was, 'I knew her too.'
And just—boom."

Chris and Jim next saw each other a month later, when they were
called in to support a search for a fallen hiker near Maroon Bells.
The hiker was Heinz Pagels, and they were told the chances of
finding him alive were remote. They looked at each other, and then
they walked up to the head of the rescue crew. "We said, 'We're
out,' " Chris remembered. "We just went in and said, 'We can't do
this.'

"It's rough out there," concluded Chris. "I've climbed Pyramid
and taken that same step that Heinz Pagels took, and I made it. And
that's another thing I'm thinking about there—how come he didn't
make it, and I made it? I climbed it in a snowstorm on Labor Day,
a year ago, and man, it was really dangerous. And you always have
this in the backcountry: People forget about the roughness of the
world."

Afternoons, we'd ride our mountain bikes. It was like a return to
grade school, the way we'd ride around, a bunch of guys and,
sometimes, girls. But the goal wasn't mischief or just killing time—it
was a workout.

There were several places you could go, but the closest—within
a few minutes of wherever you were in town—was Smuggler
Mountain. I would usually go with Paul or my lawyer friend Ted
or Richard, a housepainter, or Janie, from the photo agency, or
whoever was available: Nobody called until an hour or so before the
end of the workday, which was when the rides began.

The road up Smuggler Mountain, which comprises one of the
mountain walls ringing Aspen, was steep and unpaved, with several
switchbacks. And the further up you went, the steeper it got. Our

mountain bikes had extremely low gear combinations, which allowed you to inch up the imposing grade about as fast as a person could walk. It was harder to keep your balance at such low speeds, though, and rocks, ruts, or a slipping tire would conspire to stop your progress. Often, if you put your foot down to keep from falling, it was hard to get enough speed up to get started again. Some riders would walk till the road flattened out slightly, or even turn around and head briefly downhill, just to get back on their bikes.

The reward for this grueling exercise, after about twenty or twenty-five minutes, was a spectacular view of Aspen from a wooden platform atop the mountain, and then, of course, the trip down. Those who had brought helmets—maybe half the group—would don them at the summit, because the steep backside of the mountain meant you could go *very* fast. The trip down was perilous. The likelihood that a sudden dip or hole in the road would plunge you over your handlebars was high. You raised yourself off the seat, legs bent, to better absorb the shock of the rough roads. The bike shook like a paint mixer between your hands, and your palms needed massaging after the long drops, you'd been squeezing the brakes so hard.

Merging with a single-track path in an open valley, the route wound finally through grassy meadows and past picturesque abandoned miner's cabins. It deposited you on the smooth paved road that looped through the expensive palaces of Red Mountain.

Here you could really accelerate: The way was predictable, and joyous. The wind would quickly dry your shirt, and the evenness would soothe your jangled nerves. Only one further scary spot awaited: the super-steep hill where the road dropped down off Red Mountain to meet the Roaring Fork River. This stretch of narrow paved road, about three hundred feet long, had a pitch of 15–17 percent. Because the slightest hint of ice made it impassable, the sheriff usually closed it when a winter storm began and waited for the sand trucks. In the summer, most people on bikes walked up the hill; going down, the experience was similar to that of a giant roller-coaster plunge. You had to watch very carefully for cars ahead of you (because you would quickly catch up to them, and have to brake), cars heading up the hill toward you (which might be in your lane), and the intersection at the bottom, where a branch road fed in and where cars often collided in the winter.

Paul preceded me down this hill one evening in August. There were just the two of us and the hill was like dessert, the last thrill of a challenging ride. Neither of us wore a helmet, because they were hot and uncomfortable and obstructed the view. Paul was heavier and a fast rider; I knew he would outpace me on this last stretch, so I set off close behind, hoping any cars at the intersection would wait until I'd gone by too.

But there were no cars at all. The way was totally clear. I hunched down behind my handlebars, dropped my head, tucked my knees in to cut down air resistance, and shot down the hill. Paul was a bullet in front of me. Then suddenly, just as he crossed the intersection, I saw his bike jolt, and Paul bounced out of control off the road.

I was going so fast, it took a long time to stop and turn around. I pedaled furiously back to where Paul had entered some shrubs. He was getting to his feet, having tumbled some distance from his bike. Amazingly, he was only scraped. The same could not be said of his bicycle, however: The front wheel of the thousand-dollar machine was bent and crumpled. A new pothole, back in the intersection, was the culprit.

We carried the bike to his apartment, where Paul seemed more interested in the damage to his bike than the damage to his body. With a look of fascination, he extricated the ruined front wheel— once a thing of beauty, with its alloy rim, double-butted stainless spokes, and gracefully forged hub. The tire was mostly off, the tube hung from one side like entrails, spokes splayed from the center. It was warped, deformed, irretrievable. With a giddy laugh and a maniacal look, Paul pounded a nail into an empty space above his couch and—between a poster of the infant prince of Norway being carried to safety by two woolly courtiers on ancient nordic skis and a poster for the Telluride Mushroom Festival—he hung up the wheel. It is there to this day, and though I laughed knowingly when he put it up, I was never sure exactly what it meant to Paul. It wasn't the sort of thing you could ask about, but I thought I could guess. It was a reminder never to go so fast again, and a conversation starter. With Paul's sense of humor, it was possibly a commentary on modern art. Most of all, it was a mountain biker's Purple Heart, a trophy of victory over the roughness of the world.

Chapter VIII

You Cannot Find a Finer Home

Rebecca Orlean, the older sister of my college roommate, had a knack: She could look at almost anything—a shop window, a table setting, a photograph—and know, intuitively, the changes that would make it look better. Her tastes tended toward the expensive, but that had not kept her from taking seriously the spool-table, battered La-Z-Boy, lumpy couch, and other accoutrements of our off-campus house and suggesting with a few moments' appraisal a rearrangement that greatly improved the look and feel of the place. Her eye for good design had landed her the job of directing an antique-furniture gallery in Los Angeles; and now the busy owners had offered to sponsor a summer week in Aspen for Rebecca if she would spend a day or two scouting the work of local architects for a house they aspired to build there.

She asked if I would be her chaperon on the housing search. Her employers were wealthy (they also owned a Tuscan villa and a beach compound on Martha's Vineyard), and the excursion would be like a passkey to some of the fanciest, newest houses in Aspen. Many people would die for this chance, I knew, and because it was she who asked, I agreed to do it. But I had mixed feelings. For most of my life I had happily avoided pricey cars and showy houses. Rather than luxury, they reminded me of poverty, of the social needs ignored by millionaires. Why give someone a chance to show off his expensive toy? Travel lightly, live simply—I believed in that. But in coming to Aspen I had also decided it might be okay to take a peek.

For suggestions, Rebecca had gone to prominent architects and decorators, some in New York and Los Angeles, some local, and asked about their recent work; the socially prominent, in Aspen and elsewhere, seemed also to have contributed to her list. These people had also helped her arrange appointments to see the houses; most of the owners were pleased to show them off. The goal, of course, was to find not a huge house (though most of them were), but a distinctive, well-designed house, a house that somebody had done (or allowed others to do) "right."

Rebecca's search was not easy. New houses tended to be built by new money, and there was the perennial problem of owners having more wealth than taste: Aspen was full of white elephants. Complicit in this phenomenon was the fact that so many of Aspen's houses were *new* houses on undeveloped land—the architects and builders usually had a blank slate, down to deciding which trees to clear and where to cut the new roads. If there was a local tradition, it was one describing the shape of smaller houses, of Victorians. But Aspen's new burghers were out to build monuments, and often it seemed their premier design goal was merely amplitude, square footage on a par with their extra money. Using grand gestures, they went for mega-living rooms, for chapellike ceilings, for voluminous garages, for pools and workout rooms and walls of windows; they went for neo-palaces, for statements.

The better architects tried to tap into what they considered a "Colorado vernacular," a true local style. But anything that wasn't a miner's cabin, Victorian, ranchhouse, tepee, or cave dwelling didn't look too indigenous. And even nativist inspiration was no guarantee of success. Our morning began with visits to two frightening places that looked like log cabins on steroids. One of these monstrosities, the new house of Goldie Hawn and Kurt Russell, was sort of a 6,500-square foot exaggeration of a hunting lodge in the Tyrol, with fake ponds and sodded lawn; it looked like something out of Disney. (Colorado logs don't often grow as big as the foot-and-a-half-diameter cylinders used in its exposed walls and beams; the builder explained that the logs had been brought from Montana.)

Following that, our drive through the West End, Aspen's oldest and nicest residential area, revealed splendid peaked and shuttered houses but also a vogue in ersatz Victorians—big new houses with Victorian geometry but with clumsy detailings—prefab scrolls and fish-scale shingles and shiny brass-plated doorknobs. But at least these attempted to blend in: The real eyesores were contemporary houses plopped in amidst the older ones. It reminded her of Beverly Hills, said Rebecca, where new structures too big for their lots were being built sometimes right up to the edge of the property line, impinging on both the neighbors' privacy and the street's smaller-scale aesthetic.

Afternoon took us up to Starwood, to a contemporary house owned by a Chicago commodities broker and his wife. She was an art collector and had filled the house with some fairly good-looking Native American pottery, weavings, fetishes, and portraits. A Duane Hanson hyperrealistic cowboy guarded the kitchen, hand on his hip; the living room overlooked a nicely landscaped artificial pond and garden and then the Elk Mountains—much like John Denver's view. Everything was painstakingly clean and neat, including the windows; it was one of those houses that look like nobody could possibly live in them—nothing on the marble counters in the bathroom, no newspapers in the study, no novels by the bed, no crumbs on the kitchen counters. "As I mentioned, this house is about art," the broker's wife was saying as Rebecca sat opposite her in the living room.

An instant later, there was a little thud from the window; I looked up just in time to see a small object fall off the glass into the garden beneath. Rebecca glanced up; the woman pretended not to notice. Not really a party to the conversation, I slowly got up and walked over to the window. Crumpled in the groundcover outside, barely larger than a newborn's fist, lay a hummingbird with a ruby-red throat, still twitching. I had seen this before, in suburban buildings with big, clean windows: birds flying right into the glass. Walking around the little courtyard, glass-enclosed on three sides, I saw another, identical, victim. I returned to my seat.

Our hostess didn't say anything until we were leaving the house. As though reading my mind, she looked out the window toward the ground and said, "You know, people say you can hang a bunch of stuff up on the windows to stop them from doing that, *but I won't do it!*" I understood why not: It would be unattractive, little hummingbird warning signs amidst those grand, invisible expanses of plate glass. The house was about art.

The next house was pretty, reasonably sized, and perched atop a windy hill near Snowmass. This time the architect showed us around, and Rebecca, as usual, took lots of pictures. The one after that belonged to two prominent art collectors who lived in Houston; they had left it to the butler to give us the tour. After showing us the lay of the place, the sad-looking man returned to wiping some windows, polishing some silver. He had been to butler school, he told us; I noted he even had a slight English accent. But he was not happy, as I supposed he might be, that his employers would not be visiting for several weeks. He was alone there and not doing that which he was trained to do.

"They think they need a butler, but they don't need a butler," he said to us. It seemed rather unprofessional, him going on that way. "They don't need a butler here."

The last house we saw, shown by its caretaker, reflected the socializing patterns of the jet-setting absentee owners: It contained four separate suites for friends who might be invited to join the owners for the week or weekend. As any cab driver knew, the private-jet people brought their own parties with them.

The house, another log number, had been featured in *Architectural Digest,* Rebecca thought; it was owned by a famous Hollywood director. It had a barn with horses that wintered in Newport Beach. It contained an assortment of West-icisms: the chandelier made of a dozen interlaced deer antlers, the Pendleton blankets, coffee tables employing slabs of rock or branches of trees, leather and wood, woven this and rawhide that, bleached skulls of horned animals, fireplace hearths and exposed chimneys of local river rock, and others done in faux adobe Santa Fe–style; and at least one fanciful sculpture by a local metalsmith. Lots of houses had this stuff, but it was better done than many.

What caught my eye was the room downstairs, full of equipment for outfitting the guests. A converted wine cellar, it had shelf after shelf, rack after rack, brimming with a full range of sizes of ski and hiking boots, tennis shoes, rackets, sweat suits, ski outfits, riding gear, fishing equipment—everything a person from L.A. might need for Colorado outdoor fun. It was, in effect, a mini-department store.

I raised my eyebrows at Rebecca, but since the caretaker was hovering nearby, she only smiled. A few days later I found the magazine piece about the house, in Aspen's public library. The article quoted the wife of the director: "Actually, I am just a little embarrassed about that room," she giggled. "I knew I was going too far when I started coordinating all the outfits."

Rebecca always responded graciously to the people showing their houses, but back in the car, we were free to talk. As we pulled out of the long drive heading to the house, and aimed toward Aspen, I felt more dispirited than tired. Those were houses, not homes, I complained; they were too big, too empty; they needed people in them. Designed, built, and decorated by someone else, most revealed nothing about the owner.

I felt naive when I remembered whom I was speaking to; Rebecca, in her work, had passed through many expensive houses, in resorts and enclaves and big cities all over the country. She had seen it all, and she told me that in her case, I didn't need to worry; houses like these were not really what her employers were looking for. She had gotten some good ideas, just the same, and hadn't been surprised by the square footage, the agglomerations of expensive decor, or even the complete outdoor equipment store.

"What did get me," she confessed, "were those huge walk-in closets full of clothes that people use only once or twice a year. I mean, half the shoes in that one place had never been worn! There were all those shirts and sweaters and coats still in packages. With their labels on." They were like the butler, expensive and unneeded.

From the dirt side road, we turned onto Highway 82 going upvalley. It was evening rush hour, and on the downvalley side the cars were bumper to bumper. As they crawled along, full of workers still a long way from their little homes, we sped to Aspen on open roads.

In a small number of ways, real estate in Aspen is like real estate in other places. There is an old part of town, on the original grid of the mining town, about fifteen streets in either direction, full of single-family houses on lots, houses with their own street number. Many of these are well-preserved originals, from humble "miner's cabins" to spectacular three-story gingerbread affairs, virtually all of them renovated and many with dazzling teal, ocher, or vermillion trim. Most of the hotels and condos lie within or on the edge of this zone but are clustered especially near the base of Ajax and along Main Street. Beyond this town center are the outlying areas, referred to not as suburbs but by the name of their subdivision: Mountain Valley, Meadow Wood, Red Mountain, Starwood, or the multibuilding complexes where workers live: Hunter Creek, Castle Creek, and Centennial.

In other ways, though, Aspen real estate leaves a lot for the newcomer to figure out. My friend Ted, formerly a well-paid lawyer in Denver, discovered this when he joined an Aspen law firm in 1988 and went looking for a house: "The cheapest one there was $300,000, and it was a little shack that looked like it should be razed." Not having moved to Aspen to live in a condo, he bought two acres and a two-bedroom house downvalley for $165,000 and became a commuter. The average price of a house in Aspen, newspapers reported later that year, was over $1 million.

Here was a town where a trailer in a mobile-home park was increasingly a white-collar solution: The Smuggler, the trailer park nearest the city center, had units averaging $75,000–100,000; a town where nineteen of twenty-two policemen (including the chief) had to live downvalley, out of town—as did most nurses, most teachers, and, indeed, the city director of housing development.

Here was a town where realtors would take out full-page-color magazine spreads to advertise a single house. WHEN YOU DESERVE THE BEST asserted the banner caption of one long-running ad, unfurled across a glorious color photo of the house's balconies, with a vista of the entire valley beyond. "Starwood 77. With the best views in the Roaring Fork Valley, this superb custom home offers every amenity: 5 bedrooms, 6 baths, wine tasting room, breakfast, dining, living and great rooms, pub, library, indoor swimming pool, exercise room and expansive decks. Elegantly and completely furnished. You cannot find a finer home. $4,300,000."

Here was a town—far away from coastal real estate markets, in the middle of depressed rural America, with "spec" homes selling for up to $18,000,000. It was a place where, though banks loaned eagerly, 60–70 percent of those buying houses (according to a common estimate) did not need a loan. They paid cash.

Often, residences were sold fully furnished, down to the linen in the closets, the silver in the drawers and, sometimes, the Jeep in the garage ("All you need is your toothbrush!" read one ad). This spared new owners the bother of outfitting a place they wouldn't be spending much time in. Single-family houses averaged 5–7,000 square feet; it was like buying a very large hotel suite.

As for rentals, the classified section of *The Aspen Times* each December said it all: a trifling half-column of "For Rent/Residential" listings, and these mainly short-term, $1,000–2,000/week, and then full pages of "Help Wanted" ads, which frequently went unanswered because there was no place for seasonal employees to live.

The Aspen Times, the Aspen Skiing Company, and other prescient businesses thrived, in part because they owned apartments they could rent to their employees.

When I met him, Erik, nineteen, was delivering for a florist, but living with his mother twenty miles out of town, by Ruedi Reservoir. "Couldn't afford anyplace closer?" I asked him sympathetically.

"Not at all," he reassured me. "We rented our place in town." Their house, he explained, held seven people, each of whom paid $600 a month for the privilege of sharing its two bedrooms—or over $4,000 monthly for the landlords. "The place Mom and I rent goes for only $500 a month. We couldn't afford not to."

The town's professional class, as is true in many ski towns, largely reflected the housing boom. Real estate agents were ubiquitous—trying to scare up business in the gondola as you went up Aspen Mountain, at the table next to you at dinner (if they thought you were new), in the bookstore and the grocery checkout line. There were 120 licensed architects, around a hundred lawyers, who did a lot of work for them, and practically all the most prominent people in town—Mohammed Hadid, Dick Butera, Bill Stirling, the mayor, and deep-pocket celebrities from Martina Navratilova to Michael Douglas—were developers.

And here was a town that, despite new construction worth $100 million in 1989 and a hot real estate market amidst a national slump, had areas whose population was actually *declining* due to absentee ownership, an anomalous prosperity of neighborhoods emptying of children, emptying of inhabitants altogether. It was the lonely popularity of a celebrity.

"To know the night you have to know the day," said Luke. "To know Aspen you have to know a tepee."

Two days later, counting tenths of miles on my car odometer as Luke had instructed, I crossed a bridge over a stream and turned off the pavement onto an overgrown, barely noticeable dirt road. It ascended steeply, made a switchback as Luke had said, and dead-ended at an old Toyota wagon and a big shepherd-mix dog.

I turned off my engine. The barking mutt was especially loud in the silence of the woods, and he smelled of skunk. But Luke, appearing like a giant through the shrubs, soon greeted me and calmed the dog down; I followed his long stride a short way into a clearing in an aspen grove.

There were three tepees, actually, each made of canvas and slender pine trunks. Smoke emerged from the middle one, the cooking tepee, and I went to greet Hillery, whom I knew from the *Times*. The winsome Hillery, Luke's companion of the past three years, was cooking a vegetarian stew for our supper. Another tepee, mostly unadorned, belonged to an Argentinian friend who was in town working, and the third and most beautiful tent was their home. We ducked under a piece of the canvas that was tied up, and Luke showed me the inside. Afternoon sun passed through the canopy of aspen above and created a beautiful light through the canvas, dancing all around. There were a double bed covered with Indian blankets, a hanging Indian drum, Indian masks and feathered spears, and oil lamps. Husks of corn dangled from the sides. The floor was remarkable: It had been tamped down with linseed oil and looked so set you could imagine washing it, like linoleum. He was a purist, Luke told me, and liked being able to touch the earth.

The tepee was fifteen or twenty feet tall, and the floor about the same diameter. In the winter, they installed a six-foot skirt around the lower portion to keep the snow from melting through; it piled up deep. The Toyota they simply parked down by the highway, hiking from there up the well-trodden path in the snow to the tepees.

A chair and a stump were positioned in the sun outside, and Luke and I each took one. He was a tall man, with long brown hair, often in a ponytail, a ready smile, and a beard. He frequently wore a felt hat with a white band. In many ways the tepee, in its simplicity and Native American feel, defined Luke. "I'm a tepee hippie," he said.

Hillery was short, younger, and sort of a hippie, too; she had grown up in Aspen, and she worked part-time doing layout at the *Times*, where her mother sold advertising and was a sometimes columnist. She had long hair, usually braided, dangling silver earrings, wire-rim glasses, and cheeks that looked perpetually rosy.

I looked around. A large stack of firewood, their only fuel, sat behind the main bedroom tent; uphill, there stood a wood-fired water heater with a gravity-flow pipe leading down to an old clawfooted bathtub—"for when we're feeling decadent," Luke explained. That might be often, I thought, for Luke, Hillery, and the encampment were all remarkably clean. Four cats, nearly feral, roamed about, scaling seedlings and chasing moths and making it seem like a home.

We opened the beers I had brought. It was still possible to live on a budget in Aspen, Luke explained, but you needed luck, persistence, or ingenuity. Also helpful, it seemed, was a willingness to live outdoors. A business they ran allowed them a degree of independence: They made decorator lamps. The materials were earthy, natural: rocks for the bases, branches or sticks for the body, and shades that were either made out of bark or were the standard store-bought variety, but with a layer of colored sand glued lightly on. The lamps sold for $200–$800 in town. I thought it was funny that from the tepee, they made products for the electrified world outside, and Luke did, too.

Hillery brought us plates of stew and freshly baked bread, which we carried into the main tepee as the sun went down and the air turned cool. Luke explained that while he was glad he didn't live in town, he was glad Aspen was there.

"Along with the free-for-all decadence there's a tolerance," he said, for oddballs like Hunter S. Thompson "and like me. For me, that's what's so cool about Aspen—its contradictions. That's what's so human about it. Aspen, because of its extremes, exposes more about people than a Peoria would."

The tolerance was not always evident, however: Hillery described how, two weeks earlier, the tepees had been "red-tagged" by the county—cited for being built illegally, without permits. For a while they thought they might have to take them down. But the law was fuzzy: They paid rent to a man who owned the mining claim for the area, and by some interpretations it was legal to maintain a residence at an active claim. After negotiations, they were told they could stay on, for now. There were maybe thirteen tepees left around Aspen, they thought, though there once had been many more.

Hillery didn't share all of Luke's enthusiasm for the tepees. In the winter, she said, it was really nice to have a hot shower. They worked on the lamps in a garage in town, and travel back and forth was difficult when it was cold. And kids—"Could you imagine having kids up here? And keeping them from going into the woods?" Still, they seemed like a harmonious couple, and a few months later they were married.

When I got up to leave, the moon had risen and the white aspen trunks glowed. "On full moons in the summer we have Indian ceremonies," Luke said. They beat the drum, sang and chanted, and told old stories. "I'm a white man, but I've always appreciated the Indian life-style." *Life-style* seemed an odd word when used with Indians, but I thought I knew what Luke meant.

I felt wistful about leaving, but it was nothing compared to the feeling I had about a year later, passing through Aspen's most raging disco, the Tippler, upon seeing Hillery standing on the edge of the dance floor. I went up to her.

"Hillery? What are you doing here?" I yelled over the music.

"I don't know, what are we all doing here? Waiting for a dance, I guess," she hollered back.

"How about Luke?"

Her face clouded. "Oh, we split up. You didn't know?" I shook my head.

Hillery shrugged. We stood for a moment. I had had a couple beers.

"Was it the tepee?"

"Was it what?"

"Was it the tepee? Is that why you left?"

"No," I saw her say.

She was wearing contact lenses, I thought, and pleated pants instead of a long skirt. She didn't look as funky as before. Her female friend looked downright conventional. The music pounded and the strobe lights flashed. I thought of the moonlight and their home-made lamps.

The woods were full of wardens. Visiting Luke and Hillery reminded me of the night a tall, drunken man waved down my taxi near Little Nell's at 2 A.M. At first when he said he'd direct me to his house, I went along; he was a chef at Schlomo's Deli, he told me, and wished he wasn't so drunk, because he had to be back in the kitchen at 5:30 A.M. But after we'd passed the last house on Ute Avenue, I got nervous—there was nothing out here. Was it some kind of setup?

"Slow down, slow down," he slurred a few moments later. "It's on the right. Now. Here. Stop!" There was nothing but woods. I tensed. "How much is it?" he asked. It took him a couple of minutes to dig through all his pockets, and he paid me in change, warm, moist fistfuls of it. Then he opened his door and disappeared into the woods.

I waited a few minutes and then climbed down from the cab. He had taken a well-packed trail. I hesitated a moment, then quietly followed it up. The guy was too drunk to be a threat, but I was worried about a watchdog. About a quarter-mile in, I could see a dark-colored pup-tent with what looked like a candle-lantern burning inside. The snow was well packed all around it, but no other environmental impact could be seen: with a warm sleeping bag and a place to shower, you could do it this way. It might be the only way to hold a menial job in Aspen and get ahead.

This was the message, also, of a hitchhiker I picked up in Basalt one evening. Mac, until his recent firing, had worked as a musher at the game restaurant and dog kennel known as Krabloonik. His main duties were helping in the care of the two to three hundred huskies kept there and taking tourists out on dogsled tours near the Snowmass ski area. He had come to Aspen to ski but had done hardly any because of the long hours he had to work. "The days of the ski bum," Mac informed me, "are over." The pay wasn't any reflection of what Aspen now cost, and to actually *save* any money (after making monthly payments on his car loan) he realized he would have to reduce his fixed costs. Cutting out the Krabloonik bunkhouse fee was the most feasible place to start.

He had built a shelter in the woods. He was bound for there at the moment to pick up his last belongings. If I wanted to turn in at Snowmass and take him up to Krabloonik, he would show it to me. It seemed a fair deal, and soon we were walking a long wooden staircase down the mountain to the kennels, past the little white furballs that were puppies sleeping in the snow. He approached the grid of doghouses, each with an excited, barking, half-wild animal chained to the front of it. They were mostly either "freighters" or "racers," he told me, Ford trucks or Ferraris, and the mushers referred to them by name, as "who" ("Who are we harnessing up today?"), not "which." The dogs seemed frantic for his attention, and he spent several minutes rubbing each of his favorites, talking to them, introducing me. Then, tearing himself away, he cut across a frozen stream and onto a path across the snow—this was the way to his place. In ten minutes we were there—an old green army tent set up in a small clearing amidst the pines. Nearby was a crude lean-to, insulated with plastic sheeting and what looked like pieces of a woolen sleeping bag. A triangle of blanket formed the front door. It was his pantry and storeroom, Mac explained.

"Built it in the spring," he told me, getting wistful. Life had been better, then—a steady girlfriend, good relations with his boss, days full of the dogs he loved. "Dogsledding is a great art," he said. There wasn't much left in the lean-to: thermal socks, an Instamatic camera and several snapshots of sunsets over Mount Daly that he took while on his sled trips, liquid soap, utensils, water jugs, a leather leash. And his skis, so underutilized the past few months. Yes, Mac confirmed, he was on Forest Service land, illegally. They could fine him if they caught him. But it wouldn't be fair if they did: The ski areas were on forest land, too, after all, and it was just a matter of the big guy getting favored treatment over the little guy.

We ate dinner in Snowmass. He was thinking of leaving Aspen for a smaller town, something many disenchanted locals talked about. "The order of things is pretty set here—either you have or you have not," he observed. "Once you start having huge hotels— like the Ritz—there's not a lot of room for the little guy." The presence of big money was "polluting," he thought, the boomtown atmosphere attractive to "people who don't believe in anything but money." The female situation looked similarly bleak. "There are basically three kinds of women here," Mac opined, "tourists, married, and coke whores. You're lucky if you can find one who's not one of those."

Drugs and drinking were, to Mac, the final disincentive. Growing up in Missouri, he said, "all the wine I used to drink had animals or automobiles on the bottle." But in Aspen, you entered a different realm. Unfinished bottles of imported wines from the Krabloonik restaurant, parties with premium beers that mushers staged with money from their party fund (anybody who committed a mushing mistake, like tipping the sled, had to make a contribution)—there was always something good to drink and, after six days on the job dawn-to-dusk, always a pretty good reason to drink it. Like many people, Mac said, he had gotten to a point of drinking too much, and his only consolation was that he hadn't gotten caught up in cocaine. "It's so expensive, and it's gone in a heartbeat." To get it, people "skimp on food, clothing, morals . . ."

The drinking, I predicted, was going to be the reason he was fired. But not according to Mac. He said he had been fired because, returning to "Krab's" late one night, especially hungry, he had snuck into the restaurant building, past the watchful eyes of its many Sergeant Preston & King portraits, and into the walk-in refrigerator to take some meat for a snack. The suspicious owner, wary of late-night losses, had caught him and fired Mac on the spot.

Who could tell if that was the whole story? It didn't really matter. I drove Mac and his skis down to Highway 82 and left him under a streetlight. He would hitch a ride back downvalley to an apartment in Basalt, to the couch where he was crashing in his sister's living room—everyone's lodging of last resort.

A friend on Red Mountain had a falling out with his wife; she took their children and went to Texas to stay with her parents, indefinitely. Allen was very lonely, he had a huge house, and he asked if I would like to stay there for a while. The timing was perfect, things with Johanna being strained and my A-Frame yet undiscovered, so with my car full of belongings, I moved onto Red Mountain.

An aspiring writer I'd met at the conference, Allen was a retired insurance company owner and a wealthy man. I remembered the first time I'd tried to find his place: I followed directions to a cul-de-sac, where Allen had said his was the only house. But there were three houses. "Guess I goofed," I apologized to my companion, and began to turn around the car.

"Wait. Stop," she said. "I think it's all of them." And indeed it was, we soon discovered, an entire compound: main house, four-car garage with home office above, and rec room/cabana building overlooking the pool with caretaker's apartment attached.

It was hard to count the exact number of bedrooms in his house—there were at least seven, maybe eight; it got complicated when you considered whether to count the darkroom, the exercise room, the pool-changing room, the caretaker's apartment, and the big bedroom downstairs that a sliding door could make into two bedrooms. But at least seven. To run the place, Allen employed a caretaker, a nanny, a housekeeper, a secretary, and a cook, at an annual expense of over $100,000.

But the point is none of these. The point is, it was the best-made place I had ever lived in. Not just the biggest—and at 13,000 square feet, it was certainly that—but the most carefully crafted. The driveway gates, of corroding green copper, had been brought in from an old estate in California. The massive front doors were hardcovered oak; it took the full weight of your body to push one open. A few more steps and you were inside the domed foyer, surrounded by a skylight-lit garden (tended twice weekly by an indoor floral service). Many of the furnishings and decorations of the house, constructed in the early 1960s, had become outdated, but the basic stuff was timeless: All the doors had forged, stamped hinges and heavy brass latch hardware; the moldings were hardwood; the countertops stone or tile; the parquet floors beautifully fitted; the toilets an advanced sort of wall-mounted model that did not touch the floor. From the wall of stained glass taken from a church to the ironwork of the railings that went up the front stairs, everything was custom-made. It was as though everyone involved in its making, from the architect to the lumber supplier, had rejected the materials used in construction of an ordinary house and demanded finer.

Allen was fond of saying that he lived in a halfway house. In a way it was true: Of the five members of his domestic staff, three were recovering from cocaine or alcohol addiction. They were mostly my age, and I was slow to think of them as my servants. The first morning, when the cook—a jolly Swede—knocked on my door and asked if she could bring me breakfast, I sputtered, Certainly, if she wanted to. The housekeeper, a woman my age whom I would have considered my social equal, stopped and asked if she had cleaned my room properly and whether there was anything else I needed. "You don't have to make your bed every day," she reminded me, and it was the last day I did.

Evenings, after the cook had served dessert, cleaned up the kitchen, and disappeared, were the only times Allen and I really got to talk. It was my friend's habit, after dinner, to carry a digestive down to the outside pool, which had a tiled hot tub attached, relax in the bubbles, and talk about books before going to bed. One springtime night it was snowing, but that did not deter him. "Wear this," he said, handing me a Broncos cap. "It'll keep your hair from freezing." He switched on the series of outdoor lamps that lit the steps down to the pool, and wearing only robes and Sorels, delicately balancing our drinks, we descended.

The pool and tub overlooked the lights of Aspen; when the flurries let up, we could see these, and watch the headbeams of the SnoCats above the town, on the side of Aspen Mountain—at about our same elevation across the valley. My friend told me how, over the years, he had expanded the house to fit his growing income and growing family. The pool was once parking spaces, he explained, and the rec room building, at its end, a garage and apartment. Though the house itself was very expensive, one great expense had been the foundation engineering necessary to set the house solidly into the side of the mountain—that alone, over the years, had cost a couple hundred thousand dollars. But, Allen said, as an ongoing project, it was all worth it: He loved Aspen, he loved his family, he loved the house.

But Allen and his wife did not reconcile. A year after that evening in the pool, he had moved to Montreal, and his wife and kids to a smaller house in Aspen. The divorce settlement provided for the sale of the big house.

So the house would go. Among the many casualties of the divorce were the stable lives of the servants, and in particular that of Jimmy, the caretaker. A gentle middle-aged man, Jimmy was divorced and spent all his extra time visiting his young son downvalley. Jimmy had had a good life as caretaker: an apartment, rent free, in a beautiful area, use of a car, and a small salary. It was doubtful that he could find anything similar, and I worried about him, being dropped back into the real world. I covered for him for a few days, watering plants and feeding the three aging Doberman pinschers, so that he and his son could take a long-needed vacation.

When Jimmy came back, the house was on the market and the real estate agent was throwing an open house for other real estate agents. Tea cakes were served in the library. I passed through with Jimmy, who was nervous but thought he should put in an appearance. As I chatted with an agent I knew, I heard Jimmy pointing out the workmanship, the systems, showing them all how well it was built, explaining how long he'd taken care of it—maybe they'd put in a good word with the new owner, I knew he was thinking. Meanwhile, the agent told me the property was on sale for $3.5 million and remarked offhandedly that it was "a lot of money for a teardown."

It took me a second. "What?"

"Oh. Definitely. The lot itself is worth about two and a half, and since they won't get more than three for the whole package, it only makes sense. The new owner will want a house he really likes."

"Oh," I said. It didn't make sense to me. An image came to mind from *The Grapes of Wrath,* the scene where the growers, in front of a crowd of hungry people, pour gasoline on a huge pile of oranges and destroy them in order to keep the price high. In an era of widespread and growing homelessness, how could you destroy a perfectly good house?

Jimmy was going on about the house. I wanted to feel this wasn't just a *fait accompli,* wanted to remind the realtors it wasn't done till it was done. Maybe the house would take a long time to sell, maybe the market would be weaker when it did, and demolition would look more nonsensical. But when we walked outside, I knew I had to mention it to Jimmy.

"What?" he said, looking sharply at me. Then, "No way. I mean, come on. Three acres of scrub oak, for that kind of money? I know a guy near Glenwood, picked up thirty-five hundred acres and an eight-bedroom ranch house for *half* of that."

"Yeah, well, that's probably what I'd do, too."

We walked the dogs, letting them off the leash when we got to a dirt road, Jimmy deep in thought the whole time.

"Well, now it makes sense why they kept saying, 'Nice lot, nice lot,'" he said of the realtors. Five minutes later, glancing at the house from across the hill, he said, "But tear it down?" And ten minutes later, when we returned to the house: "Well, I never thought I'd lose my job *that* way."

Later that summer, with the house on the market, Allen and his wife left on separate trips and offered me the use of the house again for a couple of weeks. I had just started seeing Margot, a magazine editor from New York who was spending some time in Aspen, and together we moved in. The cavernous master bedroom, the master bath with its skylights and bidet, the views over the entire valley—it all was unspeakably romantic. Because it belonged to my friend and because he actually lived there, the house seemed free of the moral taint I had associated with the large vacation houses Rebecca showed me. I came to envy Allen's material success (if not his failed marriage), and wondered if, someday, I might ever come to own such an aerie myself.

Coming home from errands one Sunday morning, I came up the driveway and saw Renata, the housekeeper, waxing her Subaru. It was an old car, already dented here and there, but she explained to me that if it wasn't waxed regularly, the finish would deteriorate and the car would lose value. This was an idea I had grown up with, but given my new life and our surroundings, it seemed hopelessly quaint and middle class. I noticed, though, that my car looked filthy next to hers. The smell of car wax made me nostalgic for high school; inspired by her industry, I decided to wash mine, too, and we got to talking.

A sunny, short woman with dark eyes and brown hair, Renata had grown up downvalley. Her parents were German immigrants who still worked in Glenwood Springs as draftsman and nurse. A few months earlier, following graduation from high school, she moved to Aspen, where the jobs were better paying. Soon, she landed "the most interesting job I ever had," as housekeeper for the Fields, Ted and Susie, he the heir to the Marshall Field's department-store fortune and a Hollywood producer. It was the spring of 1988, and Field had just spent $16.3 million, plus his $5.1 million New York City penthouse for the Hemmeter house, a palace on the slopes of Aspen Mountain. It was a record price for a single family home in the United States.

My reporter colleague Jane Wilson had toured the house when hotel magnate Christopher Hemmeter put it on the market the previous fall. It had sixteen televisions, I remembered her telling me, including one in the sauna; they could be centrally controlled, to show the same thing. It had indoor and outdoor elevators, eight bedrooms, nine and a half baths, and 4,700 feet of deck space. Its sale to Field was a turn-key deal: it included all the furniture, rugs, and art, two Jeeps and two Wagoneers, and two nearby condos where Hemmeter's pilots had stayed.

But Renata wasn't wide-eyed like Jane. Handing me the hose, she went on for forty-five minutes about the house, like a sort of war veteran. She had seen it all. First she mentioned the little roll-up towelettes she had to keep the bathroom stocked with. They were washable, but the Fields "used 'em once, and threw 'em away." Also in the trash she would regularly find new women's underwear, and she and the other domestics got in the habit of sorting through the garbage before setting it out.

She knew the house was worth $21 million but had heard Field himself was worth billions. "I mean, he's so rich, he could give a million bucks to sixty different people and it wouldn't even faze him." I checked: Though the *Forbes 400* listed his wealth at only around $600 million, I supposed he still had the ability to give away $60 million. Though it would probably faze him a little.

Work there was sporadic, because the Fields had houses in three other places and were in Aspen only occasionally. When they arrived, along with them came a valet, a secretary, a nanny and, thought Renata, several bodyguards. Mrs. Field, who was only slightly older than Renata but lived in another universe, seemed to intrigue her especially; Renata told me how for months until she met her she would stare at the pictures of her around the house—"I thought she looked like a vamp," she concluded. When finally she saw Susie Field in real life, Renata felt her conclusion was right, though it remained tentative, due to Renata's awe of the lady of the house and the specific prohibition, delivered by the head maid, on speaking to a member of the family unless spoken to first. Susie Field apparently had never had the occasion to directly ask Renata anything at all.

Susie's secretary had, though, and instructed Renata to clean up the bathroom and shower every time Susie used it, "which could be up to three times a day. And she'd get really mad if I didn't do it right away.

"They gave a party the Fourth of July and spent two thousand dollars on just the invitations!" Renata continued. And they had rented condos all over town—suites in the Gant, etc.—for all their guests who came in for it.

At this point, Helen, the nanny who worked for Allen, joined us in the parking area, leaning against the hood of Renata's Subaru. "The Fields' nanny made a fortune," Renata informed her.

"I'd start tomorrow," Helen replied. But Renata shook her head.

"It's not as great as you'd think," she said. Aspects of the job had left her nervewracked. Mostly, they stemmed from the value of things inside. Renata was informed the first day that she'd have to pay for anything she broke or damaged. She quickly became terrified of the idea of knocking over the Chinese knights on horses, the Ming vases. Also, in every room there was a camera, part of the security system. Supposedly, it was only in operation when the family was there, said Renata, but who knew for sure? It was said that photos had been taken of every room, which were periodically compared with the actual way the room looked. Once when Renata inadvertently moved some items from their customary place, she was "called onto the carpet" until it was all resolved.

Renata thought her worst fears had been realized when she picked up a bottle of potpourri oil she had set down briefly on a marble nightstand. To her horror, the porous marble had soaked up a ring of the fluid, leaving a stain that couldn't be removed. Appreciating that the mistake was caused not by clumsiness but by ignorance, the supervisor had let her off on that one. But it was the sort of thing that made her dread the days she worked there. Another was the locked-in feeling: Because of the many expensive paintings, the windows stayed closed, and temperature and humidity were carefully controlled. "God, when I used to get out of there, I'd just run!" Renata exclaimed.

The house's exotica fascinated her still. She told us about a suede carpet—"yes, a leather carpet"—in one room, and of the way each of the eight bedrooms had its own wall safe or walk-in vault. Since the house was so well secured against the outside world, Renata figured these were either to protect the guests from each other, or from her.

Finally, she recalled the suede banquettes of the outside elevator, but the memory seemed to put her in a trance. "Helen, that's the dream I was going to tell you about," she said, putting down her polishing rag. "I was in the elevator."

Because the house was perched on the edge of a ski slope, the main entrance most of the year was several stories down, where you would park and enter via the outside elevator. The elevator, encased in a wooden tower that was a well-known structure around town, rose the equivalent of about four stories, where an enclosed "sky-bridge" connected it to the house. Though the house's architecture was contemporary, this singular tower evoked castles, Rapunzel, the Middle Ages.

"I was going up in that elevator, sitting on those suede seats, and *she* was in there with me," said Renata. "I was so scared I was shaking. We were sitting on those benches, and the elevator was going up—it was taking forever—and then I opened my mouth," Renata paused, mouth open. She whispered, *"And I talked to her!"* The sound of the first words out of her mouth—they had had something to do with fruit—had so shocked her that she had woken up.

I took in this story greedily: Who didn't appreciate frightening tales of the superrich? But even as I felt empathy for Renata, I knew the world had grown more complicated in the several months since I had first climbed into the cab. I too was now a resident of a mansion on the hillside. I was glad Renata was telling me this story, because it showed that even though I was living in another palatial home, she didn't consider me one of *them*. At the same time, I couldn't help wondering whether some deed of mine or Allen's wouldn't someday be fodder for a housekeeper's tale. ("He never made his bed; he'd ask for breakfast at 11:30 A.M.; he was always on the phone . . .") And I harbored an inexplicable grain of sympathy for the Fields, who could purchase the labor of anyone they wished but still couldn't buy their loyalty.

. . .

Chrissie had first glimpsed the meadow through trees on a hike soon after she moved to Aspen, in 1967. Instead of finishing the hike she had found herself just sitting there, taking it in, until sunset. Afterward she returned again and again, showing it to friends, camping there overnight. It wasn't large—maybe four acres—but soon after the spring melt, it was traversed by a brook and spangled with Indian paintbrush, buttercups, and the occasional blue columbine. A couple of logs were good for sitting on. Though the trail was nearby and a dirt road passed perhaps a quarter-mile away, no one else ever seemed to intrude into this sanctuary.

Chrissie rented in town, but three years after seeing the meadow she located the owner, put together all her money, and bought the land. Maybe someday she would build, but for twenty years it was a small, impractical investment in the wilderness; she felt good just knowing it was there.

In the meantime she worked in a camping and sporting-goods store. When Peter, a fellow employee, suggested there might be a market in leading backcountry trips for the sort of camping neo-phytes they served in the store, Chrissie agreed and together they started a business. The successful firm branched into outfitting, Peter and Chrissie got married, and Aspen grew. Ambivalent about introducing people to the pristine wilderness, they resolved that if they could educate them, perhaps some of the wilderness would endure.

Their long-term dream, Chrissie explained to me one day soon after we met and were eating trail mix on a log in the meadow, was to build a small house there and raise their family on the land. She outlined the design of the cottage for me, and in our hiking boots we traced the drive that would lead to it from the dirt road.

An unexpectedly large inheritance meant they could begin to pursue the dream sooner than expected. Construction began during my second year in Aspen, but several more months passed before I happened back by the site. The modest home I had imagined there, following Chrissie's description, had swelled into something of epic scale. The place was still unfinished, but Chrissie and Peter led me through the four bedrooms, darkroom area, nanny's apartment, guest cottage, and garage. A stable was being contemplated by the brook, Peter explained, as I wondered what sort of large machine had run over its banks.

Chrissie, during all this, would not meet my eyes. Later when I pressed, she explained how it all had escalated: In twenty-three years the land had appreciated, to her astonishment, by a factor of more than fifty. By the time they were ready to draw up plans for a house, the land was worth more than half a million dollars. "We had to build a big house—that or waste the land," she explained. She meant that to spend money on anything less than a mansion would be to construct, in effect, a spanking-new teardown.

I looked around. A grader was parked on the splintered remains of what might have been one of our lunch logs. A cigarette package lay nearby; on past visits, we would have picked it up. The problem with paradise, as my waitress friend Lanette once mused to me, is that you bring yourself to it.

It was almost the last of the Aspen A-frames. It may also have been the first of the Aspen A-frames.

The place in Aspen where I hung my hat the longest was an aging, forgotten house at the foot of Red Mountain, just above the art museum, where I lived for nearly a year. Named for its shape when viewed head-on, the A-frame had a front door of sliding glass; you stepped through it and directly into the living room, beyond which were the kitchen and bathroom. Upstairs were two bedrooms. Aspen once had several of these staples of American snow-country architecture, but most were torn down to make room for larger, sturdier houses. There were two modified, expanded A-frames left around town, but I found only one other that was "pure."

Though it was on a well-traveled street and they passed by frequently, nobody could ever remember having seen my house. This had probably helped in the long run: The house, through benign neglect, had only improved. In an area of paved driveways, it had a strip of rutted dirt. Amidst the sprinkler systems and landscaping of my neighbors, my house boasted native vegetation: sagebrush and tumbleweeds. The outside light was a meager yellow bulb, such as might be found outside a fisherman's bungalow. A rusty horseshoe hung over the front door. The key was hidden in the woodpile.

Located on a capacious corner acre of prime real estate, my A-frame, by all rights, should have been bulldozed and replaced years before. It was a living anachronism. But my landlords were two old Denver families that had bought it from three bachelors who built it in the fifties, and they planned to keep it indefinitely—not, I got the sense, through any abiding love of the antique, the funky, the soulful, not as any statement of rebellion against the status quo, but more through the power of inertia. They had it, and they would continue to have it. They'd sell it when they needed to, and the profit was guaranteed: They'd bought the place for $14,000, and the land above had appreciated to about $800,000. In the meantime, they rented it all year long, and except for high season, a few weeks on either side of Christmas, it was mine.

I became the house's umpteenth tenant when one of the owners, a woman who knew me from my childhood street, walked into the *Times* one day to place a rental ad.

"Why, it's Teddy Conover!" I heard a voice say. She was a Denver landlady of some repute, savvy in that market but less so in Aspen's; she was preparing to rent the two-bedroom house for the unheard-of sum of $600 a month.

The house had, as they say, character. Outside, it was stained green, with a green tarpaper roof. Four wooden panels above the front door, once an eye-catching orange, yellow, green, and red, had faded and chipped as a result of their southern exposure. Some loose component of the tubular metal fireplace chimney banged in the wind.

The decor was early ski house: indoor-outdoor carpet, a ski rack against one wall, dormitory-style furniture, framed posters hung against wood-veneer paneling. It had been updated in the seventies with cheap track lighting and rheostats, but otherwise it was intact. The kitchen in particular was an original: Separated from the rest of the living room by a curving bar finished in ruby-red Formica and ringed with bar stools, it sported, in matching yellow enamel, a decrepit Whirlpool dishwasher, metal cabinets and, best, an antique refrigerator built in above the counters as a faux-cabinet. The refrigerator, alas, was a decorating idea whose time had come and gone; its everyday operation was to freeze or melt everything; it could not be repaired (though servicemen charged you for trying). A baking pan sat permanently stationed beneath the dishwasher, to capture the overflow from the rinse cycle. A stereo so old it had to warm up came with the place, as did a dial phone; labels on the stereo directed the guest to frequencies for radio stations that no longer existed. A game cabinet contained a twenty-year-old board game, modeled on Monopoly, called Aspen, in which every space was a business—but only five or six of these still existed. A fifteen-year-old phone book contained similar revelations about the transiency of Aspen's commercial sector: Gone were ten of the first dozen restaurants listed in the Yellow Pages, all of the boutiques, and all of the gift shops.

The A-frame could sleep eight people, assuming only one per single bed. Five of these would be upstairs, which you arrived at by climbing a wobbly, splintered ladder. From an upstairs bed, the floors were so thin you could hear conversations in the living room beneath you as though nothing intervened. The forced-air heat did not make it upstairs; auxiliary electric floorboard units had been installed, which the landlady (because she would have to pay for it, through an arcane metering arrangement) implored me to use "only when absolutely necessary." I restricted my use to only most mornings and most nights.

Through the large front windows, there was a spectacular view of Aspen Mountain, Shadow Mountain, the lower valley—and of a large house under construction across the road. The "spec" house, which actually had been completed two years before, had been sold to an owner who wanted a complete rehab. It was undergoing renovations the entire time I was there. Fortunately, most of the house was located down a steep hill from me, out of sight, but its most persistent flaw sat in full sight. This was, namely, a sod roof, some architect's expensive New Age whimsy, which refused to stay green. Over the course of the spring, summer, and fall, I watched the brown, dead grass get replaced with new sod, receive a watering three times or so a day, slowly die, turn brown, and then get replaced once again—for a total of three times during my residency. In an act of desperation, the contractor installed a lawn-sprinkler system, halfway through, *on the roof.* Of course, the grass still died. All this spectacle I took as a vindication of my simple house. Even when three days of gale-force winds tore off a piece of my tarpaper roof and subjected my books to a drenching from the rain, the cure was simple: I went out, found the blown-off tarpaper a block away, and nailed it back on. Still, the roof saga was a small compensation for the irritation of heavy machinery starting at 7 A.M., workers' trucks blocking my driveway, the dust, the pounding, the semi-trailers—the gamut of problems familiar to anyone who has lived next to construction. Summer, regardless of what others may tell you, is above all truck season in a booming resort town.

I felt the contractor had gone too far when I awoke one morning to the sight of three men in white protective suits rooting through my sagebrush. It was like a scene from an aliens movie: They wore respirators and seemed to be taking soil samples. When they returned the next day with a big machine that drilled into the ground, I confronted them. They responded with a sheaf of literature—they were from the Environmental Protection Agency, it said, searching for heavy metals in the soil that could have been left from tailings at Stefan Albouy's Smuggler Mine, a short way up the hill from my house. Superfund legislation, if contamination was found, would pay for them to remove all the soil and replace it with good, uncontaminated soil.

My landlady phoned me a short while later to tell me the news: The soil around the house was contaminated, but she had declined the offer to dig up the entire lot and had settled, instead, on the plan to "stabilize" the "area of greatest exposure." They were going, in other words, to pave the driveway free. She sounded delighted, but I was not: If the developers didn't get you, the government would. The work had been scheduled, but not completed, when I moved out one snowy day in November, one step ahead of the "improvements."

A town of custom houses needs, of course, custom furniture. I was in the studio of a furniture designer to interview him for the *Times* and write a feature story on the custom tables, chairs, and cabinets he made. The assignment intrigued me: I imagined that if there was truly a privileged person in Aspen, it would be a craftsman or artist, someone with creative vision and the freedom, amidst a community of artists as well as collectors, to pursue it. But as we were sitting down to coffee in his little office, a client arrived unannounced, an important client. "Excuse me for a sec," he said, standing up to head her off in the studio adjacent. She bustled into the room before he could make the door.

"Imagine the surprise I just had!" she exulted, taking off her fur coat and sunglasses. He took the coat and put it on a hanger. "I opened my door, and there was Neil Simon!"

"Really?" The designer began to introduce me, but was interrupted by her excited chatter—Neil Simon had accepted a cup of decaf; Neil Simon was looking better lately. Several sentences later, we learned why Neil Simon didn't call first: He was there with a realtor, not by himself, to look at one of her houses, which was for sale.

"But we're keeping the townhouse," she explained, "renting it out till December, when we'll be back from New York." It so happened that the new renter was "a beautiful little girl" who was to be the next Charlie's Angel. The girl couldn't believe they'd rent it out with all the custom furniture, art, etc. The girl had said, "I always dreamed, if I could ever move to Aspen, about the place I'd get and how I'd furnish it. And this is it exactly!" In three minutes, I had learned the client was wealthy and socially well connected and had excellent taste.

Before the Angel moved in, though, Charlton Heston's son was staying there for a while, to work on a screenplay. "At the desk, right?" asked the artist.

"Yes, the cowboy desk!" she gushed again, turning to me but still not knowing who I was. "It was made by an inmate at the Cañon City prison," she explained. "It's very big, with wagon wheels, lassoes—"

"Carvings—" began the artist.

"Carvings everywhere!" she continued. "Hysterical, some of them, the little figures. It must have taken months or years. But I guess he did have some time on his hands!"

I thought of the prisoner, working to create something of beauty against the ugliness of life in the sad mountain prison. Would he have imagined this fate for his desk? It now functioned as a piece of superior kitsch.

The artist told her briefly about my travels with hoboes and illegal aliens. Now she noticed me again. "Did he say you were from New York?" she asked hopefully.

"No, I'm from Denver," I said.

"Oh."

But my books reminded her of something. A friend of hers was coming home and saw a guy's legs sticking out the window to her house. He ran away when the woman yelled, but was caught by police on the Hyman Avenue mall. The police evidently told her that a couple of recent burglaries could be traced to the Puerto Vallarta gang wars. "There are so many of them around this summer, have you noticed?"

At this point, I realized the guy was Mexican.

"Well, there's a very big demand for cheap labor," said the designer.

"No, they said it was the gang wars."

I said I'd never heard of the Puerto Vallarta gang wars, but couldn't imagine why they would propel criminals to Aspen.

But she meant Mexicans, more than criminals. Though the two seemed to be closely related in her taxonomy of lesser life.

I could hear the clock ticking in the artist's mind: To make it in Aspen he had to work hard, and he had a ton of stuff to do. But it was half an hour before she got around to the reason for her visit: her worry over the colors. She was having second thoughts—third, actually—about the colors she and the artist had chosen for her liquor cabinet. He put together some samples of painted wood for her in the studio, showed her how they looked together, and seemed glad when she decided they were fine.

She left. The designer breathed a sigh of relief. "I'm glad she liked them, because I already painted it," he confided. I didn't realize artisans had to cater to their clients to such an extent, I admitted. Only the very successful ones can truly call the shots, he explained: His partner recently constructed an art deco–style bed for a client in Snowmass. Just as it was installed, the client asked if he could do one little favor: rig the bed so it would wake her with the sounds of birds chirping. Somehow, he did. Ah, but there was one more thing—could he cover the ceiling above the bed with tiny fluorescent stars, in the shape of the constellations?

"Northern Hemisphere or Southern Hemisphere?" the artisan asked.

"Oh. Northern," said the client.

It was all in a day's work.

Was it science fiction or something out of the Arabian Nights? PRINCE BANDAR WILL BUILD PALACE, the headline read. The story in

The Aspen Times of July 13, 1989, went on to explain that "after one of the most bitter, divisive public hearings in recent history, county commissioners voted 3–2 Tuesday night to allow Saudi Arabian prince Bandar bin Sultan bin Abdel Aziz to build a 55,000-square-foot house in Starwood."

The hearing had been a lengthy, rancorous affair in the county courthouse, extending from 7:30 P.M. till after midnight. At stake was Prince Bandar's bid to build, on Star Mesa, next to Starwood, a vacation home just slightly smaller than the White House. The prince, who was the Saudi ambassador to the United States and a nephew of King Fahd, planned a pleasure dome of fifteen bathrooms and twenty-six bedrooms. The magnitude of this structure had taken the county off guard. Only four years before, after all, hotelier Christopher Hemmeter had startled everyone with his mega-manse, a structure of unsurpassed opulence, right on the slope. And the 21,000-square-foot Red Mountain house of Leslie Wexner, owner of The Limited stores, Henri Bendel, and Victoria's Secret (it was one third bigger than Hemmeter's)—that was the absolute limit, townspeople thought, absurdity defined. Bandar's planned vacation home was so much bigger than these two that it was beyond the reckoning of most people. There was a feeling in the air that this game of "king of the mountain" had gone too far, and people expected it would never pass the growth-sensitive board of county commissioners.

But as the final hearing showed, wealth can create its own constituency. Of the more than forty people who spoke at the meeting, most of those in favor, it was clear, stood to gain financially if the multimillion-dollar project proceeded. Already, Bandar had signed several of Aspen's leading real estate agents and lawyers to his team. His conspicuous consumption in town included such things as the rental of twelve Range Rovers during the previous Christmas season. One T-Lazy-7 cowboy, down from the ranch, testified that he had served a large catered meal and found that the prince promptly paid his bills. Builders said jobs depended on it and spoke of the need to keep their industry alive. "It's like with Wexner," one old-timer told me afterward. "Everybody in the valley had worked for him by the time he was done."

The prince had also been busy in the philanthropic realm. Aspen Mountain Rescue had received $60,000, which easily put it over its goal of $100,000 in a big fund drive. The Aspen Camp School for the Deaf had gotten $10,000. At the meeting, Bandar's main lawyer, an out-of-town guy wearing shorts and a polo shirt to the midsummer meeting, dropped another bombshell: In addition to the $250,-000 to the county for employee housing and energy-efficiency projects, money that had already been pledged, Bandar would, if his plans were approved, donate $500,000 to the county for a health-and-human-services facility at the hospital. This meant a gift total to the city of $820,000—in addition, his attorney pointed out, to $500,000 in taxes to the county the first year and $100,000 thereafter.

"It appalls me that they have to make what amounts to a bribe," objected Richie Cohen, a leading realtor. But Bandar's men weren't complaining; without any coaxing or explicit requirements, they had doubled the $250,000 they had pledged only two weeks before.

Of course, Bandar wasn't there himself, and neither were any of the wealthy individuals who owned land adjacent to his. Rather, they sent their lawyers. Occasionally, one of the landowners' lawyers would stand up and convey his client's support for Bandar. The more seemly among them spoke not of "property rights" but about the lower density represented by having Bandar's house, as opposed to several smaller ones, and of a resulting appreciation of property values. Even the representative of the Starwood owners' association gave that group's blessing, despite the estimated twenty-five hundred round trips of heavy trucks that would have to be made through Starwood in the two years of palace construction. I wondered about the legal fees being generated simply by all the lawyers having to sit through the five-hour hearing—certainly, it would be in the tens of thousands of dollars.

In the most disingenous note of the night, Dick Butera, realtor, developer, and co-owner of the Hotel Jerome, explained that the palace was good because it would benefit the little people: the children (through school taxes), the construction workers, and other wage earners, the charities.

Given Aspen's history of concern over growth, I felt sure the naysayers at the meeting would at least number as many as Bandar's supporters. But they were in retreat: Antigrowth leader Joe Edwards's suggestion that new houses be limited to 2,500–3,000 square feet was greeted with howls of laughter by those in the hearing room. And the mood in the room turned palpably sour when Paul, stepping from his objective role as reporter, offered his own public comment in the form of an original song:

> *Oh, I just want a little home upon the mountainside*
> *A place where I can get away, a place where I can hide*
> *I need a place to call my own, a haven and retreat*
> *A humble little homestead, 55,000 square feet.*
>
> *I have a rich old uncle, perhaps you know King Fahd*
> *We have peculiar customs that Westerners think odd*
> *It is ordained that boys and girls should never really mix*
> *And that is why my bathrooms must total 26.*
> ("No waiting," offered Paul in an aside.)

The audience responded with scanty applause and lots of glaring. "I ought to break that guitar over your head," one outraged realtor hissed at Paul on his way out of the courthouse.

The hearing was the first time I ever felt sure Aspen was in a steep decline, not because the house was approved, but because no one could even muster a laugh about something as unbelievable as Prince Bandar's palace.

The importance, of course, was all symbolic. Because of its location, no one would be able to see Bandar's house from their car; it was only visible from mountaintop or airplane. But it marked a vast change from the days, mostly in the early seventies, when Aspen had first developed an antigrowth consensus. Faced with subdivisions encroaching on pastureland and, in particular, the appearance of three large commercial/condominium structures too big and too ugly to blend in with Aspen's small-scale beauty, local government started passing an array of growth-control measures. Restrictions were placed on the teardown of existing structures. The height of all buildings was maintained at three stories. Buildings and areas were zoned to existing uses. Areas of the county were allotted annual increments of additional beds, which could not be exceeded, to keep growth in check. Signs (neon had been prohibited since the fifties) were further regulated by code. Approvals were required for a wide array of "improvements" and additions. A comprehensive growth-management plan was enacted to put the brakes on breakneck development. The politics were billed as progressive, though at its heart the movement was conservative: Those already there wanted to keep Aspen exactly the way it was.

"We have the power to make this community whatever we want it to be," said activist county commissioner Dwight Shellman, an est graduate. And indeed they did affect the community, preserving Aspen's pristine Victorian look and instilling an ethic of central planning, anathema to the frontier mentality of most Western towns.

But to the chagrin and amazement of the antigrowth activists, there was an unexpected result: Things looked the same, but they got much more expensive. Pitkin County, 80 percent of which was federally owned forest, didn't have a lot of room to grow in the first place: Aspen was sort of like Manhattan, a strictly delimited tract of land beyond the borders of which you could not build. The growth-control rules effectively decreased building opportunities even more. By the eighties, demand for Aspen land was so intense that locals, people who had lived in Aspen their whole lives, could find no place for their kids to move and in fact were being lured into selling by the insane prices their houses were commanding. An avalanche of money flowed into the town, and the town was helpless against its advance.

Of course, anyone living in one of the 99 percent of American small towns in decline during this period might not be inclined to sympathize. Most towns were dying a death of slow attrition as businesses moved out and young people failed to return. But in fact, Aspen's dislocation was not so different from the feelings sensed by people elsewhere as the last department store shut down, the last coffee shop became a 7-Eleven: This isn't still our town. It's not the place we knew. In Aspen you knew it because there was nowhere to buy underwear and socks. Finding a parking place became impossible. The old post office became an Esprit store, the Elks Lodge a Hard Rock Café, Crossroads Drug a Banana Republic.

Ironically, during many years of frenzied construction, parts of Aspen shared something else with other small towns—a sense of emptying out. This was because people who lived in town sold their houses to people who would not live in town—to people who came only on vacation. The result, it is now commonly acknowledged, was the death by abandonment of certain tony neighborhoods, such as the town's West End and Red Mountain, where by a common estimate over half the dwellings are not inhabited at any given time.

This semiabandonment, this conquest by absentee owners, was a condition of community for which no precedent existed in the area. In the boom-and-bust cycles so familiar in the West, towns either waxed or waned. The way Aspen was booming was new, and peculiar. People were rattled by the absentee castle-builders.

Teddy talked about this as he cut my hair one day. He had a house-sitting job on Red Mountain and thus benefitted from absentee ownership, but something still felt funny to him. "You know what I heard?" he asked me. "I heard Wexner flew over the foundation of his house after they poured it last week and decided from the plane that it wasn't in quite the right place. So he told them to move it a few feet." He shook his head as I held mine very still, wary of his scissors.

"Twenty-one thousand square feet, right?" I said.

"Twenty-one thousand square feet," said Teddy. "I don't get it. I mean, am I missing something? What did he build it for? Not to use it—he won't be there more than two weeks a year. Why'd he build that thing?"

A month later, I heard two older, wealthier, and more sophisticated observers ask the very same question. Fritz Benedict, age seventy-four, the artichect of many Aspen's most tasteful houses, who had introduced me to Elizabeth Paepcke—an *eminence grise*— was having breakfast at the Wienerstube with me and his old friend Denver engineer Tom Cole, who owned a pricey unit in the Fifth Avenue condos near the slopes and had been coming for years. Fritz was telling about an acquaintance of his, an oilman from Midland, Texas, who was building an 8,000-square-foot house on Red Mountain. He already had, in addition, "one of the Ford houses" in Maine, a place on Cape Cod, and possibly others. Tom put down his fork. "Now, why is he doing that?" he demanded.

"It's an ego thing," Fritz concluded. "It's so he can show his friends. It's also so he can show the town. This is an 'in' place right now, and he wants to have a presence here." They shook their gray heads and looked at their plates. Partly, this was a question of manners, of the differing values of old money and new. Partly, it was the perennial reaction of old-time Coloradans on seeing their lives once again influenced by big money from the coasts: The development of Colorado has almost always been a result of outsiders' designs. But what you could talk about were the practical things: "Can you imagine owning so many places, having to deal with all the things that can go wrong, all the personnel things?" Fritz asked. Tom countered that it wasn't really a hassle, that whatever went wrong, a person wealthy enough could "throw money at it," and make it go away. But the question remained: Why did they build them?

The key was: It was not about shelter. It was about money. You built them because you could build them. You built them because they gratified your sense of self-worth. You built them because, like having a beautiful wife, it was a way of telling the world you had made it.

Fritz was party to a celebrated dispute that arose from all the new building. He had sold a large parcel of land in Hunter Creek Valley, a scenic and nearby area popular with hikers, mountain bikers, and cross-country skiers, to a Florida businessman, who constructed an immense edifice practically astride one of the two trails used by locals for years to gain access to the valley. The businessman, Tom McCloskey, declared the trail to be on his property and closed it. Protests from locals were loud and angry, with a group called Friends of Hunter Creek filing suit against McCloskey and McCloskey filing suit against the county. Some people blamed Fritz for not having foreseen the conflict and taken steps to provide an easement for the trail. ("I should've thought of it," he told me. "I'd do it differently now.")

But the same phenomenon was occurring everywhere. Within a few months, one old-time landowner declared that too many cross-country skiers were disrupting his peace and closed the popular Owl Creek/Government trail between Aspen and Snowmass; another claimed all the naked hippies in the natural hot springs near his house offended him, and filled it with boulders; and the protest against another trail closure, on Shadow Mountain, resulted in the arrest of Aspen's chairman of the planning and zoning commission. This was a flashpoint of anger between locals and the new landowning class; its reductio ad absurdum was contemplated on the bathroom walls of *The Aspen Times*:

MCCLOSKEY BUYS HOUSE ON MAROON CREEK. SEZ ACCESS TO THE BELLS QUESTIONABLE.

MCCLOSKEY BUYS HOUSE ON HWY 82, SEZ ACCESS TO ASPEN QUESTIONABLE.

I picked up a hitchhiker one day, Steve, a Snowmass property manager. His job was to look after the houses of absentee owners, of which there were scores around Snowmass. Most of them, he said, were empty forty-five weeks of the year. Yet they had to stay heated so the pipes wouldn't freeze; and their swimming pools, as a rule, were heated continuously—not drained—so they'd be ready for use when the owners arrived. "In fact, there's one pool," he told me, grinning, "that I've never seen anybody in . . . except me."

I envied Steve. And yet, I wondered, how was it possible? I had been in Amsterdam, where not only did empty buildings have to be securely sealed against break-ins by squatters desperate for a place to live, there was a legal mechanism by which the squatters could gain the right to stay if they had lived there for a given amount of time. Dutch society saw housing as something scarce and precious, and subject not just to the property rights of the owner but to the interests of the commonwealth. In any third world country, houses as nice as those in Aspen would be surrounded by fences and guarded by dogs. Aspen had a tremendous housing shortage, and yet break-ins at secluded vacation homes were relatively rare: Workers would first live in the woods or out of their cars. Rather than feel a right to something a rich man had built, most of Aspen's working class aspired only to be rich enough to own such a thing themselves.

A left-leaning poet friend of mine from out of town saw the county's approval of Bandar's house as a fatal error on the part of the Aspen establishment. "It's a time bomb," she predicted, a grotesque symbol of overindulgence and the concentration of wealth in the hands of a few. "That place is going to become a rallying point for the have-nots."

It was an intriguing thought—often I had mused whether the next revolution would be started by resort-town workers, those who toiled double shifts on minimum wage in order to serve strangers many, many times richer than themselves, and lived as outsiders in towns owned by the absentee wealthy. But though it might have been just, it didn't seem likely.

A more persuasive vision of the future was offered to me by the eccentric old miner named Ed Smart. Smart was a curious man who believed that Aspen's original wealth—mining—would also be its future wealth and who had spent much of his life accumulating mining claims in the valley. Perhaps, like many miners, he believed that the only true wealth was tangible, something you could hold in your hand—silver, say, or gold. Aspen's wealth, the wealth of hype, being intangible, was illusory, and "someday soon it will end, the great slot machine of the mountain will come crashing down," he predicted, shaking a finger at me.

There seemed to me a chance of that. Boom and bust has been the history of the West, and Aspen's first life, and death, offer a cautionary lesson to the present: The rug can be pulled out, they say. A thoughtful person can't imagine something this trendy without imagining its absence. How Aspen might fade, nobody could know—maybe skiing would fall out of vogue. Maybe some technological advance would change the picture, the way transportation improvements spelled doom for the old resorts of the Catskills and opened up recreation in Vermont and the Caribbean. More likely, maybe another fashionable spot would eclipse Aspen as the landing place of the rich and famous.

Sometimes I would think about this. Who, then, would heat the scattered pleasure domes? What would become of the swimming pools? I could imagine in Aspen a version of the formerly splendid neighborhoods where I had lived in Dallas and Denver, enclaves full of mansions that were surrounded by poverty, exclusive areas fallen on hard times, mega-homes divided into many little apartments for a greater number of poorer people. I remembered lying in my bed in one such apartment, looking at the elaborate dentil work along the ceiling, the marble fireplace, the old pedestal sink that had once been part of a different architectural and social configuration. What was it like then? I wondered. Who were the people who lived here? How many rooms did each of them have? Will the Hemmeter mansion have its working-class inheritors, grandchildren of Renata, who will think the same thoughts? Will they stop to wonder at the wall safes in their little living rooms? Will the fragments of suede carpeting recall for them the days of past glory? Will they see the splintered redwood decks and wonder, in the way you can't help but wonder when seated in the Wheeler Opera House or looking out through the window frames of an abandoned miner's cabin, Who was it that preceded me here?

Chapter IX

Nothing Gold Can Stay

Nature's first green is gold,
Her hardest hue to hold.
Her early leaf's a flower;
But only so an hour.
Then leaf subsides to leaf.
So Eden sank to grief,
So dawn goes down to day.
Nothing gold can stay.

—ROBERT FROST

One of the strange ironies of Aspen is that even among those who continue to love the town, there is a constant discussion of when Aspen began to go downhill and whether it now is ruined. This discussion usually takes as a narrative model the Book of Genesis, with Paradise created fresh in the late forties and fifties and Innocence lost gradually ever since. Walter and Elizabeth Paepcke are like Adam and Eve, the first in the Garden, and greedheads from the outside world play the Serpent. It is a battle of good and evil for the soul of Aspen.

When Aspen began to "delaminate," to borrow a ski-shop phrase, is a matter of considerable interest to the Aspen-identified. Among the decisive blows recalled by pre-sixties Aspenites are the paving of Independence Pass, on Aspen's Denver side, which allowed for easier access (Tom Sardy); the legalization of condominium ownership, which cleared the way for more buildings and more people (Bil Dunaway); and the death of Walter Paepcke and departure of the Aspen Institute (Elizabeth Paepcke). Death knells tolled by sixties people include the paving and guttering of downtown streets around 1965; the installation of the first traffic light in 1973 (there now are five); and the opening of a Kentucky Fried Chicken restaurant the same year. More recent proclamations of the End of Aspen include the gutting and renovation of the Hotel Jerome in 1985; the construction of the Silver Queen gondola (which made it possible to get to the top of Ajax in one ride) in 1986; the construction of the Ritz Carlton Hotel (which is big enough to open Aspen to convention business and further obliterate the traditional off-season) in 1988–92; and the arrival of many Hispanic workers, especially Mexicans, to fill the quickly expanding market for unskilled labor, beginning in the mid-eighties.

Though Aspenites don't like to mention it, the murder-by-car-bomb of drug dealer Steven Grabow in 1985 also seems significant. In a town of celebrated murders (ski racer Spider Sabich, by singer Claudine Longet; abusive heir Michael Hernstadt, by Keith Porter; proprietor of Dr. Feelgood's Head Shop, with an M-14), it stands out by signaling the ways in which Aspen's self-perceived innocence was a thing of the past.

Dark-haired, olive-skinned, and handsome, Grabow was a ski instructor once featured on the cover of the local phone book. Selling drugs was a faster route to prominence, however. Widely known as a cocaine dealer, he was ostentatious with his wealth, owning several cars, a condo, and a house on Red Mountain; my father once entered a shop where Grabow had just bought several Rolex watches. A federal grand jury indictment placed him in the awkward position every indicted dealer knows: Associates wondered whether he might trade knowledge of co-conspirators for a lesser charge. Apparently, someone powerful thought it likely. One day after indoor tennis at the Aspen Club, Grabow climbed into a borrowed Jeep (his own had been seized), turned the key in the ignition, and was gravely wounded by a bomb that had been placed under the seat. He crawled a fair distance across the parking lot before expiring, his blood staining the white snow. "Whoever put that there," said an investigator at the time, "knew exactly what he was doing." The murder suggested that Aspenites weren't immune to outside evils, that there could be horrifying consequences to actions that were locally condoned.

A more gradual death might be said to have been suffered by something known as the Aspen Idea. With the apparent hope that it might revive the high-minded legacy of the Paepcke era and help Aspen rediscover its purpose, the editor of boosterish *Aspen Magazine* asked me to write an article entitled "Whatever Happened to the Aspen Idea?" The idea, as originally articulated by Walter Paepcke, was essentially his vision for Aspen, a plan "for man's complete life . . . where he can profit by healthy physical recreation, with facilities at hand for his enjoyment of art, music, and education." Moving around town in the summer of 1988, however, you didn't seem to meet many people who were spending much time thinking about things like education, or who had even heard of the Aspen Idea. My search into its fate led down an interesting path.

The phrase Aspen Idea had been adopted by the Aspen Institute, Paepcke's brainchild, as its own. In fact the institute hired a University of Chicago professor, Sidney Hyman, to write a book by that title, *The Aspen Idea*, which traced the history and growth of the institute. The institute and the town parted ways in anger, however, after the antigrowth city council vetoed the institute's plan to build a large hotel on its Aspen Meadows land. With a few parting shots ("Trying to run something of a serious nature in a town that is dedicated only to fun is probably one of our permanent problems," said chairman Robert O. Anderson. "Imagine trying to run a great university in Las Vegas."), it moved its headquarters to Maryland, retaining only a token presence in the town of its birth. As Sidney Hyman explained to me, "The Aspen Idea is a portable idea. It can be done anywhere. You're really looking not for the sybaritic life but the good life. The good life is contemplative."

Townspeople, though resigned to the exit of the institute, were not so willing to part with the Idea. Hearkening back to Paepcke's view, *The Aspen Times* in 1979 called it "the very foundation upon which present-day Aspen is built." Mayor Bill Stirling told me, "It's not an amenity, it's at the very soul of the town. It's the focus, the nexus, for what I think sets Aspen apart and gives it, fundamentally, its unique flavor." And Sears Roebuck heir Edgar Stern, chairman of the powerful Aspen Valley Improvement Association, said the Aspen Idea is a term "used to identify the unique and idealistic yet practical and realistic character of life achieved in the Aspen valley."

As Aspenites redefined the Idea, it appeared to have less to do with thinking and more to do with, as Edgar Stern put it, the "character of life achieved in the Aspen valley." To Stern and others, the Aspen Idea couldn't have unfolded anywhere else—only in Aspen. And it didn't have much to do with education. To them, the Aspen Idea concerned life-style.

Life-style is a much-hated word. It connotes things like light beer, living room sets, and split-level houses—not *life* but consumer choices, the superficial trappings of life. It's an empty portmanteau, a TV word (". . . of the rich and famous").

And yet in certain ways life-style is what the Aspen Idea, and Aspen itself, has turned to. I first started thinking about life-style and Aspen when my "hair stylist" (Would Walter Paepcke have submitted to a "hair stylist?") told me he had left Brooklyn and come to Aspen in order "to start a whole new life-style." Didn't the phrase used to be "start a whole new life," I thought to myself? Would he have said, "In a previous life-style, I was a stockbroker?" Just as consumer culture has grown to the point where people increasingly define themselves through the things they buy, so have we come to define ourselves through the choices we make in the ways and places we live. A story from the in-flight magazine on board a United Express flight to Aspen featured a piece on "three couples [who] boldly leave Chicago in search of a new life-style in the Colorado Rockies." Since so few people were born in Aspen, and since the odds of getting rich there still are not great, people come to Aspen as an exercise of choice.

The result is that Aspen is less and less a community—a group of interdependent people who share in discussion, decision making, and moral sensibility—and more and more a life-style enclave. Their ways of appearing, consuming, and recreating make them different from people with other life-styles, but Aspenites are not especially interdependent, they have a fractious politics, and they come from everywhere. It's still a paradise, and it attracts many pilgrims, but the life-style paradise that is Aspen today has features Paepcke never could have imagined.

. . .

It's a common problem, but a vexing one: which restaurant? Paul and I can take an hour away from the *Times* for lunch, but where do we go? Lauretta's, we went to yesterday, In & Out, the day before, and Wednesday's special at Nature's Storehouse is one we don't like. I had dinner last night at Pour La France, Paul just went to Szechuan Garden, and if we get a burger at the Red Onion we'll be tempted to get a beer, which is a bad idea. Clark's Deli has nowhere to sit, the Aspen Mining Company will have a wait, Toro's went out of business, La Cocina is too much food, but the Cantina . . . well, that might do. Deciding took us only about five minutes, which is pretty good. Other decisions are harder.

Such as, which ski run? Gentleman's Ridge is supposed to be decent, but North Star and those others are all skied off, and do we want to have to go down those? Ruthie's? Ruthie's would be okay. For the thousandth time this year. Or we could do Bell Mountain, face of Bell, there might be some powder left. But why does it even have to be Ajax? How about Snowmass? I haven't been to Snowmass in a while. Snowmass has some good cruising, and we could wear our telemarks. That Elk Camp lift has good stuff off it. Buttermilk, if there was new snow—avoid the crowds. Highlands doesn't take the SkiCo pass, so forget Highlands.

Choices—choices make all the difference, and change has brought choices to Aspen. Which mountain bike, which trail, which party, which bar, where to dance, which of the sushi restaurants, which of Aspen's two morning dailies, which jacket, which skis to demo, which running shoes, *which?*

My friend Ted throws a barbecue party and I bring hamburger while Margot brings chicken; but when we get there we see that others have brought orange roughie, mahi-mahi, elk steaks, bratwurst, tofu patties, pork ribs, and a strip steak. If this weren't so funny we might feel embarrassed. My hamburger, I feel, represents the Ford Escort of the choices I could have made: standard, functional, boring. Having money gives you choices, and the choices carry a heavier symbolic weight. "In affluent societies," says Thorstein Veblen in *Theory of the Leisure Class,* "the economic struggle is substantially a race for reputability on the basis of . . . invidious comparison." This may be true when I'm the only one with hamburger. But for those with designer meats, what's going on here has less to do with one-upmanship than with making a personal statement, identifying yourself—expressing your *taste*. Style is everywhere in Aspen.

While I'm covering the Coors Classic cycle race, waiting for the pack to whoosh by on Galena Street, Claire sidles up to me and starts talking about the guys from the Aspen Cycling Club who are ogling the race from behind the ropes across the street. "Gear fetishists," she says, "like you see in Boulder."

"What do you mean?"

"You know—guys who spend all their money on equipment, who think the measure of a man is how many specialized types of athletic shoes he's got in his closet," she says, and more: "You can practically generalize about them. They're forty-year-old guys who leave their wives and their girlfriends because they're *afraid of losing their life-style.*" I note a tone of malice; she explains she used to date one of them.

"What do you mean, their life-style?"

"Oh, you know—the time spent on exercise, the occasional fling, hanging out with the guys every Thursday evening, the whole thing. They freak out when they think of losing it."

Imagine, I think, a life-style so precious . . . the town is jealously cultivating a separate set of values about what's important in life. It's not, for the most part, about pursuing careers, raising kids, leaving your mark on the world. It's about riding with the guys on a beautiful Thursday evening.

Decisions.

It was a Sunday morning in spring, and the sheer white curtains billowed out with cool wind. I woke up to find Marciela already awake, chin on the pillow, staring ahead. I knew what she was thinking about; we had been talking about it.

Raised in Argentina, she had come to Aspen from college in Scotland and graduate work in Paris. Alluring, quick, and well-to-do, her waters ran deeper than those of most people you met in Aspen. She had lived with her family in Argentina until they emigrated and was now one of the few international people you meet who have an identifiable center about them. She had wanted excitement, but not necessarily of the passing kind.

After a while in Aspen she had found a boyfriend, but though they had been steady for three years, Marciela would not move in with him. Instead, she bought a condo in his building. He was well known, and through him, and then on her own merits, she became friends with a wide variety of interesting people. All was fine until, two months before, he had decided it was time to get married and have children. His insistence threw her into a tailspin of confusion, and in her struggle to figure things out she began a series of torrid affairs. She felt guilty and deliciously out of control. She wanted to get away and think. She liked me, and I liked her. I touched her arm. She turned over and stared at the ceiling.

"Ted," she said. "There are too many choices."

"What do you mean?"

"There are too many choices. You can do anything, meet anyone, go anywhere."

"I know."

"There are no rules. It is horrible. It is poison."

This was true in no arena more seductively and dangerously than relationships. There were scads of good-looking young people in Aspen. With so many to choose from, it seemed shortsighted to commit too irrevocably to one: Who knew when you'd meet someone who'd fit you just a little better? Would Joan suit me better than Maggie? Gina better than Ann? The incentive for working on a troubled relationship was also less: Why fix the old car when, for just a little pain, you can get a brand new one?

In New York I had met a friend of Marciela's. She was about to return to her native Scotland after a four-year stint in London, a time in Los Angeles, and a summer in Tuscany. Her greatest advantage and greatest problem were her beauty and love of adventure. She was appealing to, among others, very wealthy men. A French baron had flown her to the Greek isles; her villa in Italy had belonged to a count. She had once been to Aspen to visit Marciela, and ended up the date of a hot young screenwriter at Don Johnson's Christmas party. They had invited her back the year after, and she had gone. She asked me if I knew a hip book editor in New York; Marciela later whispered they'd had a fling. The three of us went out one night with another man, Richard, from Aspen, and dressed up, the women took New York by storm.

She had traveled a faster lane than Marciela and, a little bit sooner, had lost her way. She was going back home. Estranged from her family, she wanted to make up with them, remember who she was, have them help her remember who she was. Richard, from Aspen, wondered why she had regrets. "When the prince wants a kiss, kiss him," he said. Marciela objected that the goal of having kids and a family, leading a healthy life in a certain kind of community, rarely goes with the fast lane life. Richard shrugged.

In Aspen, we were far from our parents. Since almost nobody grew up there, nobody had parents around. That was part of the cruise-ship atmosphere: More than in a city, somehow, you sensed the joy of not having a bedtime. Of eating, drinking, doing exactly what you wanted. Of being naughty.

Though an overabundance of choices was Marciela's complaint, it was the threat of curtailed choices that had brought her to the edge of crisis. Not much limits your choices the way marriage does, except having kids, which often follows. It was one of those damnable choices that limit your other choices. Her boyfriend was turning up the pressure, trying to force a choice. Did she have to limit herself yet? Did she want to? Did she owe herself more fun before getting married, did she need to get it out of her system? Would there be another chance? Was making a limiting choice the best way to solve the problem of too many choices? Or were you better off to absent yourself from the land of boundless choice?

In Aspen, the sight of people grappling with choices, from where to eat to whom to sleep with to what to do with the rest of their lives, is a commonplace. Unless you've experienced it yourself, it's easy to dismiss Aspen's as a spoiled kid's dilemma: *Poo-o-o-or little rich kids, can't decide where to have dinner.*

But as Marciela got up and padded softly to the bathroom, I saw a friend who was trying to make the best possible life for herself. The path was fairly untrodden—her mother, certainly, had never walked there. Her friends who had stayed home, married immediately, and found spouses and careers had not walked there. Privilege had created a sort of frontier, an unexplored territory of how to spend your life. In a way I once would not have admitted, it took a kind of courage.

Despite the progressive politics that became a part of the fabric of Aspen during the sixties and seventies, in terms of local change, Aspen adopted the firmly conservative stance of beautiful places everywhere. With something as "good" as Aspen is or was, you don't want to risk change. What all the dates for the Death of Aspen have in common is a dislike of the results of having more people in paradise. Paradise, one might conclude, is inherently selfish.

I began to think along these lines one quiet afternoon when I paid a visit to my friend Karin. Karin had come to Aspen with her husband in the seventies, and one of the ways they supported themselves was through real estate speculation: He would buy a raggedy condo, she would fix it up, and they would resell it. With prices rising, they had made a tidy bundle, and the house where they lived, with its indoor pool and valley view, reflected it. Karin had since divorced her husband and moved on to other interests, including a strong one in the New Age. As we sat drinking coffee in front of a roaring fire, she told me she'd been reading *Black Elk Speaks* ("Being the Life Story of a Holy Man of the Oglala Sioux"), a book that I later found shelved in both the fiction and nonfiction sections of libraries. She was angered: The book described vividly how the Sioux and their traditional ways had been violated by the Wasichus, as they called white men. They were "dirty with lies and greed," said Black Elk, for "the yellow metal that they worship and that makes them crazy."

"All the new people who are ruining Aspen are exactly like the Wasichus," Karin declared. "They want nothing more than to make money, and their lives are based on money."

I suggested that anyone who wasn't already rich when they arrived had to make money some way—and hadn't she and her husband made a lot of money in Aspen?

"That's different!" she cried—they were fixing Aspen up, not destroying it. The Wasichus considered themselves to be builders, too, I countered, and like it or not, we were all Wasichus. In the big argument that followed, Karin and I resolved nothing, and parted with the friendship bruised.

In many ways, this is the history of America. Immigrants—and we are all immigrants, American Indians simply having arrived long before the others—who have made lives here have quickly, perennially forgotten that they too were once recent arrivals. To the more long established immigrant, the recent immigrant is not a newer version of himself but something else entirely: an interloper. In a place that considers itself paradise, interlopers mean change and pose a particular threat.

Aspen is certainly different now, but so is everything. When I was away from Denver at college, I would return home every Christmas to find a new skyscraper gracing downtown. It wasn't always pleasing, but I learned to accept it: I was growing, the city was growing. In America, and especially the West, you get used to this: Change is built-in, and without it things (American things, especially) lose their vitality. There are thousands of small towns across America where change occurs more slowly; most people appear to wish to leave these places. Resorts, apparently, have a limited shelf life—Acapulco and Atlantic City are overbuilt and ruined; the Catskills long ago lost their cachet. Aspen may be on the downside of the resort-town cycle. Then again, others are predicting a thriving future for small towns based around universities or upscale recreation, as cities deteriorate and fax machines, modems, and Federal Express make it possible for professionals to do business effectively from the middle of nowhere.

Originally called Ute City by white men (after the inhabitants who had to be chased away), the camp on the Roaring Fork was renamed Aspen by mining promoter B. Clark Wheeler. The quaking aspen, or *Populus tremuloides,* a member of the poplar family, is so called because of the way its pale green leaves tremble in the summer breeze. (The flattened stem of the leaf is perpendicular to the plane of the leaf surface, and the joint between them is very flexible.) It makes sense that the name Aspen did not occur to the first white settlers, because at the time there were probably few aspen around: The aspen is a successional tree, which rapidly invades sites from which other trees have been removed. Early miners, needing wood for mines, houses, and railroad ties, denuded many of the mountains around town, and the appearance of aspen trees, so striking in the fall with their hues of gold and red, was one quick result.

Something happens to aspen groves, however. As the trees, with their beautiful white limbs, grow tall, their shade blocks out the direct sunlight that they require to reproduce themselves. The shade is just what seedlings of climax forest species such as Engelmann spruce and lodgepole pine need, however, and they will gradually replace the aspen as the ecosystem returns to a climax forest.

The phenomenon of change in Aspen thus inhabits its very name. Certainly, there have been changes for the worse since the miners noticed the unexpectedly lovely consequence of their environmental devastation, but also, perhaps, some changes for the better: One of the things that changes, it seems, is the idea of a paradise. A silver baron's capital is different from a skier's heaven, and a hippie hangout from a Hollywood East. And yet Aspen, the place, has served all these purposes. As one paradise has lapsed, another has flowered. Paradise, one might conclude, has not been lost. It has simply changed hands.

"It is easy," Joan Didion has written, "to see the beginnings of things, and harder to see the ends." Aspen began for me early one winter in ways I clearly recall. The first of my trial separations began a year and a half later, under circumstances that are more difficult to describe. What I know is that each departure was for me a sort of moral correction, a stepping back from myself in alarm to ask, "What are you doing?"

Others can point to a proximate cause for their leaving: a divorce, a firing, a romance or business opportunity elsewhere, a rise in rent, drug debts, a desire to return to school. My waitress friend Lanette has bought land in Telluride and is considering a move there; she has a good situation in Aspen, but I think she is looking for the way things used to be. Others find that in a town the size of Aspen it doesn't take long to bounce too many checks, break too many hearts, burn too many bridges. It is the way of the West: Life becomes difficult, so you move on. You may long for a bigger pond. You may yearn to go home. You may, like my friend Barry, have become too tangled in the threads of lunacy and excess that are part of the fabric of the place and wish to disentangle yourself in a place less crazy, before Aspen ruins you. All of these things can happen. Perhaps nobody ever understands the real reasons. Looking back, though, you have to finger the likely suspects.

The first I remember like a bright sun after you close your eyes. It was the annual Aspen/Snowmass *Food & Wine* Classic, a bacchanalian extravaganza sponsored every year by *Food & Wine* magazine. One objective was to introduce vintners to restaurateurs, but the main goal seemed to be to drum up enthusiasm for going out to eat and drink. Members of "the trade" were there, but outside gourmets could buy a ticket for $250. At the *Times,* it was one of the plum assignments, so to speak, because your ticket to the three-day event was free, and there was practically an infinite amount of good food and wine to consume.

I started Friday morning with a chardonnay tasting at the Paradise club. I dropped in to a cajun cooking demonstration with Alex Patout at the Isis Theater, listened briefly to a lecture on "Emerging Wine Regions" at the Jerome, and arrived at the "Grand Tasting" at the tent that covered half of Wagner Park in time to sample several varieties of cabernet, a nice merlot, and a little burgundy. My ticket didn't get me into the "Dining Out with the Winemakers" dinners that were being held around town, so I walked home unsteadily, made a sandwich, and fell asleep. The next morning I caught "California Cuisine with Bradley Ogden" at the Stage III movie theater, had another chardonnay tasting at the Paradise, audited "Wine: Is It a Good Investment?" at the Jerome, and heard "Restaurant Critics Speak Out" at the Isis Theater. Falling asleep around 3 P.M., I woke just in time to make the "Ten Best Chefs of the Year" dinner at the Grand Champions athletic club, where I remember a speaker's dais lined with eight or nine jeroboams of Mumm Cuvee Napa.

The next day, Sunday, organizers gave me a gift pack that included free samples of caviar, cheese, sausage, B&B liqueur and, new from the makers of Grand Marnier, a very sweet liqueur made of passion fruit, called La Grande Passion. I was up the next morning for "Mouthwatering Moments with Jim Dodge" at the Isis and another chardonnay tasting, and then returned from lunch just in time for the finale, the "Dessert Extravaganza" under the big tent. White-covered table after table offered an overwhelming selection of bonbons, truffles, cheesecakes, trifle, mousse, raspberry tarts, tiramisu, chocolate ganache cake, petits four, poached pears with blackberry couli, and even some cookies. People who were already quite red-faced and fat began shoveling these into their mouths so quickly I was hard-pressed to fill my own plate. The grass underfoot, meanwhile, had been mashed into a chocolate- and wine-spattered mess. I backed away from the feeding frenzy in order to keep my china plate balanced and was accosted by a California entrepreneur who had cooked up a special sweetened version of pâté de foie gras, which she offered me on a tiny water cracker.

"The real stuff, from the goose?" I asked, delicately placing the concoction on my tongue. She explained that yes, true pâté such as the substance between my teeth was made from the livers of over-stuffed geese. The geese were overfed because then their livers got overbig with deposits of fat from all the excess coming into their bodies; *foie gras,* in fact, meant "fatty liver." I tried to write this down and eat another cracker while listening to her, said thanks, and moved on. Next table down, I accepted a fluted glass of sauternes, and then another. The dessert-wine tables, like the tables of all the wines offered at "Grand Tastings" both days before, had bowls where you could pour out any wine you didn't want to drink. Today, the bowls all looked to me as though they were full of spit. I drank my second glass down. Pâté—the last time I'd heard it discussed was by Elizabeth Paepcke at the design conference, where she compared Aspen itself to an overfattened goose, nearing a death by richness. I downed a third glass of sauternes and then, blanching, ducked through an opening in the side of the tent and, next to a pine tree, threw up.

I noticed some changes in my attitudes. I was tiring, for example, of joie de vivre, of the stylized, commercial fun of a resort town. All of Aspen's skiing, nightlife, and celebration seemed tantamount, some days, to the commercial rejection of sorrow. I remembered my cab-driver friend who said he came to Aspen "for all the good times to be had. What else is there to life?" Well, the rest of the range of human emotions, to begin with. Aspen tried to institutionalize the idea of being upbeat, but after a while it just didn't ring true. Nobody really wants to smile, wave, and say hello every day. My friend Bo Persico, a counselor at Aspen Mental Health, said many of his clients were simply people who saw constant whoopee all around them and felt out of joint: Why aren't I having fun? they asked. Some days I didn't want to party. Some days I wanted clouds.

I was missing a sense of the ordinary, of junk cars and old people and vacant lots and fat guys with no style. There was a pressure to always look good, and it could be tiring. In my darker moods, I saw "dig me" written all over people who did dress stylishly; and an *Aspen Magazine* ad for itself—"the magazine that captures Aspen as you know it and love it"—made me even feel I was an out-of-place denizen of a "dig me" town.

Other days I "knew it and loved it" a bit too much. Pleased with

Aspen and myself, I almost felt sorry for a Denver lawyer I knew, an associate of my father's, upon seeing him and his wife in the lift line at Snowmass. He was wearing blockish, outmoded glasses and a long nylon parka, belted in the 60's style. He was important in Denver, but Aspen had a way of demoting the fashion retro; why would he choose to come up here, I wondered, and embarrass himself?

Not long after, my father and stepmother came up from Denver for the weekend and took me to lunch. Over the years, I knew, they'd considered buying real estate—a small house or condo—in Aspen, but my father had always felt it was too expensive, that you paid too big a premium for the name. My reaction this time was something along the lines of, well, you pay a certain price to play in certain leagues; are you willing, or not? I saw hurt in their eyes, but didn't realize why until months later, when my stepmother told me I had made them feel timid, like hicks, failures.

These negative feelings about the town and myself had ripened and been joined by others by the time I went to Barbi Benton's annual pajama party several months later. I had forgotten about the *Food & Wine* Classic, or thought I had. In the excitement of heading to Barbi's, I wasn't thinking about much else. Since my fervid teenage years I had been acquainted with Barbi Benton, whose button nose and generous bosom were regularly shown to good advantage in the pages of *Playboy* magazine. She had been Hugh Hefner's girlfriend (ergo, the pajama party, a throwback to Hef's annual extravaganzas at the Playboy Mansion West). Since then, she had married a developer named George Gradow and moved to Aspen. The party the year before—held at the Aspen Art Museum—had been something of a disappointment, a friend who had been there told me, due to the fact that Barbi had recently given birth to their first child and had not been in her usual fighting trim. In fact, the party had not been "pajama" at all but had been a "luau"/Hawaiian theme party, which had allowed the hostess to wear a grass skirt high up around her waist.

But this year the pajamas were back, and so was Barbi. Margot and I left our car with the valet, handed another fellow the pillows and blankets we'd been instructed to bring, and arrived on the deck outside the mountaintop home to a strange tableau. A throng of mostly middle-aged people, many of them local movers and shakers, were dressed in pajamas and negligees, slippers and robes. A hostess handed us candy-striped cotton nightcaps and served us champagne—in little half-pint milk cartons, with straws. We moved onto the deck with some trepidation—did we really want to see all these people in their nightclothes? Yes, was finally the answer, we did.

It is easy to meet people dressed in pajamas, and soon we were talking to a tall, rounded gentleman who apparently marched to the beat of a different drummer: Robeless, he was wearing a caftan. No, he hadn't gotten it just for the party; he had several. It was ideal for everyday wear around the house, he explained, because in a house with . . . he paused. "Servants?" I asked. He adopted the word gingerly . . . with servants, with a robe or pajamas, you always have to worry about things . . . becoming exposed. But not with a caftan. We nodded knowingly.

Like Barbi's husband, George, this man was a developer. Later in the evening, Margot would observe that "all the men are developers." Those invited seemed to be prominent mainly in this developer way. A well-known friend later told us she, too, had been invited but "threw the invitation away—I've never even *met* Barbi Benton!"

From the aerielike vantage of the deck, we could see down the valley, where a storm had been building since we arrived. As the wind picked up, we held fast to our nightcaps, filled our plates with a last helping of lobster-claw casserole and mushroom caps filled with steak tartare from the buffet, and headed quickly to the entrance to the white canvas party tent set up on a little knoll above the house.

Inside, there was a carpet of sheets and comforters, and everyone's pillows had been distributed all around. A New Age keyboardist and a guitar player were busily providing mood music. There was an easel set up near them, too. I recognized other guests as they entered the tent, hair mussed by the gathering winds. There was Joanne Lyons, owner of the Joanne Lyons Gallery, and Carol Ann Kopf, of Carol Ann Jacobson Realty, both with their husbands (Kopf's was a largely built developer named Don Kopf, and inevitably nicknamed by some locally as Dumbkopf.) I was pleased to see Frank van Damm, let's call him, a local character with long white hair and a genius's distraction about him, whom I had come to recognize as a token freak/mascot of a lot of these fancy parties. Strangely, he seemed to be enjoying himself enormously. He told me he was working on a new computer that was going to revolutionize China. "Re-revolutionize China?" I asked in jest, but he didn't get it. We chatted about how unpleasant town had seemed that summer, with so much building and so many new people, chatted about Bandar's big house—typical old Aspenite antigrowth conversation. But it felt strange then to see him so jolly amidst all the people who were the instruments and direct beneficiaries of the growth.

The rain began to fall in sheets, it thundered, and we worried about the metal tent poles we were sitting right next to, atop the high mountain. The world would not mourn our loss, I thought to myself, should lightning hit and paramedics arrive to discover us all in the tent, full of wine, champagne, lobster claws, and silk pajamas. But soon I noticed a more immediate peril. Water falling on top of the tent began to form a large pool, making the roof sag between the tent posts. Alerted, our hostess found an umbrella, stood underneath, and poked at it, but was too short to reach. The computer genius came soon to her aid, however; he put her on his shoulders and positioned her under the great bulge. She had center stage now. Reaching up with both her arms, she nicely began to expose her gallant rounded bosom, naked beneath her little frilly top. "Ooooh!" she chirped disingenuously, noticing it.

Her husband began a little dialogue, preliminary to the festivities. It was about the games we were going to play at this slumber party—Trivial Pursuit, Reminiscence (about pop-culture history), and Pictionary—and, especially, about the prizes. "The first prize, which *may* be available, is a 1989 Jeep Wagoneer," he said, immediately grabbing everyone's attention. Was this really possible? Were these two out to make Aspen party history? "Second prize," he continued, "is a week or two's trip to Hawaii, for two." Third prize was a pear-shaped diamond, and he mentioned the carats. No one really knew whether he was joking or not. A sample question might be the first word in the Bible, he said. "In!" cried a couple of people. "Or the last word," he said. "What was it?" The group was silent. "Oy," he said. He prattled on with the microphone, the guests his captive audience and money his main topic.

"Eat all you want, it's paid for!"

"Waitress! Would you bring more hot chocolate?" Then, as an aside to us, "They'll bring the hot chocolate when we pay the caterers!"

More wine? someone asked. "There is no more! You guys get what you paid for!"

Guests reshuffled their pillows and blankets as several leaks began in earnest from the canvas above. Joked George, "For twenty dollars more, we could have got the waterproof kind!"

We struck up a conversation with a decorator from the coast who also appeared to feel a bit out of his element. Our talk immediately turned catty as we began to discuss the plastic surgeries around us: apparent cheekbone implants here, lip augmentation there, plain old facelifts, which opened wide the eyes and made slightly crooked the lips. My date quoted Woody Allen: "They never look younger. They just look surprised."

Our host began a game of Trivial Pursuit, reading out the questions over the mike and keeping some kind of point tally for correct answers. With the decorator, we felt we were a sort of brain trust, but because we were at the back and pandemonium reigned, we never seemed to get called on. I was trying to answer "Name the Welsh national vegetable" at the top of my lungs ("Leek! Leek!"), but to no avail. An old guy with curlers on offered "parsnip." "Wrong!" cried George. "I guess nobody gets it!" The game continued, George and Barbi arguing over how many points a given question should be worth. Finally, the winners were named—the moment of truth. What would the prizes be?

"The loan didn't go through!" George screamed. "So instead of the diamond, for third place, Ellen Graves, we have . . . a rubber sheet!" There was lots of laughter, though actually Ellen didn't look too amused. Second prize, to Carol Ann's husband Don Kopf, is . . . a pair of support hose, husky size! And the first prize, a pair of incontinence diapers, went to a socialite financier. There was more laughter, but it had an edge: In a bizarre way, George had been toying with his audience. It was a money fetishist's prick tease, and a mocking of old age. At least a couple of the guests were old enough to, conceivably, be in need of the joke prizes.

Cocoa with marshmallows and schnapps was served, and the lights went down as the New Age keyboardist rose to tell bedtime stories. But her warm-up tale was a real bore, and though she had the mike, she didn't have the floor: Guests kept up their private conversations and began drifting out the door of the tent, where the rain had by now mostly stopped. When finally she finished a long story to very scattered applause, George took a vote about who wanted another tale . . . practically nobody. The party began to end.

We drifted through the house on our way out. Built by a wealthy Polish architect/disco promoter/ski instructor, the place was known locally as the Magic Mushroom house. Circular and made of stone, it had a central atrium hung with scores of plants, most of them on beams up high. The master bedroom was entered through a hole in the stone wall, up a little ladder. Inside, it was entirely filled by a round water bed; above was a huge skylight. It was cavelike, as was much of the house, including the tub (deep and lined with river rocks) and shower (rough stone walls). A stairway led up to more; along its walls was a gallery of needlepoints, all signed "Barbi," many from the early seventies, many of them representations of big breasts. In the hallway on the way to the bathroom were other photos of Barbi; my favorite had her in profile, in front of the pyramids, a study in geometry. Windows revealed a large workout room downstairs, with color-coordinated vinyl pads.

We picked up our bedding and waited for the car. Going to a pajama party in Aspen was like being in a theme within a theme; when you got out, where were you? On top of disoriented, I felt sullied. I was not proud to have gone. It was unseemly to cut down your host, and yet I had joined the ranks of those who slam Barbi. How many times in Aspen had I heard her made fun of? "When she was pregnant, she walked all over town with blond hair in long pigtails." Or, "The best way to kill a party is to invite the two of them, Barbi and George." And yet I was sure that most of her detractors, if invited, would show up at her party, if only to tell friends later how terrible it was. Such was the ambivalence of life in Aspen. You wanted to cut down certain prominent people to buttress the integrity of your own taste, of your own soul. And yet there was nothing so delicious as being welcomed into the fold. George's attitude of contempt began to make more sense: He had invited to the Magic Mushroom House a nest of snakes who were his friends.

. . .

I felt increasingly deserving of contempt as the months of my second year in Aspen went by. There was the day some people I'd known at the *Times* went lift scavenging: climbing the hills beneath the chair lifts to look for goodies dropped by skiers in the snow, now that the snow had melted. Everything from lip balm to cocaine packets to fifty-dollar bills was lying there, they said, waiting to be discovered: Did I want to come? I sneered silently and declined, thinking it sounded rather déclassé, an Aspen equivalent of the "canning" my hobo acquaintances used to do.

There was the day I attended a morning slide show on sustainable agriculture in the third world and then an evening dinner with Alison at a fancy restaurant called Gordon's. In the middle of the entree, she flirtatiously flung some baby peas toward a friend at the next table and things shortly escalated into a regular food fight, with jicama, prosciutto, and mâche flying through the air. As I lay in bed that night, images of starving kids met others of spoiled brats tossing fifty-dollar tuna steaks and made me wish for a confession, something I could say or do to be able to get some sleep.

Marciela was invited to a weekend house-party at an estate on Vancouver Island; did I want to come as her guest? Also present would be X, Y, and Z, names I knew from *People* magazine. Oh, and W, who might be looking for a story like one of mine to make into a feature film. It was expensive, and I wasn't entirely comfortable with an idea of a nationwide elite of people who flew in for house parties or with the companion concept that there are really only four or five hundred important people in the world, and if you hang out in the right circles, you will meet them all. The idea of this painless promotion to the fast track was a seductive one. Was it a harmless perk of my life in Aspen or a sort of death? I said I couldn't go.

Finally, the writer William Kittredge gave a reading in town. He spoke of eating oysters at a beautiful seaside resort with his woman friend, the two of them "cultivating the notion that it was possible to live without guilt amid the pleasures of paradise." The minute he said it, some pieces fell into place.

It all went back to my discussion, early on, with my landlady Johanna and how she sensed my disapproval of her life. What was the moral imperative, she had asked in so many words, that said she should not live in Aspen? How would the cause of world justice be furthered if instead she lived in Topeka? Why shouldn't someone with the chance to do it explore the good life?

I hadn't known the answer, and the longer I'd stayed in Aspen the less I tended to think about it. But the hard questions don't go away. I shifted uneasily in my chair as William Kittredge spoke of "people who've collapsed into serving their own selves and pleasures." Was he reading this in Aspen *on purpose?*

On an individual level, I thought, many of the early pilgrims to Aspen could be congratulated on having taken charge of their lives, gone west to a new place to try to find something better. But taken on a community level, the meaning of Aspen had changed. Aspen was a symbol of money, of the leisure class gone into retreat, of private dreams pursued in sweet oblivion to the world's struggle. To live there was somehow to be a part of that.

Between Barbi's party and some new attitudes, including a desire to mock my hosts, I knew I was losing my innocence. The result of Adam and Eve's seduction, their loss of innocence, was that they had to leave Paradise. I was thinking it might be time for me to do that, too.

Still, I vacillated. Novelist Thomas McGuane once called Aspen "one of America's top petting zoos," but to me it seemed more like a circus, a specialized world offering much of interest that the outside world did not. There was a fright about leaving: Where would you go next? What could be as interesting?

These thoughts filled my head as I headed for Denver one Sunday morning, wondering, first, about whether going to church would do me some good and, second, about a story I had read over breakfast in the *Aspen Daily News.* A house even bigger than Prince Bandar's had been proposed. Actually, it was two house plans that had been submitted, one by O & R Horsehauling, Inc., and another by 533, Inc. (shell corporations traced by a diligent reporter to Saudi prince Abdul Aziz al Ibrahim, a major financial supporter of Mohammed Hadid who would eventually take over his Ritz hotel project), the first nearly 30,000 square feet and the second over 40,000. Savvy city planners had noticed the two houses were a sort of architectural reflection of each other, and they suspected the owner planned to join them with some kind of tunnel or covered bridge, rendering him a house of effectively 70,000 square feet—

larger than the new permitted maximum for a single house. Having just seen an aerial photo of Prince Bandar's nearly finished 55,000-square-foot house, which looked like a big swollen tick, this news caused a sort of giddy sensation in me.

My mind wandered over the FOR SALE signs along Highway 82, and I began thinking about how smart it would be to get together enough money to buy a little real estate now or, failing that, a new car to replace my crummy old Honda wagon—say, a Jeep Cherokee 4.0-liter, red, with a sunroof. It seemed surprising, also, that I had gone this far through adulthood without owning a leather jacket. They were expensive, sure, but maybe it was time. It was time.

I was meeting my old friend Tracey for dinner in Denver. We went to a little neighborhood restaurant, Señor Pepe's, a Mexican place I'd been going to forever. It was one of those places you go to when you're not interested in surprises, an old standby.

We sat and chatted, ordered beers. As we caught up, I said it was good to see her. I looked around. There were some couples, some families, some kids. It all looked very gray and middle-class. There was no glamour for miles. "Tracey," I said, clearing my throat. "Maybe next time we could go someplace a little more interesting."

"What do you mean?" she asked. I tried to explain, but the look on her face showed she wasn't getting it. What I wanted to say was that Señor Pepe's, which used to seem ordinary in a familiar, neighborhood kind of way, now struck me as ordinary in a rather dull way. But that sounded somehow impolite. I said it anyway.

"What's happened to you?" she asked, visibly upset.

I was confused. Though I had never thought of it that way before, I knew immediately that Aspen had happened to me. Her tone was that of a witness to moral decay. It was more complicated than that, of course. Experience had happened to me, temptation. I had been seduced, but it was always too simple to blame only the seductress. I said something about Aspen, and she said I ought to come home. Other friends thought so too, she added: Everyone talked about how I had changed. In the *Odyssey*, this step was dramatic but rather too simple: Ulysses' friends marched into the land of the Lotus Eaters, grabbed the men who'd fallen under their spell, dragged them to the boat, chained them to a bench, and sailed away. Eventually, they were delivered back home.

Two things, it seemed to me, were left out of that story. First, the

Lotus Eaters were blamed: No fault was placed on the men. And second, those men weren't the same anymore. If their boats were to dock in that paradisaical land again, they would no doubt be the first ones up the beach. It was, in some ways, too late to go home.

Still, you had to try. Friends these days lack the chains to perform good deeds like that, but I had other allies. I had memories of the food-and-wine extravaganza. I had the pajama party. Tracey's concern was like a cry from my fellows. We ordered coffee and skipped dessert.